MODERN DRUMMER® Legends

RUSH'S NEIL PEART

Subscribe to *Modern Drummer*: moderndummer.com/subscribe

For fun and educational videos, subscribe to the
"Modern Drummer Official" YouTube channel

Modern Drummer Publisher/CEO **David Frangioni**

Managing Director/SVP **David Hakim**

Editorial Director **Adam Budofsky**

Art Director; Layout and Design **Scott Bienstock**

Front cover photo by Sayre Berman

Back cover photo by Mark Weiss from the book
Crash, the World's Greatest Drum Kits available at Amazon.com

Published by:
Modern Drummer Publications, Inc.
315 Ridgedale Ave #478
East Hanover, NJ 07936

Special thanks to the entire *Modern Drummer* and Hal Leonard teams;
Don Lombardi, John Good, Scott Donnell, and the DW Family.

To the millions of Neil Peart fans and *Modern Drummer* readers in the world, this one is for you!

Contents

In The Limelight: Neil And Modern Drummer

Neil Peart's ten appearances on the cover of *Modern Drummer* magazine span the years 1980, when he was five albums and several tours into his historic run with the Canadian progressive-rock band Rush, and 2020, the year of his passing. It's an unprecedented feat. No other drummer has come close to appearing so many times on the front of a major drum publication, certainly not the world's most recognized one.

It's no secret that in person Neil was far from an attention hog. It's one of the great ironies of his career, given how absolutely ravenous his following was for every beat, fill, solo, and lyric he contributed to Rush's music. But just because Neil was perhaps the world's least clichéd rock star, it doesn't mean he didn't value the access he had to the eyes and ears of his legions of followers.

Peart's fans have always been highly appreciative of the time and effort he put into choosing the exact right words and constructing the perfect musical accompaniment to the most complex songs commercial radio has ever embraced. During the classic-rock era, when the opening strains of a Rush tune unexpectedly leapt out of a radio speaker, it was a special feeling, an acknowledgement to us music geeks that our teenage dreams of rock stardom *and* sophistication could come true. Hero worship gets a bad rap most of the time, but Neil fans didn't so much pine for groupies, private jets, and endless parties as they daydreamed about making concept albums in the best recording studios, playing intricate drum solos in the world's greatest arenas, or holding court Buddha-like on a mountaintop as a sea of drummers hung on their every word. Neil represented a pinnacle of sorts: a renaissance man who rocked righteously but whose nickname "The Professor" seemed completely apt. The fact that he was one of *us*…well, let's just say it was the perfect shield against anyone who was dumb enough to trot out some hackneyed "drummer joke" in our presence.

When Neil died this past January 7 at the age of sixty-eight, many of the world's greatest drummers reached out to the *Modern Drummer* office, asking if we could include their thoughts on the great drummer in the tribute issue they knew we'd immediately begin working on. Their words are presented here, as they were in our regular monthly issue this past May, under the headline "Remembering Neil." (We took a slightly different approach here, weaving the quotes throughout the nine other NP/*MD* cover stories that make up the bulk of this special Legends edition.)

While observing the drum community over my more than thirty years at *Modern Drummer*, something that always impressed me about Neil was how broadly his influence spread. Sure, he was by far the most influential drummer on players in heavy and progressive-rock bands—that made sense, given Rush's music. But his influence permeated *so* much more of the drumming community, and I had a hunch that if we threw out a fairly wide net and approached players who worked in styles that were different from what Rush was known for, their impressions of Neil might be valuable. And *boy* were they.

In fact, some of the most astute observations and heartfelt remembrances came from the indie, country, world-music, and jazz drummers we contacted. For so many of them, Neil was their entry point into drumming, their first and therefore most important musical role model. And while his performances hooked them when they were at their most impressionable age, as they grew up, even if their musical tastes and experiences went in radically different directions from Neil's, the words of wisdom and encouragement he shared whenever he sat down for a *Modern Drummer* interview continued to be important, and revelatory, and sustaining. It's a legacy that drummers—no, that *music*—won't soon forget.

Adam Budofsky
Editorial Director, *Modern Drummer*

April-May 1980

Karen Lacrombe

The First MD Cover Story

"The Neil Peart interview was a story we pursued for many months," said *Modern Drummer* founder Ron Spagnardi in his editorial accompanying Neil Peart's first *MD* cover story. "A talented and opinionated artist," continued Spagnardi about the then-twenty-seven-year-old drummer, "Neil is not impressed by mob fan adulation, and maintains a philosophy indicative of the seriousness with which he views his drumming." In this fascinating interview, Neil, still early in his career, touches on themes that would crop up throughout the magazine's subsequent conversations with him, but also betrays a certain guilelessness that would fade in later years as he evolved into the "professor" that his fans came to know and love.

Interview by Cheech Iero

MD: Do you enjoy the hectic schedule you keep on the road?

Neil: To me, it's just the musician's natural environment. I won't say that it's always wonderful, but it's not always awful either. As with anything else, I think it's a more extreme way of life. The rewards are higher, but the negative sides are that much more negative. I think that rule of polarity follows almost every walk of life. The greater the fulfillment that you're looking for, the greater the agony you'll face.

MD: During your soundcheck, you not only use the opportunity to get the proper sound, but also as a chance to warm up and practice a bit.

Neil: Well, soundcheck is a nice time to practice and try new ideas, because there's no pressure. If you do it wrong, it doesn't matter. And I'm a bit on the adventurous side live, too. I'll try something out. I'll take a chance. Most of the time I'm playing above my ability, so I'm taking a risk. I think every day is really a practice. We play so much, and playing within a framework of music every night, you have enough familiarity to feel comfortable to experiment. If the song starts to grow a bit stale, I find one nice little fill which will refresh the whole song.

MD: Refresh it for the rest of the group as well?

Neil: Sure, for all of us. We all put in a little something, a little spice. The audience would probably never notice, but it just has to be a little something that sparks it for us. And for me the whole song will lead up to that from then on, and the song will never be dull.

MD: How did you become involved with Rush?

Neil: The usual chain of circumstances and accidents. I came from a city that's about sixty or seventy miles from Toronto. A few musicians from my area had migrated to Toronto and were working with bands around there when they recommended me

as someone of suitable style. I guess they tried a few drummers, but we just clicked on both sides. There was a strong musical empathy right away with new ideas they were working on and things I had as musical ideas. Also, outside of music we have a lot of things in common.

MD: Where has this tour taken you?

Neil: Well, this isn't really much of a tour. By our terms, most of our tours last ten months or so. This one is only three or four weeks. This is just a warmup as far as we're concerned. We've been off a couple of months. We took two weeks of holidays and then spent six weeks rehearsing and writing new material. After that kind of break, we just wanted to get ourselves out onstage. That's the only place where you really get yourself into shape. Rehearsals will keep you playing well, and you'll remember all your ideas and learn your songs and stuff. But as far as the physical part of it, the feeling of being on top of your playing, you've got to have the road for that.

MD: This is a warmup for what?

Neil: The studio.

MD: At what studio will you record?

Neil: We will be going to Le Studio, which is in Montreal. We'll record there and mix at Trident in London.

MD: When the members of Rush are composing a piece of music, is the structure determined by the feedback you receive from one another?

Neil: Yes, to a large extent. It depends really on what we're coming at it with. Often times [guitarist] Alex [Lifeson] and [bassist/singer] Geddy [Lee] will have a musical idea, maybe individually. They'll bring it into the studio and we'll bounce it off one another, see what we like about it, see if we find it exciting as an idea, and then we get a verbal idea of what the mood of it is, what the setting would be. If I have a lyrical idea that we're trying to find music for, we discuss the type of mood we are trying to create musically, what sort of compositional

skills we'll bring to bear on that emotionally. The three of us try to establish the same feeling for what the song should be. Then you bring the technical skills in to try to interpret that properly and achieve what you thought it would.

MD: Your role as a lyricist has drawn wide acclaim. How did you develop that particular talent?

Neil: Well, that's really hard to put into focus. I came into it by default, just because the other two guys didn't want to write lyrics. I've always liked words. I've always liked reading, so I had a go at it. I like doing it. When I'm doing it, I try to do the best I can. It's pretty secondary. I don't put that much importance on it. A lot of times you just think of a lyrical idea as a good musical vehicle. I'll think up an image, or I'll hear about a certain metaphor that's really picturesque. A good verbal image is a really good musical stimulus. If I come up with a good picture lyrically, I can take it to the other two guys and automatically express to them a musical approach.

MD: The tune "The Trees" from your *Hemispheres* album comes to my mind.

Neil: Lyrically that's a piece of doggerel. I certainly wouldn't be proud of the writing skill of that. What I *would* be proud of in that is taking a pure idea and creating an image for it. I was very proud of what I achieved in that sense. Although on the skill side of it, it's zero. I wrote "Trees" in about five minutes. It's simple rhyming and phrasing, but it illustrates a point so clearly. I wish I could do that all of the time.

MD: Did that particular song's lyrics cover a deeper social message?

Neil: No, it was just a flash. I was working on an entirely different thing when I saw a cartoon picture of these trees carrying on like fools. I thought, "What if trees acted like people?" So I saw it as a cartoon really, and wrote it that way. I think that's the image that it conjures up to a listener or a reader. A very simple statement.

> "There's a lot of different kinds of drumming that turns me on. It could be a simple thing; I don't think that my style really reflects my taste."

Karen Lacrombe

MD: Do all of your lyrics follow that way of thinking, or have you expressed a more philosophical view in other songs that you have written?
Neil: Usually I just want to create a nice picture, or it might have a musical justification that goes beyond the lyrics. I just try to make the lyrics a good part of the music. Many times when there's something strong that I'm trying to say, I look for a nice way to say it musically. The simplicity of the technique in "Trees" doesn't really matter to me. It can be the same way in music. We can write a really simple piece of music, and it will feel great. The technical side is just not relevant, especially from a listening point of view. When I'm listening to other people, I'm not listening to how hard their music is to play, I listen to how good the music is to listen to.
MD: When you listen to another

drummer, what do you listen for?
Neil: I listen for what they have. There's a lot of different kinds of drumming that turns me on. It could be a simple thing; I don't think that my style really reflects my taste. There are a lot of drummers that I like who play nothing the way I do. There's a band called the Police, and their drummer plays with simplicity, but with such gusto. It's great. He just has a new approach.
MD: Who are some of your favorite drummers?
Neil: I have a lot. Bill Bruford is one. I admire him for a whole variety of reasons. I like the stuff he plays, and the way he plays it. I like the music he plays within all the bands he's been in.

There were a lot of drummers that at different stages of my ability I've looked up to, starting way back with Keith Moon. He was one of my favorite mentors. It's hard to decide what

drummers taught you what things. Certainly Moon gave me a new idea of the freedom and that there was no need to be a fundamentalist. I really liked his approach to putting crash cymbals in the middle of a roll.

Then I got into a more disciplined style later on as I gained a little more understanding on the technical side. People like Carl Palmer, Phil Collins, Michael Giles—the first drummer from King Crimson—and of course Bill were all influences. There's a guy named Kevin Ellman who played with Todd Rundgren's Utopia for a while. I don't know what happened to him. He was the first guy I heard lean into the concert toms. Nicky Mason from Pink Floyd has a different style. Very simplistic yet ultra-tasteful. Always the right thing in the right place. I heard concert toms from Mason first, then I heard Kevin Ellman, who put

all his arms into it. You learn so many things here and there. There are a lot of drummers we work with…Tommy Aldridge from the Pat Travers Band is a very good drummer. I should keep a list of all the drummers that I admire.

MD: Do you follow any of the jazz drummers?

Neil: I've found it easier to relate to the so-called fusion [drummers], actually. I like it if it has some rock in it. Weather Report's *Heavy Weather* I think was one of the best jazz albums in a long time. Usually technical virtuosity leaves me completely unmoved, though academically it's inspiring. But that band just moved me in every way. They were exciting, and proficient musicians. Their songs were really nice to listen to. They were an important band and had a great influence on my thinking.

MD: What drew you towards drums?

Neil: Just a chain of circumstances. I'd like to make up a nice story about how it all happened. I just used to bang around the house on things and pick up chopsticks and play on my sister's playpen. For my thirteenth birthday my parents paid for drum lessons. I had had piano lessons a few years before that and wasn't really that interested. But with the drums, somehow I was interested. When it got to the point of being bored with lessons, I wasn't bored with playing. It was something I wanted to do every day. So it was no sacrifice. No agony at all. It was pure pleasure. I'd come home every day from school and play along with the radio.

MD: Who was your first drum teacher?

Neil: I took lessons for a short period of time, about a year and a half. His name was Paul, I can't remember his last name. He turned me in a lot of good directions and gave me a lot of encouragement. I'll never forget him telling me that out of all his students, there were only two that he thought would be drummers. I was one of them. That was the first encouragement I had, which was very

important to me. For somebody to say to you, "You can do it." And then he got into showing me what was hard to do. Although I wasn't capable of playing those things at the time, he was showing me difficult rudimental things, and flashy things—double-hand crossovers and such. So he gave me the challenge. And even after I stopped taking lessons, those things stayed in my mind and I worked on them. And finally I learned how to do a double-hand crossover. I remember thinking how proud I would be if my teacher could see it.

MD: Did you study percussion further with other instructors?

Neil: Well, it's relative. I think of myself still as a student. All the time I've been playing I've listened to other drummers and learned an awful lot. I'm still learning. We're all just beginners. I really like that Lol Creme and Kevin Godley album [*L*]. The [title] stands for "learner's permit" in England. And that album is so far above what everybody else is doing, yet they're still learning. I really admire them.

MD: When you were coming up, did you set your sights on any particular goals?

Neil: My goals were really very modest at the time. I would get in a band and the big dream was to play in a high school. Ultimately, every city has the place that's the "in" spot where all the hip local bands play. I used to dream about playing those places. I never thought bigger than that. For every set of goals achieved, new ones come along to replace them. After I would achieve one goal, it would mean nothing. There's a [theater] in Toronto called Massey Hall, which is a 4,000-seat hall. I used to think to play there would be the ultimate. But then you get there and worry about other things. When we finally got to play there, we were about to make an album, and thought about that.

MD: Your mind was a step ahead of what you were doing at the present.

Neil: Yes. I think it's human nature not to be satisfied with what you were originally dreaming of. Whatever you were dreaming of, if you achieve it, it means nothing anymore. You've got to have something to replace it.

MD: Describe your feelings, walking onstage and looking at an audience of 35,000 screaming fans.

Neil: Any real person will not be moved by 35,000 people applauding [for] him. If I go on in front of 35,000 people and play really well, then I feel satisfied when I come off the stage. I'm happy because those 35,000 people were excited. If we're in front of a huge crowd and I have a bad night, I still can't help being depressed. If I come offstage not having played well, I don't feel good. I don't see why I should change that. Adulation means nothing without self-respect.

MD: You feel you must satisfy yourself first.

Neil: I never met a serious musician who wasn't his own worst critic. I can walk offstage and people will have thought I played well, and it might have even sounded good on tape, but I still know I didn't play it the way it should be. Nothing will change that.

MD: Do you feel there are certain things that contribute to a particularly good or bad night?

Neil: I don't think there is anything mystical about it at all. I just think it's a matter of polarity. I go looking for a lot of parallels. I find it in that, because certain nights it is so magical, and the whole band feels so good about how they played. The audience was so receptive and there's feedback going back and forth and good feelings generated by the show. That has to be the ideal. That particular show might happen five or six times out of the whole 200-show tour. But that is the ideal show. Every other show has to be measured on those standards. Our average is good. We never do a bad show anymore. We have a level where we're always good. Even if we're bad, the show will be good.

Somerset Maugham, I believe, said, "A mediocre person is always at his best." And that's true. If you play really great one night, you're not going to be great every night. As far as my experiences go anyway, I've never known any musician that was. I'm not. Some nights I'm good and some nights I'm not good. Some nights I think I stink. I think it's just a matter of knowing that you have an honest appraisal of what your ability should be and know how well you've lived up to it. To me, there's no mystery about that at all. You know inside.

MD: What type sticks do you use?

Neil: I use light sticks generally. I've [played] butt end for as long as I can remember. It gives me all the impact I need. When I'm doing anything delicate, I play matched grip with the bead end of the sticks.

MD: So you use both matched and traditional grips depending on the feeling of the music.

Neil: Yes, both. I go back to the

fixed or re-rigged somehow. But if you break a bass drum head, the show stops. We once had to stop in the middle of filming *Don Kirshner's Rock Concert* because I broke a bass drum. So we stopped and fixed it. That's all you can do. It doesn't happen anymore, because of that idea and because [drum tech] Larry [Allen] keeps an eye on the heads and changes them.

MD: Who mikes your drums?

Neil: Our sound man, Ian [Grandy], chooses the mikes and positions them.

MD: You have your own monitor mix during live performances, correct?

Neil: Yes, Larry mixes that. That's really just my drums in a separate mix, because we have front monitors.

MD: Are the monitors on your left and right side just feeding you the drums?

Neil: Yes. All I hear is myself coming from those monitors. The front monitors give me all synthesizers and vocals, and when it comes to guitar and bass, they're right beside me. There are only two other guys; I'm fortunate in that respect, so I don't

MD: Do you use a pitch pipe, get the note from the keyboard, or just hum the note you're after?

Neil: I've been using the same size drums for several years, and I just know what note that drum should produce. When you combine a certain type of head with a certain size drum, I believe there is an optimum note, which will give you the most projection and the greatest amount of sustain. With the concert toms I just go for the note. I have a mental scale in my head. I know what those notes should be. By now it's instinctive. With the closed toms, I start with the bottom heads. I'll tune the bottom heads to the note that drum should produce, and then tune the top head to the bottom.

MD: How often do you change the heads on your drums?

Neil: Concert tom heads sound good when they're brand new, so they get changed a bit differently. They last through a month of serious road work. The Evans Mirror heads are used on the tom-toms and take a while to warm

> "I don't understand the people who would look at my drumkit and say, 'All you need is four drums.' That makes me as mad as looking down on someone who has only four drums."

conventional grip when I have to do anything rudimentary, because that's the way I learned it. It's not the best way. For anybody else learning, I wouldn't advise that. I've seen a lot of drummers who could play a beautiful press roll with matched grip.

MD: Why do you tape the top shaft of the bass drum beater so heavily?

Neil: That's an interesting trick that other drummers should know about. I break a lot of beaters off at the head, because the whole weight of my leg goes into my pedals. And I always break them where the felt part of the beater meets the shaft. They break right at the shaft, and then the shaft goes through the head. If you put that roll of tape on there, you'll never break your drumhead. In fact, I can still get through half a song if I have to, until the beater can be changed. The worst thing that could happen in a show would be for your bass drum to break. Anything else could be changed or

need them in my monitors. I have direct instruments to my ears, which to me is the best. I'd rather have that than to fool around with the monitors. And the stuff the other guys need in their monitors I get indirectly, because it's pointing at them, so I also hear it. I know a lot of drummers who prefer to have the whole mix in their monitors, and in some cases need the whole mix in their monitors.

MD: Have you ever worn earphones while playing live?

Neil: No, not really, they fall off. I even had a lot of trouble in the studio keeping them on. I went through all kinds of weird arrangements, getting the cord out of my way. It's just not worth it, I like to hear the natural sound.

MD: What are your thoughts on tuning?

Neil: Concert toms are pretty well self-explanatory. I just know the note I want to achieve and tighten them up.

up. It takes a week to break them in. I don't change those much more than every six weeks or so. They do start to lose their sound after a while. You start to feel they're just not putting out the note they should be. Then you say, "I hate to do it, but let's change the heads."

I like Black Dots when they're brand new. I used to use those on my snare, and the Clear Dots also sound good when they're brand new. But the Evans heads don't. It takes a while. I've gone through agonies with snare drums. I guess most drummers do. I had an awful time, because there was a snare sound in my mind that I wanted to achieve. I went through all kinds of metal snares, and I still wasn't satisfied. It wasn't the sound I was after. Then my drum roadie phoned me about this wooden Slingerland snare. It was second-hand. Sixty dollars. I tried it out and it was the one. Every other snare I've tried chokes somewhere. Either

very quietly, or if you hit it too hard it chokes. This one never chokes. You can play it very delicately, or you can pound it to death. It always produces a very clean, very crisp sound. It has a lot of power, which I didn't expect from a wooden snare drum. It's a really strong drum. I tried other types of wooden snare drums. I tried the top-of-the-line Slingerland snare drum. [But] there's no other snare drum that will replace it for me.

MD: What kind of finish does your kit have?

Neil: It's a mahogany finish. The Percussion Center in Fort Wayne, Indiana, where I get all my stuff, did the finish for me. I was trying to achieve a rosewood. At home I have some Chinese rosewood furniture, and I wanted to get that deep burgundy richness. They experimented with different kinds of inks, magic marker inks of red, blue, and black, trying to get the color. It was very difficult.

MD: What has been done to the inside of your drum shells?

Neil: All of the drums with the exception of the snare have a thin layer of fiberglass. It doesn't destroy the wood sound. It just seems to even out the overtones a bit, so you don't get crazy rings coming out of certain areas of the drums. You don't get too much sound absorption from the wood. Each drum produces the pure note it was made to produce as far as I'm

concerned. There's no interference with that either in the open toms or the closed toms. The note is very pure and easy to achieve. I can tune the drums, and when I get them to the right note I know the sound will be proper.

MD: Why do you use same-size double bass drums instead of two different-size drums to achieve two different bass voices?

Neil: I'm not looking for different sounds. My double bass drums are basically for use with fills. I don't like them to be used in rhythms. I like them to spice up a fill or create a certain accent. Many drummers say anything you can do with two feet can be achieved with one. That just isn't true. I can anticipate a beat with both bass drums. That is something I learned from Tommy Aldridge of the Pat Travers Band. He has a really neat style with the bass drums. Instead of doing triplets with his tom-toms first and then the bass drums, which is the conventional way, he learned how to do it the other way, so that the bass drums are anticipated.

MD: Giving it a flam effect?

Neil: In a sense. It has an up sort of feel. You could just be playing along in an ordinary four-beats-to-the-bar ride and all of a sudden stick that in. It just sets that apart. When you listen to it on the track, it sounds strange. It really works well and it's handy in the fills. You can be in the middle of a triplet fill and all

of a sudden you can leave your feet out for a beat and bring them back in on the beat. It's really exciting.

I like to interpose two bass drums against the hi-hat too. There are a few different things I do where I throw in a quick triplet or a quadruplet using the bass pedals and then get right over to the hi-hat. I'll complete my triplet and by the time my hand gets over to the hat, my foot is already there. So you'll hear almost consecutive left bass drum and hi-hat notes. If you want a really powerful roll, there's nothing more powerful than triplets with two bass drums. I could certainly get along without two bass drums for 99 percent of my playing. But I would miss them for some important little things.

MD: Did you go to the Zildjian factory to select your cymbals?

Neil: No, I must admit I've cracked so many cymbals, that would be futile. I just know the weights that I want to get, and if I have one that's terribly bad, I'll take it back. I go through an awful lot of crash cymbals. I hit them hard and they crack, especially my 16" crash, which is my mainstay, and my 18" crash.

MD: Where do you buy your cymbals?

Neil: From the Fort Wayne Percussion Center. I actually haven't seen their store in many years. Most of our business is done by them shipping the merchandise out to us, or [owner] Neal Graham comes out from the

REMEMBERING NEIL

To truly have your own voice on an instrument is one of the greatest achievements a musician can have, and Neil Peart had just that. He also had his own voice as an author and lyricist who was a master storyteller, an architect of dreams, a teacher, a sage, an explorer—and I think the outpouring of grief that was experienced at the news of his passing went beyond just the loss of a fellow drummer. We "knew" him through his written words, whether

it be from the music or his nonfiction work. The loss of his person was felt on a profound level. He inspired millions as a wordsmith extraordinaire, and his playing "just sounded cool." And by that I mean, you can't just decide to be cool. Cool is. Or it isn't. And his playing was cool and spoke to musicians and the layman alike. The Rush records were always mixed with the drums equal in the blend—you never had to listen while squinting from the edge of your seat to decipher what he was

doing through a cacophony of reverb or a wall of other instruments. His playing, like it or not, spoke with the clarity of his written words.

I only met him once. We were working right next to each other at Ocean Way in Los Angeles. He was recording the "Hockey Night in Canada" theme and I was recording with Brian Wilson on his Gershwin record. Sabian's Chris Stankee pulled me next door to meet him, and there was a full big band and a film

crew, along with the actual Stanley Cup trophy. I found him to be kind, engaging, and warm. After a while he was asking me all the questions in our conversation—about what I was doing, what it was like working with Brian Wilson, and whatever else was coming up in my schedule.

One of the definitions of the word "gentleman" is someone who makes you feel at ease, accepted, and in good company. Neil was a gentleman indeed. I wish I would have had the store. He brought me my new drums a couple of weeks ago. I know he has a lot of imagination; if I want something crazy, he'll come up with it. If I want crotales on top of the tubular bells, or a temple block mounted on top of my percussion, he can do it. When you present him with an idea, he thinks of a way to achieve it. He never let me down in that respect. He built my gong stand. The gong stand mounts on the timpani and is attached to the mallet stand.

MD: With the extensive setup that you use, I'm wondering why you don't use electronic percussive devices.

Neil: It's a matter of temperament

Karen Lacrombe

really. I don't feel comfortable with wires and electronic things. It's not a thing for which I have a natural empathy. It's not that I don't think that they're interesting or that there aren't a lot of possibilities. But personally I'm satisfied with traditional percussion. I have distrust for electronic and mechanical things. I've got enough to keep me busy, really.

When I look at my drums, the five-piece setup is the basis of what I have.

I might have hundreds of toys, but for me most of my patterns and most of my thinking revolves around snare drum, bass drum, hi-hat, and a couple of tom-toms. But there's more to it than that. I can add a lot more. I don't understand the people who are purists or fundamentalists, who would look at my drumkit and say, "All you need is four drums." That makes me as mad as looking down on someone who has only four drums. I'm not afraid to play on only four drums, but there's more that I can contribute to this band as a percussionist.

I'm certainly not a keyboard percussion virtuoso by any means,

nor do I expect to be. I just want to be a good drummer at this point in my life. Having eight tom-toms to me is excellent, because I can do that many more variations of sounds. So you're not hearing the same fill all the time, or the same sort of patterns. There are different notes, different perspectives of percussion. To me it sounds like a natural evolution. I couldn't understand anyone who would look at it with bitterness, or reproach, because

I don't neglect my drumming because of that. When I'm not busy drumming, I have something else to do. And the guys show me the notes to play and I play them. I know Carl Palmer spends a lot of time on keyboard percussion, and I admire him for that. He's getting quite proficient. Bill Bruford's getting amazing on keyboard percussion, because he's devoted the time and the energy that it takes to become a proper keyboard percussionist. I admire that to no end. I spend a lot of time thinking about composition, and drumming has to be the prime musical force. I spend a lot of time working with words. I look at that as a simultaneous education while I'm refining my drumming skills.

MD: Do you use lyrics as a guide to your drumming?

Neil: Not after the fact. Once we have agreed on the musical structure and arrangement, it then becomes a purely musical thing. Obviously, if there's a problem in phrasing I might have to rewrite the structure. But for the most part I forget about the lyrics and listen to the vocals. Getty's interpretation is really when it becomes an instrument, so there's a way I can punctuate the vocals or frame the vocals somehow musically.

MD: What are some of your thoughts on soloing?

Neil: I guess there are mixed feelings. How musical it is depends on the drummer. I find it very satisfying. I guess a lot of drummers do improvise all the way through their solo. I have a framework that I deal with every night, so I have some sort of standard where it will be consistent. And if I don't feel especially creative or strong, I can just play my framework and know it will be good. But certain areas of my

chance for another encounter with him, but I'm grateful for the lovely one that I had. I wish he would have been able to enjoy his retirement, especially after living through such unimaginable tragedy. He was an important figure during my school years in real time '76 to '82, basically *2112* through *Signals*. *Moving Pictures* and *Signals* can catapult me back to junior high school in my mind more powerfully than a photograph. I think many of us feel that way, and his contributions to music and literature will live within us all.

Todd Sucherman (Styx, sessions)

The first big concert I ever attended was Rush during their *Roll the Bones* tour. It was the first time I saw a band in an arena, and it was the first time I ever saw a live drum solo. Needless to say, it blew me away. It sparked a lifelong flame that I've carried through my career to this day. Neil was one of my absolute biggest influences, and his drumming inspired so much of how I've developed as a drummer. He was and will always be a pillar of this fantastic drumming community for countless reasons. But one specific reason in my mind is that he was and will always be at the center of so many

conversations between drummers— and non-drummers—of all ages, all skill levels, and all styles of music. He brought people together because of drumming and helped them fall in love with this incredible instrument. Neil Peart was the "gateway drummer" for me and many others, and he'll continue to be that kind of legend for the rest of time.

Matt Halpern (Periphery)

My first concert was Rush at the Cow Palace in San Francisco, 1980, on the *Permanent Waves* tour. I was twelve. My older brother had

first played me *2112* and *A Farewell to Kings* when I was ten. It was "Xanadu" that got its hooks in me first. Neil's multipercussion sound world and his effortless odd time signatures fascinated me. It was so cinematic. His lyrics were the script. Lying on the floor listening to it in the dark or staring at the gatefold sleeves had a profound impact on my life that I would only come to realize much later, when I transitioned from being a drummer in a band, living in the limelight, to being a film composer. Once-mystical devices like the vibraslap, crotales, temple blocks, orchestra chimes, and

continues on page 12

MODERN DRUMMER

> "When I do an interview, I'm looking for [one] that's going to be stimulating, and I'll get right into it. Just sit for hours and relate. That's an ideal, like an ideal show. It doesn't happen that often."

solo are left open for improvisation. If I feel especially hot, or if I have an idea that comes to me spontaneously, I have plenty of room to experiment. I try to structure the solo like a song, or piece of music. I'll work from the introduction, go through various movements, and bring in some comic relief. Then build up to a crescendo and end naturally. I can't be objective. Subjectively, I enjoy doing it and like listening to it. It's a good solo. Non-drummers have told me it's a nice drum solo to listen to.

MD: Do you have any advice for the young drummers with aspirations of someday playing in a musical situation similar to your own?

Neil: I used to try to give people advice, but the more I learned, the more I realized that my advice could only be based on both my values and my experiences, neither of which are going to be shared by very many people. I would say to them, "Go for what you're after." I can't get much more complicated than that. I don't feel comfortable telling people what to do.

MD: Have you ever taught private students'?

Neil: No, I haven't. I've been asked to do clinics, which I'm interested in but fearful of. But I would like to get into doing that, relating to people on that level. I like to talk about drums. I like to talk about things I'm interested in. For

me to talk about things I'm honestly interested in—and obviously drums is one of them—is foremost.

MD: What are your thoughts on interviews?

Neil: I won't do an interview for a promotional reason. I do them because I like to get my ideas out. Sometimes I can talk about something in an interview and realize that I was totally wrong. And I'll have had the opportunity to air those thoughts out, which most people don't. You don't have conversations with your friends about metaphysics, the fundamentals of music, and the fundamentals of yourself really. When I do an interview, I look for an ideal. I'm looking for an interview that's going to be stimulating, and I'll get right into it. Just sit for hours and relate. That's an ideal, like an ideal show. It doesn't happen that often.

MD: Before setting up your kit, Larry Allen cleaned and polished each cymbal to a high gloss and cleaned all the chrome. Does he take this great care as per your instruction, or is this something Larry does on his own?

Neil: That's a reflection of Larry's care. He takes a lot of pride in having the set sparkle and the cymbals shining. On his side I relate to that, but it doesn't affect me really one way or the other.

MD: Do you hear a difference in the brilliance of the sound when your cymbals are clean instead of tarnished?

Neil: No, not really. It's hard to justify really. To me a good cymbal sounds good, and a bad cymbal doesn't sound good. That's the way I feel about it. My 20" crash has a very warm, rich sound with a lot of good decay. I don't think dirt would improve that.

MD: Some drummers feel that as the cymbal is played, gets dirty, and gets tarnished, it takes on a certain character all its own. Do you think it is really the aging process that is the factor?

Neil: Yes, I think age has something to do with that. But the cymbal is metal—how can dirt make it sound better? If you don't want the decay, stick a piece of tape on it. It'll do the same thing dirt will do. It may be true that dirt is a factor. But it won't give it a warmer sound by definition, because the note of the cymbal is still the note of the cymbal.

MD: The dirt will only affect the sustain.

Neil: Exactly. So if you want a shorter sustain, get it dirty. My cymbals are chosen for the length of decay that I

REMEMBERING NEIL

continued from page 11

tubular bells now play an everyday role in my film music.

As a high school sophomore, I was given an English assignment to write and send a business letter to any business that interested me. Since the only business I cared about was drumming, I wrote to Neil Peart and sent it in care of *Modern Drummer*. I wasn't expecting a reply, but there in my mailbox right around Christmas vacation 1982, roughly nine months later, a postcard from Neil arrived.

I couldn't believe it! I stood by the mailbox in disbelief, reading and rereading Neil's handwritten responses to my questions. I must have read it a hundred times that day. I promptly wrote him back, and again nine months or so later he replied with another handwritten postcard! In both incidences Neil stressed to find and be myself. To "try and do everything, and find out what you do best!" Obviously, based on my questions, I was trying to imitate him. I was fourteen and had no idea who I was. I wanted to sound like him, but it hit me and it stuck, perhaps because he underlined the word

"you." It may have taken me a while to find my own voice (still in progress), and I certainly borrowed from Neil along the way, but that was the best career advice I was ever given. I have never forgotten it. I pass it along to any hungry musician that asks me for advice.

The inspiration, compassion, and personal encouragement that Neil so graciously gave to a fourteen-year-old kid from rural Northern California has helped fuel my passion for music and quest for originality to this day.

Thank you, Neil Peart. You will forever be in my heart, in my hands, in

my feet, and in my ears. Rest in peace.
Brian Reitzell (film composer, percussionist)

In 1981 I was a brand-new drummer. My ears were searching for inspiration. I had heard "The Spirit of Radio," but it was still a bit of an underground thing here in L.A. Seemingly out of nowhere *Moving Pictures* dropped, and like most drummers I was flabbergasted. Brave, technically challenging, musically beautiful, sonically delightful, this record changed the game. I was already a fan of Phil Collins, so odd

want. And a certain frequency range. The amount of decay is especially crucial.

MD: Tell me about that Chinese cymbal you're using. It sounds great!

Neil: I had an awful time trying to get into China cymbals. I bought an 18" pang, just looking for the Chinese sound. It had a good sound and I found myself using it for different effects. But it's almost a whispery, electronic sound. When I listen to its sound in the studio or on tape, it sounds like a phaser. It has a warm sort of sound, but it didn't have the attack I was looking for. So I got the Zildjian China-type, which had that but also a lot of sustain. Larry picked this one up at Frank's Drum Shop. It was made in China. It's a 20" with a little more bottom end to its sound.

MD: For the size of your setup I was somewhat surprised to see you using 13" hi-hats. Why 13s?

Neil: I've always used 13s. I use a certain hi-hat punctuation that doesn't work with any other size. I've tried 14s, and every time we go into the studio, our co-producer, Terry Brown, wants me to use 14" hi-hat cymbals. I've tried them. I'm an open-minded guy. But it just doesn't happen for me.

MD: Are they conventional hats?

Neil: Just conventional, regular old hi-hats. We work with a band a lot called Max Webster, and their drummer and I work very closely, listening to each other's drums. Webster told me not to change that hi-hat, because for any open hat work or any choke work, it's so quick and clean. It just wouldn't work with 14s. The decay is too slow.

MD: Are you talking about that particular pair of 13s or any 13s?

Neil: Well, any 13s for me. I've gone through about three sets of 13s in the last eight or nine years, and they've all sounded good. When I found myself to be one of the only drummers around using 13s, I tried others, but either my style developed with 13" cymbals or the 13" cymbals were an important part of my style.

MD: You are using Evans heads on your toms.

Neil: Yes. The Evans heads have a nice attack, which gives a good bite from the drums. At the same time, you never lose the note. I play with a lot of open drums, open concert toms. But my front toms and my floor toms are all closed with heads on the bottom. I never lose the note on account of that. With certain types of acoustical surroundings, open drums just lose everything, all you hear is a smack. I get that with my concert toms. I hear that with other drummers. If you're in a particularly flat hall, or if the stage area is particularly dead, it kills the note of the drums. I think it's easier to get a good sound with open drums. I've been talking to people about this lately and developing a theory. I think that perhaps, especially with miking, it's easier to get a good sound with open drums. But I think that a better sound can be achieved with closed drums. A more consistent sound. I think that over a range of hundreds of different acoustical surroundings, closed drums have a better chance of sounding good more often. That's just a theory. It depends on a number of things of course. I open up my bass drums in the studio, but I leave the toms closed.

MD: Yet for your live performance, I see you have left both heads on the bass drums. Why?

Neil: I think I get a rounder note, and a more consistent bass drum sound. And our sound man's happy with both heads on. We just have a small hole in the front head and a microphone right inside.

MD: I noticed you use a microphone under your snare drum.

Neil: Yes, I use an under-snare mike for the monitors only, which Ian doesn't use out front. I don't use the over-snare mike in the monitors, because I'm getting all of the middle I need out of the drum itself. It's the high end that gets lost in the ambient sound of the rest of the band. The high end gets lost first.

MD: What about in the studio?

Neil: In the studio sometimes both, but usually the top.

MD: In the studio, do you use one mike to catch the snare and the hi-hat, or is that done separately?

Neil: Just one mike on the snare alone, and the hi-hat has a separate mike. It's a logistical thing. We have to go for close miking. Just about everything is individually miked. There are three overheads to cover the cymbals, one separate overhead for the China-type. I have a certain set of long, tubular wind chimes that have to be heard at a particular point, so they have a mike. There's a mike for the timpani, there's two mikes for the orchestra chimes, and they also pick up the crotales. There's also a separate mike for the glockenspiel. If I want to try to inject that much subtlety into our music, the glockenspiel has to be miked closely or it won't exist. It's crucial. Miking is a science that I can't talk about with much conviction. I don't know a lot about it other than a few bits of theory I picked up in the studio. As far as live miking goes, I'm pretty ignorant, I must

---

meter wasn't new, but this was different. It felt comfortable. Every day in the bedroom, testing my mother's patience, I worked on "YYZ," "Tom Sawyer," "Red Barchetta," and "Limelight." Not sure why I needed to know these songs, but determined all the same. Then one day I was asked, almost forced, to play at my junior-high talent show. I accepted, but it's as if my classmates chose the song. It had to be "Tom Sawyer." If you can play "Tom Sawyer" then you're a pro. Never mind the gigs I was already doing. I was being put to the test. Play it I did, and the kids loved it. There is something about playing in front of your friends that can play games with your nerves.

Neil set the bar so high, it seemed or seems unreachable, but he did it with grace and humility just to give us hope. Now with a career entrenched in the progressive-rock scene, I understand why I had to know those songs. I was in school with the Professor.

Jimmy Keegan (Pattern-Seeking Animals)

During the last three and a half years, Neil faced this aggressive brain cancer bravely, philosophically, and with his customary humor, sometimes light and occasionally dark—all very characteristic of him, even given the serious situation and the odds handed to him at the time of the diagnosis and subsequent surgery. But he fought it.

His tenacious approach to life served him well during these last years, and although he primarily kept his own counsel, he retained his dignity, warmth, compassion, understanding, and generous, deeply inquisitive nature, which never deserted him. He was cogent right up until the end, and miraculously, he really had no pain—a blessing for which we were all profoundly grateful.

The outpouring of love, respect, and appreciation from every imaginable quarter for this beautiful man and extraordinary, singular talent, graced with a mind like no one I have ever met, is touching beyond words. To those that had to guard and hold onto this information closely for three and a half years, for obvious and protective reasons—his wife, Carrie, daughter, Olivia, his loving family, bandmates, friends, and colleagues—they have my undying admiration.

continues on page 25

admit. I'm just trying to get my drums to sound good to me, and then it's up to the sound man to make them sound good in the house.

MD: Could you tell me a little about your recent album, *Permanent Waves*?

Neil: There's quite a variety of things this time. We didn't have any big ideas to work on, so it's a collection of small ideas. Individual musical statements. We got into some interesting things, and some interesting constructions too. We built a whole song around a picture. We wanted to build a song around the phenomenon called Jacob's Ladder, where the rays break through the clouds. I came up with a couple of short pieces of lyrics to set the musical parts up. And we built it all musically, trying to describe it cinematically, as if our music were a film. We have a luminous sky happening and the whole stormy, gloomy atmosphere, and all of a sudden these shafts of brilliance come bursting through and we try to create that musically.

There's another song, "The Spirit of Radio." It's not about a radio station or anything, it's really about the spirit of music, when it comes down to the basic theme of it. It's about musical integrity. We wanted to get across the idea of a radio station playing a wide variety of music. "The Spirit of Radio" comes from the radio station at home called CFMY, and that's their slogan. They play all great music, from reggae to R&B to jazz to new wave, everything that's good or interesting. It's a very satisfying radio station to me. They have introduced me to a lot of new music. There are bits of reggae in the song, and one of the verses has a new wave feel to it. We tried to get across all the different forms of music. There are no divisions there. The choruses are very electronic. It's just a digital sequencer with a glockenspiel and a counter guitar riff. The verse is a standard straight-ahead Rush verse. One is new wave, a couple reggae verses, and some standard heavy riffing, and as much as we could possibly get in

there without getting redundant.

Another song, "Free Will," is a new thing for us in terms of time signatures. I mentioned before that we experiment a lot with time signatures. I get a lot of satisfaction out of working different rhythms and learning to feel comfortable.

MD: What time signatures are you using during this tune?

Neil: We work in nearly every one that I know of that's legitimate. All of the fives, sevens, nines, elevens, thirteens, and combinations thereof. There were things on the last album that were twenty-one-beat bars by the time they were completed. Because they had a seven and a six; a five and a four; or seven, six, seven, six, seven, six, five. I get a tremendous amount of satisfaction making them feel good. I don't think that you have to play in 4/4 to feel comfortable.

MD: How did you develop your understanding of those odd meters?

Neil: I remember figuring out some of Genesis's things. That was my first understanding of how time signatures were created. And I'd hear people talking about seven and five, and if they played it for me I could usually play along. But I didn't understand. I finally got to understand the principle of the common denominator. Once I understood it numerically, I found it really easy to pick up the rhythm.

Then you take on something just as a challenge and turn it into a guitar solo in 13/8 and find a way to play that comfortably and make changes. As I would change dynamically through a 4/4 section, there would be certain ways that I would move it, try to apply those same elements to a complicated concept.

I think Patrick Moraz put it best. He said, "All the technique you have in the world is still only a method of translating your emotions." So we're coming back with that acquired technique. There's a lot of truth in Moraz's statement, because now we're

finding out as we have gone through all those [that] some of them honestly were technical exercises. You have to say that sometimes you get excited about playing something just because it is a difficult thing. And certain times we would get into the technical side of it but become bored with it. Now we're finding out how to bring those technical ideas back and put them into an exciting framework. We have a song that's almost all in seven and has some alternating bars of eight, and the chorus that goes into it again is in four. It's all very natural to play. I can play through the whole song and I don't count once. The only thing I count are pauses. If I'm stopping for eight beats or something, I'll count that off with my foot. But when I'm playing, I just don't count, unless I have to for meter reasons.

This is probably a common experience, but slower things for me are the most difficult to keep in meter. If I'm playing really slow straight fours, I count that, but if I'm playing really fast in thirteen, I don't dare count, I just play it. We were talking earlier about music taking patterns as a musician. I think it does that. I have a program in my head that represents the rhythmic pattern for a thirteen, or a seven, or a five. And I can bring those out almost on command, having spent a lot of time getting familiar with them.

It's so exciting when you start to get it right the first few times and you're putting everything you have into it. That's the ultimate joy of creating. That joy is such a short-lived thing, most of the time you don't have time to enjoy it. Most times when I write a song, the moment of satisfaction is literally a matter of a few seconds. All of a sudden you see it's going to work and you're going to be happy with it, and then—*bang*—you're back into working it again. You're thinking, "How am I going to do this?" Whether it's lyrically or musically, the moment of satisfaction is very fleeting.

A Life Changed Forever

A *Modern Drummer* reader spoke for many when he penned this tribute to his hero.

Have you ever experienced a moment when you realize your life has changed? A moment that you will forever remember for the rest of your life? Something where you know, right then and there, that your life will never be the same again? A true defining moment. That is what happened when I heard my first Rush song, and the drumming of Neil Peart.

It was during the Christmas break of 1982. I was riding on a high-school bus, returning from one of my first winter track meets. This was an incredible transitional time in my young life. Having been brutally bullied from third grade on, my life was just starting to normalize in high school. For the first time I was part of a school team, and though I had yet to forge strong friendships, I was making acquaintances, and for the first time people were actually cheering for me when I ran races. This was a far cry from being jeered, or worse.

The 1980s were the age of the boom box—huge portable stereos—and we were allowed to bring them to track meets. Blasting them at the back of the bus was a sacred teenage ritual of the time.

I was sitting midway in the bus, lamenting a less than stellar performance in the JV heat of the mile, when something caught my ear. The sound was coming from the boom box owned by Paul Quandt, who was sitting with his friend Rory Martin. The two were "copiloting" the device, the largest in the high school I think, which earned them the seat of honor, i.e., the last seat on the bus. You know, where the cool kids sat.

The song was "The Camera Eye," and by the time it was over, I knew my life had somehow changed. Musically the song was unlike anything I had ever heard. It was the exact opposite of the pop songs of the day. It was over ten minutes long, contained more shifts in tempo than I could keep track of, was sung with a voice that threatened to crack the windows of the bus, and had drum rolls that seemed to move through hyperspace.

Before it ended, I had moved to the back of the bus, a location I had once feared. Somehow I knew it was okay, since I was coming to partake in the music being offered. By the time it was over, the guys (I don't remember any girls back there) were cracking jokes at my newly discovered "air drumming" skills. But this was also different. I inherently knew they were laughing with me, not at me. I also wasn't the only one air drumming that night.

This turned out to be the start of me becoming friends with upperclassmen, and put me on a path to actual friendships for the first time since moving to my mother's hometown six years earlier. Not only did the music and drums affect me, but through the years, Peart's lyrics spoke to me in a way I never thought music could.

Within a year, I would go to my first Rush concert with these people (Dave and Ron), and the love of that band would be a common bond with my college and lifelong friends. The best man at my wedding, Keith, and our friends Todd, Jay, Kevin, Pat, Ken, and more all went to Rush concerts together.

In fact, my first Rush concert was in 1984 (the *Grace Under Pressure* tour) and I never missed a tour after that, concluding with the R40 tour in 2015, Rush's last. Along the way I graduated from air drums (my mother would not allow drums in her house) to drumming magazines, catalogs, buckets, and more. When I graduated with a master's degree, my wife agreed it was time for a drumkit. Though I've never played in a band, I've introduced countless people to drums. In fact, I introduced my nephew at the ripe old age of one. Three pictures that tell the story are one of him at age one on my lap at the drums; one of him at his first Rush concert with me (*Clockwork Angels* tour), and one of him winning a statewide award for drumming during his senior year in high school. He continues to play, and lord knows he's far better than me.

Thirty-eight years ago I was discouraged and alone, but to quote another Canadian musician, Rik Emmett from Triumph (who were greatly influenced by Rush), "Music holds the secret, to know it can make you whole."* My life changed that cold, bleak winter night, and Neil Peart has touched every part of my life since then, and only in the most positive of ways.

Neil Peart died on January 7, 2020, and a small part of me died as well. I know many who feel the same. I am left with the gift of thirty-seven years of original music that continues to enrich my life to this day. And as Neil wrote so eloquently years ago…

Everyone would gather
On the twenty-fourth of May
Sitting in the sand
To watch the fireworks display
Dancing fires on the beach
Singing songs together
Though it's just a memory
*Some memories last forever***

Al Prescott
Westford, Massachusetts

* from "Hold On," by Triumph, lyrics by Rik Emmett   ** from "Lakeside Park," by Rush, lyrics by Neil Peart

April 1984

Moony, Hemingway, Simmons, And All Points Between

In his second (and longest) *MD* cover-story interview, conducted on the last day of Rush's five-concert series at Radio City Music Hall in September of 1983, Neil grapples with fame, addresses critiques of his lyrics, and embraces electronic drums.

by Scott K. Fish

Dino Safari

MD: Rereading the lyric sheet from *Signals*, it's easy to think of you as the Mark Twain of rock lyrics, writing about Huckleberry Finn or Tom Sawyer type characters.

Neil: Well, that's certainly something that I relate to strongly. I basically come from a standard background like that. I grew up in the suburbs, but at the same time, most of my relatives had farms. So every summer or holiday I'd be out at the farm.

I always had a very simple outlook on life as a response to that. When I first got into the big time, I did, and still do, find it very hard to relate to. I love playing drums and I love traveling. But I find a great deal of difficulty dealing with everything that surrounds that. Fame, for me, is embarrassing. It's not something I get arrogant about. I don't feel like people are bothering me. But at the same time, I get embarrassed if strangers walk up to me on the street who think they know me. I just get embarrassed, tense, and uncomfortable.

MD: Why?

Neil: Because it's *unreal!* But it's something that I can never hope to tell people or convince them of. They think they know me. They *don't* know me. They don't know anything about me. They're strangers. It just makes me defensive.

I like meeting people. I like people. One of my favorite subjects to think and write about is the human race. So I'm not any kind of a misanthrope—a person who hates human beings. I'm not reclusive to that extent. But I am a private person, and I'm basically shy with people I don't know, especially when I can't meet them on equal terms. If I can meet someone's friend, or even a stranger, person to person, I get a kick out of that and I enjoy it. But I feel differently when somebody comes up to me with an attitude that I'm something special, or thinks that they know something about me, or that—as I read so often in letters—"You and I have a lot in common." How do *you* know? I struggled a long time to figure out why it bothered me so much. When I first joined the band, nobody knew who I was, because I wasn't on the first album. There'd be kids hanging around backstage to see Alex and Geddy and not paying any attention to me. But still, *the situation* would make me feel uncomfortable because it's not a real relationship. It's not any kind of a situation you can base a friendship on. You can't start a friendship with somebody who thinks you're a plastic figure on some kind of pedestal.

MD: You don't think that you've changed from the kid who was on the farm?

Neil: Certainly, in that I've broadened. But I don't think that I have changed my essential nature. I still get excited by and enjoy the same things. I understand things a lot better now, I guess. Thirty years of experience gives you a greater understanding. But I don't think I've become any of the dangerous things that this situation can make you become. That's something that was a conscious effort for

all three of us. We didn't want to become rock 'n' roll clichés. We didn't want to become isolated people who would feel totally alienated from the human race. That's what the song "Limelight" is about—the alienation that fans try to force on us. People force us to protect ourselves. They force us to check into hotels under false names. They force us to have security guards to keep people away from us. That was a real shock for us, and it was a real hard thing for us to give in to.

In the first four or five years that we were on the road, if I wanted to, I'd walk out of the hotel, walk through the city to the gig, and walk in the back door. After the show was over, I'd walk out the back door and walk back to the hotel. I'd get up in the morning and go to work. Then I'd finish work and go back home, just like a normal person. I love that. I love it more because I can't do it anymore. I resent the fact that I can't do that now. It's all because of an unreality that, I guess, was started in the early days of Hollywood, where they created these people who were supposed to be demigods. Then rock 'n' roll picked up on that as a marketing tool to make musicians larger than life. It's something that I try to fight, but you can only fight it so much, because it's such an ingrained thing in society that somehow entertainers and celebrities are different from everybody else. It's something I detest. I really hate it. It's totally unnatural, it's totally unreal, it makes everyone uncomfortable, and it makes everyone alienated.

MD: Do you think that's what killed Keith Moon?

Neil: He's a bit of a special case. Jimi Hendrix might be a better example of someone who pushed and pushed and alienated so greatly. For a lot of these people it's a weakness of character that they possess. A lot of people feel uncomfortable about fame. Fortunately, when we were first starting and opening for different bands, we saw the ways that people dealt with it. There are basically two ways: You can either try to avoid it, or you can play it as a role. We saw bands play it as a role. They'd walk out after the show and say, "We love you! You're wonderful! You think I'm great? I think I'm great too!" That's the choice you have for dealing with it without going crazy.

I try to hide from it, basically. I stopped having my picture taken. I stopped being a public figure because I don't want to have a famous face. I spent all my life learning how to play drums and loving it. Having famous hands is okay, even though that carries its own set of pressures and insecurities. But having a famous face? That's nothing. I mean, what's your face? I didn't work all this time for my *face*. I don't think about writing songs for the sake of my *face*. And I didn't spend the last seventeen or eighteen years playing drums to make my *face* famous. I resent that whole mentality.

I remember saying out loud one day, "I hate being famous." That was the crux. Yes, you want to be successful in any profession, but take professional architects or doctors. They

don't have thousands of people chasing them around all the time and people they don't know running up to them on the street. Yes, you want to be successful for the sake of independence. There was a point we reached that was successful enough for the record companies to leave us alone because we were selling enough records. And there's a certain balance you reach when all of these things become equal. And that's wonderful; that's a great period.

But when it goes beyond that, people expect and demand so much of you because you're not human anymore. "What do you mean you don't feel good today?" It's so frustrating. Maybe eight days out of ten you don't mind meeting people and signing autographs. But maybe one night you don't want to deal with strangers, you don't want to see people, or you feel sick. You're physically sick and you're only doing the gig because you're a professional. You're only going to the gig to do the job. Period. Do you think people understand that? No. If you come out and say, "I don't feel well. Please leave me alone," they react with, "Oh, wow. Mr. Bigshot. Mr. Big Star. You're too good to deal with us." I just don't understand that. I don't have that alienation from my side. I still get a pleasure out of answering letters from people. It's a thing I can do on *my* time, on *my* terms, and I can feel good about it. When I'm home I'll write fifteen or twenty postcards usually, and answer the mail, which I mostly get forwarded from *Modern Drummer*. It's a positive thing on both sides. I feel good about it, and the person who receives it is going to feel good about it.

In England, where life is even more narrow and circumscribed than here, and those people have nothing to live for but their favorite group, you can't even open the curtains in your hotel room. You cannot walk out of the hotel. I wouldn't dream of going for a walk in the afternoon because there'll be fifty people outside the hotel. If you open your curtains, there'll be people staring in at you—shamelessly staring into your life. And that's the kind of thing

that infuriates me.

MD: Was there ever a time where you were at a crossroads of pursuing either your writing or your music?

Neil: I verge on that from time to time right now. I started as a lyricist totally by accident. I'd literally written two songs just for fun before I joined this band. When I joined Rush, it was actually my predecessor who had written most of the lyrics in the past. Neither Geddy nor Alex was very interested in doing it. I thought, "Well, I've always been interested in words and reading and so on. I'll give it a shot." I did a couple of things that the guys liked, so it encouraged me to keep going. Now I really enjoy it and get a lot of fulfillment out of it.

Over the years I've developed a stronger and stronger interest in prose writing. I've pushed myself as a lyricist, just as I did as a drummer, to constantly explore new areas and use different constructions, rhyming patterns, and rhythms. There's a lot really in common between being a lyricist and being a drummer. You're dealing with mathematical rhythms and phrasing, and you can use the same freedoms of stretching bar lengths. All of that comes into play in writing lyrics. It's a thing that I still enjoy doing very much. But I have found myself a bit constricted by verse. Lyrics, or any kind of versified poetry, is very concentrated. You have to take things, filter them down, and filter them down. Every word has to be of very strong value. The better I've gotten, the fewer words I use, because those words become of greater value. I've seen that reflected in the best of the modern prose writers too—specifically the American writers of the '20s and the '30s.

My favorites of that era are, first, Theodore Dreiser and Sherwood Anderson, and then F. Scott Fitzgerald and William Faulkner. Hemingway is one of my very favorites, and I like John Steinbeck and John Dos Passos. It's the golden age of literature, I think, as recognized by most people. If it's not, it certainly is by me. That's what I respond to; I would really like to emulate that someday as a prose writer. But I realize that, as long as I'm in Rush, Rush is the first commitment. There's no way that I can split that 100 percent commitment.

I've tried to devote a week or two every year purely to being a writer. That's when I've done some of the articles for *Modern Drummer*. I've also worked on short stories and started on theoretical novels and so on, just to see what I'd like to do and to see what I do best. I've done enough now to know that I would like to give it a stab. And if I could complete one good short story, I'd feel like a real writer. But to do a novel or a series of short stories takes a 100 percent commitment, and I don't want to compromise what I'm doing as a musician by any means.

But at a certain point as a musician you reach the law of diminishing returns. To me, improvement has always been the measurement of how well I'm doing. At the end of

every tour I can say, "Okay, I've learned this and this specific rhythmic idea, and I've improved this much." Then we do an album and that's like final exams. A record defines you at your absolute best. With everything that you can do technically, the studio can represent you at a better-than-human perfection. So for me, on the tour following an album, I'm trying to live up to *that* set of standards. And every night I go onstage trying to play every song as good as it is on the record. That's just a totally involved commitment.

But with the law of diminishing returns, I've gotten to the point now where my level of improvement has slowed down. It was easy when we first got together. We weren't that good, and *I* wasn't that good. So it was easy for us to improve, and we improved by leaps and bounds. Every album was a major step in terms of progressing as a band and as individual musicians. We've gotten to the point now—no false humility or arrogance—where we are pretty good as musicians, and we've gotten good at writing songs and interpreting them. We can take a particular mood or emotion that we want to express, and we have enough technique, empathy, and pathos now that we can do it. I find that at the end of the tour now, where I used to have five or six new rhythmic areas that I would explore during that tour, now I might have one or two. And I might only learn one or two new things because of that law of diminishing returns. So it has become a little less fulfilling in terms of progression.

I'm still very satisfied when I walk offstage thinking that I played well. And I'm still very unhappy and frustrated when I walk offstage thinking that I haven't played well. But the progression isn't as vast now. Consequently, the gratification isn't as immediate, and it isn't as constantly renewing. So I think there will come a time when I'm as good as I can ever be and I'll have to say, "Okay, I can live on this for a while"—like a lot of musicians do. They work themselves up to a certain level and then they survive on that level for as long as they can. I don't think I would work that way because I have another goal. Writing has become another goal for me. I can measure my improvement in writing as I used to be able to do with drumming five or six years ago, and that's exciting. I get that buzz from writing now that drumming has always provided me with. So there's a bit of a conflict now, even though my commitment is really 100 percent as a musician. But in the back of my mind there's a future goal: I really want to, one day, write just one good short story.

MD: What would you like to write about?

Neil: I want to write about being a musician, because it's never been done. People outside music, who are good writers, have tried to write about it. But because they are writers and not musicians, they don't really understand the essential mentality of it and the gears that make it move. They don't know what it's like to really be a musician. So I would like someday to refine my ability and technique as a writer to be able to express what it's like to be a musician. I would like to write about being a young musician playing at a high school dance, and I would like to write about a really successful musician in the middle of a tour at this level. It's a hard thing to be able to find a way to write about that in a literary sense. I don't want to write popular "pop" stories as a musician. I want to be really great at it. I want to reconcile my experience. When you start, the only thing to write about is what you know. Then, as your technique develops, you can try to write about something you don't know anything about.

If people could understand what it's like to be a musician—if they would understand that a musician is someone who gets up in the morning, goes to work, finishes work, and goes home—it would get rid of that alienation. There's that elemental thing. I've done a lot of other jobs. I wasn't born with a silver spoon in my mouth, and I didn't become a professional musician overnight. When I was eighteen, I went to England with musical motivations and goals. But when you go out into the big world, as any adult knows, you're

musician necessarily, because there are other things that I can do, and other things that are satisfying to do. Music is something that I would never stop doing. I'm sure I'll never stop playing drums. But at a certain period in my life it will not be the focus. It'll be a hobby. And in some ways it's a nicer thing to play drums for the *joy* of it rather than because you're *obliged* to.

Let's face it: Out of a tour of 150 or 200 shows, not every one of those is going to be *exactly* where I want to be that night. There have been times where I've been onstage thinking, "I'd rather be anywhere in the world than here," and other times when I've been sitting onstage saying, "I'd rather be here than anywhere else." There are extremes. Again, as with any job, some days you like it and some days you hate it. That's another thing people don't understand. They think it's always a wonderful joy, everything is looked after for you, you don't have to worry about a single thing, and it must be wonderful to sit in front of people who love you. It just doesn't work that way. No one's life is perfect. There is no paradise.

> "I like meeting people. One of my favorite subjects to think and write about is the human race. But I am a private person, and I'm basically shy with people I don't know, especially when I can't meet them on equal terms."

in for a lot of disillusionment. So while I was there I did a lot of other things to get bread in my mouth. When I came back from there, I was disillusioned basically by the music "business." I decided that I would be a semi-pro musician for my own entertainment, would play the music that I liked to play, and wouldn't count on it to make my living. I did other jobs and worked at other things, so that I wouldn't have to compromise what I liked to do as a drummer.

There's a choice there. If you're a musician you can say, "I don't care what I have to do. I'm going to make my living as a musician." Therefore you'll be happy to play in any kind of band as long as you're playing your instrument. I know musicians like that, and I don't knock it. There are two different kinds of personalities at work there. I know people who want to be session musicians because they don't like to travel. They like to stay at home, and they like the familiarity and the security of that. So consequently, yes, that's the perfect place for them to be.

Conversely, there are people who think that it's incumbent upon them as a matter of pride to make their living as musicians. To me, it's a matter of pride to play the music I love. That's the essence of it. So I never felt that it was a compromise to have a day job in order to pay my bills, and at night, to work in a bar band that played the music I liked to play or just to put a band together in my spare time that played music I liked. I don't care about being a professional

I worry about a lot of things. I carry the world on my shoulders sometimes. It's almost like the joke Woody Allen made in *Annie Hall*: "As long as I know there's somebody in the world suffering, I can't be happy." It's true. There's a compassion in that. Sometimes I think about a city like New York. There's an exciting, glamorous aspect to New York, and there's a tremendously sordid, horribly brutal, disgustingly inhuman side to it too. And when I go by those buildings I think, "Okay. Here's a building where 500 people live or work. What are their lives like?" They come here every single morning and fight their way through the war of rush hour. They go to that little office and do meaningless things all day. Then they fight their way back home again at night and watch TV or go to a bar and get drunk. Then they come back the next morning. You have to respond to that. You have to be compassionate about that. You have to say that time, as a moving, circular thing, sometimes runs people down and ruins people's lives.

One of the new songs that we've done, "Between the Wheels," says, "The wheels can take you around/or the wheels can cut you down." There are those two things. A lot of people *aren't* run down by time, and they aren't pushed by time. They're just in the middle. Everything rolls right by them.

MD: But isn't that their choice?

Neil: Well, it'd be nice to think so. If you take a hard-line,

libertarian mentality about it—yeah. You could say that. But a lot of times it's circumstances, or whatever intangible thing you call it. Fate. There's a thing I'm fond of quoting that's been attributed to Ernest Hemingway, although I've never been able to nail it down, and I've read all his books. "There are no failures of talent, only failures of character." It refutes that statement, "There are a thousand good musicians in the world and you just happened to get lucky" or, "There are probably drummers in India who are better than you, but because they're in India, they'll never get anywhere."

With a lot of the great musicians that I know who didn't get anywhere, there's a reason why. Either they can't live with themselves, or no other musician can stand to work with them. It's a flaw of character. It's not the fact that they're not talented. They're great. They're emotive, they move people, and they have everything that great musicians need to have. But nobody can stand to live with them in the way that a professional musician has to live with other musicians. It's a tremendously insular, familial kind of world.

MD: If they realized the character flaw, could they change it?

Neil: Do you think that's possible if someone has a little pool of poison in their mind that causes them to take it out on someone else whenever they're feeling a little insecure?

MD: I think they could do it. It's more difficult for some than for others.

Neil: There's always a price to pay, too. I have a little poison pit like that: temper. When I was a teenager, I recognized that I had a bad temper, and set out consciously to control it and keep it back. Consequently, yes, I do that. When I get angry, I don't yell at people. I don't freak out. But I pay for that inside. I carry that with me, and I get knots of tension through the course of a tour—through the course of any situation where I have to deal with people on a daily basis and there's constant interaction. And it hurts me. It makes me uncomfortable where I don't need to be uncomfortable. It makes me nervous when I don't need to be nervous. But I probably wouldn't have been together with these two guys for nine years if I hadn't learned to control that. You can't just build the foundation for the kind of relationship that we have, based upon swearing at each other. You have to base it on respect, and you have to maintain that respect. You can never afford to lose control at somebody. You might feel remorse for it and say, "I'm sorry I did that." It doesn't matter. It's always there.

Our band has a very special relationship. I see a lot of other bands at our level, and they literally are never together except when they have to be. They'll even be recording an album and never all be in the studio at the same time. And when they're on the road, they don't travel together. They have different dressing rooms. I couldn't go on in a relationship like that. We have an equal share in everything. We collaborate on the arrangements. If I write something

they don't like, they say so. If I can fix it so they'll like it—fine. If I can't, I keep it in my notebook.

You have to open yourself up. When I bring a new idea to those guys, it's a very vulnerable thing. I'm a bit tense about it because I'm baring my soul. "Here's something I worked on and believe in. What do you guys think?" If they like it—great. But if they have doubts of any kind, there's a bit of insecurity and vulnerability involved there. It's incumbent upon them—or me in the opposite circumstance—to be very careful about that. You have to say, "There's something about this that doesn't ring true." It's important to be *specific* too. They can say, "I like what you're trying to say here, but a couple of lines are a little bit obscure or could mislead people. A cynical person could read something totally different into it." I have to respond to that and say, "Yeah, that's true," and I go back to the drawing board. There's a give and take that's really critical to us. We're very rare in that respect.

Almost every successful band you can think of has *one* person. That person either writes all the songs, or if that isn't admitted and they say that the songs are written by the whole band, there's one member who really is the original essence of that band. That person gives them their character, direction, and originality. That's got to be really hard to live with. That's where all these solo albums, musical differences, and euphemisms of modern rock 'n' roll come about—because of that ego conflict of, "I'm not happy to be *just* a guitar player, drummer, or whatever. I want to be *the* main one."

So the democracy that we've been fortunate enough to have is a real democracy in that sense. Majority does rule, but it's always the majority of interested parties. It's never one person. It's always a congruence of different people's ideas. Then you can say, "No, that's not a good idea," throw it away, and no one's feelings are hurt. Everyone has agreed upon it. Everyone has given something to it, and everybody agrees that it's no good. That's fine. But when one member brings something in and everybody else is negative about it, that causes tremendous conflicts. In a lot of bands today, the problem is that they all don't have equal abilities or equal input.

MD: And yet in some bands the whole is greater than the parts.

Neil: The synergistic idea—that's certainly true of us. The important thing about that, again, is that we are all equal as musicians. We all make the same number of mistakes. We've all grown at the same pace. We've all been very, very concerned about progressing. We all want it to get better and better.

Fortunately we all get better at the same pace. I've been in other bands where everybody *wanted* to get better, but half the band was getting better a lot faster than the other half.

That causes a tremendous rift. We've all had an equal input in the writing and in the day-to-day business of running the band, and we've all improved at the same rate. But we make enough mistakes to be human—enough that we can be equal, and we can all laugh about it. That's important because I get embarrassed when I make a mistake. I hate making mistakes. It's the worst thing. When I make one, I can't laugh about it immediately. At first it's like, "Oh, shit." And then I have to try to get myself back into the flow and try not to over concentrate, because that makes you

overcompensate, and that just makes you make four or five *more* mistakes.

When we walk onstage, we try to just set the flow. The thing should just flow out of you in a natural sort of way. In the middle of that, if I do something by accident—like a drumstick breaking at the wrong time, which puts me in the wrong place—that just makes me uneasy and embarrassed. Then suddenly I do another stupid thing and then another stupid thing. Then it's like, "Get me away from here!" But in the normal course of things, each of us has breakdowns. And it's not hard for any of us to admit it, because it's not always the same guy. It's not always me saying, "Oh, I made a stupid mistake again. Sorry, guys. Let me play again tomorrow night and I'll try to do better." It's important that none of us feel downgraded by it. That equality is very important.
MD: A lot of your lyrics are said by many to be inspired by Ayn Rand.

Neil: Yeah, that's sort of a convenient post to latch on. It's like the science fiction label. I'm not as big an Ayn Rand fan as I'm made out to be. Our album *2112* happened to be based around, in a coincidental way, the circumstances of one of her stories. I gave due credit to that. I realized that, as our story progressed about the rediscovery of creative music in the future, her story happened to be about the rediscovery of electricity in some totalitarian future. I didn't set out to adapt that story into a musical format. But the story of *2112* developed, and *then* I realized that it paralleled the circumstances of her story.

So it's an easy thing for people to fix on. The song "Science Fiction" happened to be set in the future. I happened to have done two or three other pieces that were set in the future. Out of all the pieces we've written and out of the ten albums we've made, perhaps a total of two and a half albums have had to do with the future or anything that could be called science fiction. If people aren't really into your music, but they're forced to write about it, then they pick up on what they can get easily: superficially. It's the whole labeling aspect that any number of musicians of whatever school have complained about.
MD: In Harry Shapiro's book *A-Z of Rock Drummers*, he alluded to many of your lyrics as being "fascist."
Neil: I've never written anything political. I'm an apolitical person really. If I'm interested in anything, I'm interested in the philosophies that bring about those political schools of

thought. I don't write about politics. Sometimes I write about philosophy. Ayn Rand, for instance, has been categorized as being a fascist writer. Consequently, if I admit any influence from her....

John Dos Passos was known as a radical left-wing writer in the '20s. "The Camera Eye" was directly influenced by him. But at the same time, nobody calls me a Communist. I'm influenced by these people because they're great writers, not because of their politics. I am an Individualist. I believe in the greatness of individual people. That's not anti-populist or anti-human. When the lights come on behind us and I look out at the audience and see all those little circles, each of those circles is a person. Each person is a story. They have circumstances surrounding their lives that can never be repeated.

In the song "Entre Nous," the introduction says, "We are secrets to each other/Each one's life a novel that no one else has read." That's the essence of it, really. All those people have a whole novel about their lives—the time they were born, how they grew up, what they did and what they wanted to do, their relationships with other people, their romances and marriages—all those things. And they *are* individuals. That's what I respond to. They're not a mob. They're not a crowd. They're not some lower class of degenerates. They're individuals.

I'm always playing for an individual. I don't play for the crowd—for some faceless ideal of commerciality of some lowest common denominator. It's a person up there every night, who knows everything I'm supposed to do. If I don't do it, that person knows it. It's like I have a judge on my shoulder, in the old Anglo-Saxon way, who watches everything I play. If I play it right, my judge says, "Not bad." And if I play it wrong, it's, "You jerk." That individual is the person I play for every night.

If you play for a crowd, then you pander, basically, to a mentality or a lowest common denominator. You basically say, "If I play something simple but make it look good, then these people are going to be impressed. We'll shoot off a bunch of pots and wear flashy outfits and all the other stuff." That's fascism, basically. The rest of the world is a mob and you're the only individual. But if you have the values of any decent musician, you could never play for "a mob." Then you don't become a musician. You become some kind of entertainment marketing director. It's not musicianship anymore.

MD: How do you feel about the kids who come to your concerts wasted?

Neil: Well, it's sad. I don't know. You can never really understand the reasons for it. I can't say that I could sit with those people and necessarily carry on a conversation. It's a sad thing.

MD: You don't feel that your music contributes to that?

Neil: No, I don't think I can take that responsibility. I have the responsibility subsequent to that judge on my shoulder. If I walk offstage thinking that I haven't pleased that objective standard, I feel bad. If I walk offstage feeling that I haven't played very well or didn't really live up to any set of standards, then I feel very badly indeed. On the other hand, regardless of whether the whole audience is wiped out of their minds, if I go on and know that I'm really living up to my own standards and playing to the standards I go onstage with every night, then I feel good about it. I can't judge by the fact that somebody in front of me is really drunk, but thinks it's great. You can't go by that.

MD: When a person listens to your albums or attends your concerts, do you have an ideal that you hope they can walk away with?

Neil: Sure. You have the ideal listener. The person I play for every night is *that* person. We make a record for the person who buys it, goes home, puts on headphones, sits there with the lyric sheet, follows along with every word and hears every note that we do, understands what we're trying to do, and understands whether we've achieved it or not. Yes, there is an ideal listener who probably doesn't really exist. But he or she is the person that you aim for.

It ties exactly back to the standard we aim for. I think it does have a subliminal effect on people. The fact that we are so well regarded as a live band has to reflect that set of standards. Regardless of whether we're playing in Igor, Indiana, or if we're playing at Radio City Music Hall, the same amount goes into that show every night. I walk onstage with the same mentality and the same urge to really do well. It's a fundamental truth about us, and I think it has to do with the fact that a lot of people consider Rush first and foremost a live band. That's wonderful. The essence of a musician is a live performer—a person playing an instrument onstage.

When you make a record, it represents only one performance. But when you try to duplicate that performance, that can be hundreds and hundreds of times. Some of the songs that we're playing now are five, six, seven, eight, and nine years old. You have to bring something fresh to them every year. And you have to play that with true conviction every night. We've dropped songs that were very popular and that people expected us to play forever. There comes a day when we have to say, "We have nothing to say with this song anymore. We can't play it with conviction." Otherwise it becomes like a joke—like we're taking advantage of people or we're pandering to them. We can't do that, so we drop the song. And we take a lot of flak for it. People say, "Well, why didn't they play more *old* songs?" It's because we can't do that honestly. We can't play "Fly by Night" or "Working Man" anymore with any conviction.

There are some songs that do survive. They are challenging enough or self-representative enough that we can say,

"Yes, that song still represents how we feel as musicians, as people, and we're still proud and happy to play that." But there are other things that you grow out of. There are things on our last album that we've grown out of already and we'll never play again. It stands to reason that there are things we did six or seven years ago that are still relevant to us and we still get joy out of playing. Consequently, the audience gets pleasure out of it. So there's both truth and beauty there. And that's the important thing. You can't say, "Well, these people have been listening to this song for eight years and they expect you to play it. You've *got* to play it." That's a lot of people's mentality. We get that pressure, sometimes, directed right at us. "Why didn't you play that song?" Because we can't *honestly* play it for you anymore. If we played it, it would be a lie. And you don't want us to lie to you. We don't lie to our audience on any level. When we make our records or play in concert, that same set of standards comes to the stage with us. We're not there to play a role.

MD: You've mentioned Keith Moon, Michael Giles, and Bill Bruford as influences. Have you ever met any of those people?

Neil: No, actually I never met any of my real drumming idols.

MD: If you had the opportunity to sit down and speak with them, what would you ask them about? Would you ask about equipment?

Neil: Probably not. I might discuss it with somebody I work with on a regular basis, such as the drummer from a band that we tour with. Drummers automatically seem to have some kind of affinity for each other, so we might talk about equipment and technical things, given an already existing personal relationship. But if I met another drummer I respected, we'd probably talk about books, movies, sailing, or any point of interest that we had in common, because at a certain point, especially when you do become well known, you get tired of it. There was a time when I was happy to sit and talk about drums all day and all night. But you can only say the same thing so many times.

When you already have a friendly relationship with someone, you wouldn't talk about the prosaic everydayness of, "Yes, I use a Clear Dot Remo head on my snare." You'd talk about, "Well, how do you think it would affect my snare sound if I used a different type of head?" You'd talk about *theoretical* things, or you'd talk about other things. One of my very best friends is a drummer who's very classically schooled, and also grew up in Africa, so he has that whole different input on things. He can give me a whole different insight, and we'll talk about that in theory. We don't talk about what kind of pedals we use, but we'll say, "Well, I've been trying *this* lately and it didn't really work for me. You try it and see what you think." Equipment will become a fact of everyday life, like dishwashing detergent or car wax.

There was a time, like I said, when I'd always be glad to talk to a drummer anytime. But you can only hear so many times, "Hi, I'm a drummer like you." And from the way people say it, you're supposed to be impressed by that and you're supposed to welcome them into your life—invite them home for supper and all that—just because they're drummers.

MD: I think statistics have shown that there are three million drummers.

Neil: There you go. I'm supposed to have a brotherly affinity with three million people. And that ties in perfectly with the fact that I'm also supposed to have some kind of affinity with the two million people who buy our records.

A lot of people think that the equipment is an integral part of the style, when really the equipment is only an expression. It's not an influence. It doesn't affect the way I play. It's an expression of the way I play. I choose my drums and equipment because of a vision I have inside—because of a goal I'm trying to achieve in expression. It's not what kind of hammers and nails you use; it's the vision you have of the perfect thing you want to build *with* those tools. I can't imagine that carpenters spend much time talking about different hammers and nails, or that doctors talk about scalpels, or auto mechanics talk about different wrenches. That's got to be pretty limited. I have to think that, when auto mechanics get together, they're more interested in the completed car.

That's an essential analogy that really holds water. If I met one of those drummers, we might talk about reggae music. I'm not interested in becoming a reggae drummer by any means, but it happens to be a rhythmic area that I respond to strongly. If I met another drummer who said, "I love Bob Marley, Jimmy Cliff, and Third World," then we'd have something to talk about right there. We wouldn't talk about what kind of snare stand is the strongest.

I've just come to understand that recently because equipment was always very interesting. I've always had an

REMEMBERING NEIL

continued from page 13

Apart from his deeply gifted, genius talent and prolific output, which he brilliantly displayed through music, lyric, and prose writing, and that staggering storehouse of knowledge across an array of subjects in multiple fields, he remained a kind, gentle, considerate, and modest soul and a consummate gentleman. I think I speak for all, known and unknown to him, to say he will be deeply missed, eternally loved, appreciated, and remembered for his many invaluable contributions to music, art, and the written word. Those will be forever celebrated.

Thank you, my dear friend, for passing this way. We are all richer for your presence and light in our lives.
Doane Perry

It's extremely hard to put into words exactly how much Neil Peart meant to me as a fan, a drummer, and lastly a friend. It's even harder now, as I write this on the heels of yet another stellar drummer, major NP fan, and good friend Sean Reinert's passing, one week after Neil's. So this piece is written also with Sean in mind, because Sean influenced tons of up-and-coming metal drummers, the way Neil touched us as players a few decades prior. And both men were stellar human beings and kind souls who I miss very much as I type this, trying to hold the tears back.

Neil Peart is my favorite drummer and always will be, and my first-ever contact with him was when I wrote him a fan letter in care of *Modern Drummer* back in 1985, which was a kind of secret way to contact the ever elusive NP that some of us heard about as kids in the '80s. I was lucky; he got my letter and returned a postcard packed with all the answers to my questions, and he wished me "all the best." The fifteen-year-old kid sat in his driveway—actually it's still my driveway—looking at "The Golden Ticket": "Oh, I can't wait to show all the drummers in band tomorrow," I gloated, and boy did I. That postcard sat on my dresser for about three years before I went off to Berklee, and I sealed it in a photo album for preservation.

Many years later, after I became a "known" drummer, I had mentioned to drum tech Lorne Wheaton at a

continues on page 26

affinity for drums as a physical thing—the combination of circles and lines, the way drums look, the way they're made. There is something about that that's good. I've always been really interested in hardware. I try to always investigate new things, and I try to be interested in new equipment.

MD: What was your role in the creation of Tama Artstar drums?

Neil: Basically, when we were mixing our live album, we had a lot of spare time. I don't like just sitting around. They had an old set of Hayman drums sitting around the studio. I thought, "I'm going to restore those." I took them all to pieces, cleaned all the crud off, and put them back together, got new heads for them and tuned them. Once I had restored them, we recorded a couple of demos, and they just sounded so great. They had so much pure tonality. I put the heads on them that I normally use, and I tuned them the way I normally tune. The only difference was that the shells were very thin. I equated that with violins or guitars. It's the thinness and consistency of the wood that gives the character of the sound, its resonance and the true quality of a classical instrument.

I started thinking about why drums keep getting thicker. Why does it give you status to say, "I have 12-ply drums"? That was just people barking up a tree. It was saying that more is better—that thicker is better. That's wrong. When you have a resonant acoustical instrument, the wood has to resonate. Therefore, the thicker and denser it is, the less it's going to resonate. So I wanted to get a thinner-shelled drum. I knew Tama didn't make one, so I talked to Neal Graham at the Percussion Center. He's kind of my equipment mentor as far as that goes. I talked to him about my theory that thin drums will sound better. We talked about it a bit and I thought, "Well, I could go to Gretsch or the other traditional companies that still make thinner shells." Neal said, "Well, I'll talk to Tama and see what they'll do." They were cooperative enough to make me a 4-ply version of their normal 6-ply set,

and they asked me to keep quiet about it. They did have the quality I was looking for. They were more resonant, and their voice was throatier somehow. "Voice" is the operative word. They had more of a voice; they were more expressive.

I expressed my gratitude to Neal Graham, talked to Ken Hoshino at Tama, and said, "These are great—just what I was looking for. You really should consider making them for jazz players. The jazz purists have stuck with Gretsch and the old-style thinner shells for that reason. They want that. They don't want big, thick, heavy, dead-sounding drums." We talked back and forth a bit, and then I heard that they were going to market them as a series of special shells. Ken Hoshino brought me the basic layout of that ad with the picture. The copy hadn't been written. He asked, "What do you think we should put there?" I said, "I've run into problems with that with other companies. I've given them a quote to work from, and they misquote it or twist it around to make it a little more favorable. This time I'll write it myself." I thought I'd try writing an advertisement about *why* I wanted this kind of drum, why I think they're great and how it all came about. They were glad to have me do it, I guess.

One of the statements I made in that ad copy was about listening to old big band drummers and the old records, where they were basically recorded with only one microphone. That microphone was also picking up the whole rhythm section and probably half of the horns. There is a character to those drums. You can hear when they hit it hard, as opposed to when they hit it quietly. You can hear the energy in there. With modern close miking and noise gating, you lose all that. The difference between me hitting my snare drum quietly and whacking it to death in the studio gets minimized. The dynamics get lost and it's frustrating. I hear my drums a certain way. It's the sound I'm trying to get on records. It never seems to be captured by microphones regardless of different techniques we've tried.

On *Moving Pictures*, I had a PZM microphone taped to my

REMEMBERING NEIL
continued from page 25

NAMM party in 2006 or 2007 that I would really love to meet his boss, if it was at all possible, and he told me, "Next time we come through, text me. Don't worry, he knows who you are." "What! Neil knows who I am?" "Yes, dude, trust me, he knows who you are!" I was floating on air just knowing the fact that maybe I might have been on his radar. The next time Rush came through town, thanks to Lorne and Rob and Paul from Hudson Music, I was in the dressing room,

with my wife, shaking hands with "The Professor." (Here come those tears….)

It was the moment I'd waited my entire life for. Mike Portnoy had told me a few hours prior, "Don't talk about drums unless he does first," but I knew this very important tidbit of info going into the meeting. So did Neil talk about drums? Not only did he talk about drums, he showed me what he was working on with Peter Erskine at the time on his practice kit. This is when he's supposed to be warming up, but no, he's taking that precious time before his show to show me what he's working on. Blew my mind, still

does just talking about it. After that I pulled out my Slingerland Artist model snare for him to sign, and he goes, "I used to play one just like this." "Yes, sir, I know, that's why I have one!"

It was one of the greatest days of my life, and every tour after that he always took care of me with tickets and passes for any show I could make it to. Even when I was on the road, he would extend the invite down to my wife and family. I was now in the "inner circle."

On another tour, we sat in his dressing room discussing his book *Road Show* and the death of Dimebag

Darrell from Pantera, whom he writes about in that book. Neil never knew that I was on that tour with Dime and Vinnie up until a day prior to the shooting, and he knew how much talking about this was kind of upsetting to me, because obviously he knew I might not be sitting there talking to him if that had happened a day or two prior. He put his giant hand on my shoulder and said, "Let's talk about something else." He knew he'd struck a nerve, and he wanted our meeting to be a happy one. I told him I was very happy he wrote about my friend, and I told him how much his

Dino Safari

chest to try to capture *my* perspective of the drumset. Yes, it added to it and it helped to apply that special dynamic that I hear. But still, I've never heard my drums recorded the way I hear them.

MD: Did you change the miking techniques in the studio when you used the Artstar drums?

Neil: No. In the studio we try to cover all angles. We use close miking, but usually there are also several different types of ambient miking. When it comes down to the mixing stage,

we'll try different combinations of the close miking and a bit of the different ambiences from all of those other mics.

MD: Have you ever tried no close miking—just room mics?

Neil: We've done that for special effects. On one of our earlier albums, there was a part that was just drums. We used one microphone about thirty feet away from the drumset. It sounded great, but we couldn't blend it with other instruments. It's so ambient and so big sounding that there was no room for anything else. In that case, it was

friendship meant to me. I never once said to him, "Dude, you're my favorite drummer." I didn't have to. When we left him to do his warm-ups, I thanked him as usual, went to shake his hand, and then he brought me in for the "Bubba hug."

The last time I spoke with him was over the summer. Michael (Neil's longtime righthand man) had called me to ask a few questions about something, and I said, "Hey, is Bubba with you?" and he goes, "Yeah. he's in the other room." I just told him, "Give him a hug for me." A few minutes later the text "big hug back" came in. That's

how I want to remember my hero—not because he was one of the greatest ever to pick up sticks, but because he was a genuine, awesome guy.
Jason Bittner (Overkill, Shadows Fall)

There are two events in my life that led me to choose drumming as a career. First, seeing Gregg Bissonette give a drum clinic in January of 1989, and second, seeing Rush on the *Presto* tour on June 22, 1990. I will never forget the feeling that these two events gave me at twelve and fourteen years old. They were both overwhelming experiences, and I

remember after both saying to myself, "That's it. I want to do that for the rest of my life. I want to be those guys." The Rush show sealed the deal for me.

I became completely obsessed with Rush, learning every note of every tape, wallpapering my room with posters, getting all of the tour books, pins, and patches, constantly writing down all of the albums in chronological order anywhere I could—usually on friends' notebooks. To me there is absolutely nothing in the world like seeing them live. (I got into Frank Zappa around the same time, but sadly, was never able to see

him live.) I was lucky enough to see Rush live twenty-four times, and each one was a truly magical experience. I get goosebumps even thinking about going to see them.

Like so many others, Neil's influence runs deep to the core of who I am. I would not have become a professional musician if it were not for Neil's profound influence on me. Which means I would not have gone to Indiana University, where I studied music. Which means I would not have met my wife, possibly not become a father, and probably not live in Los Angeles. My life revolved around Rush

continues on page 28

okay because it was just drums; the other instruments were *incidental* to the drums. But there's just no way, when you create that big of a sound, that you can squeeze other things in there as well and still maintain the integrity of that sound.

It's generally acknowledged that drums are the hardest thing in the world to record. That's almost a cliché by this point, but it's true. It's so hard to get drums to sound like they really sound.

MD: Are there any drummers you've heard on record where you've thought, "I wish my drums could sound like that"?

Neil: No. I think that we have achieved as good as what I've ever heard from anybody else. But that doesn't mean that it's the ultimate. On *Moving Pictures* or *Signals*, at its best, the drum sound is as good as I've ever heard anywhere, given the character. If you have a dinky little guitar and keyboards and stuff, and nothing to interfere with the drum sound, then yeah, the drums sound more present. But then it's just a matter of what else you're including them with.

See, my drums always sound wonderful on basic tracks. When they're first recorded and there's just bass there and a guide guitar, the drums sound incredible. But as soon as you start putting in a big guitar sound, a big keyboard sound, a big vocal sound, and try to make everything work together, which obviously is the most important thing…. See, the crucial, number-one point is not to make the *drums* sound good. It's to make *everything* sound good. When it comes to that point, the sound gets lost.

MD: Why?

Neil: Because there are so many things fighting for the same space. In modern music, a big guitar sound covers a broad frequency range, from the high end to the very bottom. Consequently, a good guitar sound will mask all of that from the drum sound. It's a bit of a struggle, really. When you hear a band that has a small guitar sound or a narrow keyboard wash over the top of the drums, then yes, the drums can speak through, perhaps closer to their true representation.

MD: Are you still using your Slingerland wood snare with the Artstar drums?

Neil: Yeah. It's ironic, because it's not even the top-of-the-line Slingerland. It's their second one down. I don't know what it's called. I bought it secondhand for sixty dollars. It was the first wooden snare I ever owned. I'd always used metal ones before that and had never been totally satisfied. Then we picked up this wooden snare and it was perfect. It was *the one*. Then I thought, "Well, if this isn't even the top-of-the-line wooden one, I must be able to get something better." So I got the top-of-the-line wooden Slingerland, and I've tried several of the wooden Tama ones. I even have the twin to that sixty-dollar snare behind me for the other kit. Everything's identical, but it just doesn't sound the same.

I think somebody who had this snare before me did a modification on the bearing edge of the snare side. Someone filed the bearing edge where the snares go across. It's murder on snare heads because it makes the tension very uneven, but the snare never chokes. I can play it however delicately or however hard, and it will never choke.

MD: Have you ever had Tama try to duplicate that drum?

Neil: No. Basically I've just tried what Tama makes. They either sound good loud or they sound good soft. None of them have the versatility that my snare has. I haven't pursued it that much because my snare makes me happy as it is. I'm not looking for something better, really.

MD: Is the inside of the snare Vibrafibed?

Neil: No. I've never fooled around with it. I was even afraid to get it painted. For a long time it was copper colored. When I had the black drums or even when I had the rosewood Tamas, it didn't matter so much. It looked okay. When I got the red drums, the copper started to look a bit tacky, but I was even afraid to get it painted because disassembling it, painting it, and putting it back together might have affected it.

I think Slingerland probably still makes that snare. I still

REMEMBERING NEIL
continued from page 27

and Frank. RIP, Neil, and my deepest condolences to his family and friends.
Ryan Brown (Dweezil Zappa)

A good friend in high school named Mark Casey once gifted me every Rush album (on vinyl) from *Rush* to *A Show of Hands*. That's fifteen records! At the time, Mark and I were in a punk-rock band together, but he said, "I see that you're getting serious about the drums. Check this guy out!" The songs were fascinatingly long, and complex, with multiple time signatures. But still,

everything made sense. Neil Peart's drum parts were remarkably well thought out. The sounds were crisp. The patterns were super creative. Then I got a chance to see the band live on the *Presto* tour. Neil pulled off every single note without a hiccup. And as I looked around, I found myself sitting in an arena filled with fans air-drumming all the signature fills, accents, and breaks.

Shall we take a moment to talk about Neil's lyric writing? Unique and intelligent! For a teenage listener trying to find his or her way in life, "Subdivisions," "Freewill," and "The

Spirit of Radio" were such thoughtful masterpieces.

Although Neil and I endorsed many of the same drum/cymbal/head companies, I regretfully never got to know him. I always felt an urge to respect his privacy, which I was told was an essential part of him. But from what I've been told by close colleagues, Neil was one of the kindest, most humble people in our drumming community. He was also a total legend. While we strive to make ripples in the world of music, Neil Peart was a massive shockwave. Thank you for everything, Neil.

Brendan Buckley (Shakira, Perry Farrell, Tegan & Sara)

Neil changed the world of drumming forever. What an amazing player; what a fantastic band. He was a good friend and an incredible man. We used to play double drums at my house, and I remember asking him one day, "What do you feel like jammin' on today?" He replied, "Can we just focus on playing in 3/4?" So, we played tunes that were jazz waltzes in all the tempos we could think of, and we traded and had a blast expanding vocabulary in 3/4. He was always

have one of their top wooden snares too. It's good. I have a Gretsch wooden snare, and it's also a good wooden snare.

Whenever I've had a set of wooden drums, of course, because they're wood, no two drums are exactly the same. Drums number one and number two would be great, but number three would be a little bit deader. With the Vibrafibing, I don't lose the tonality *or* expressiveness of wooden drums, but it evens out these inconsistencies. Consequently, my four closed tom-toms all have the same timbre to them. They have the same effect when I hit them. That's the big advantage. It doesn't really change the sound so much as it makes all the drums sound like they belong in the same drumset.

This summer, I introduced an alternate drumset into my regular drumset. I'm using Simmons drums, but I didn't want to incorporate them into my regular drums. I didn't want to

patterns that I would normally play, because they don't work. Those drums will not speak in the same way that I can make a 9x13 double-headed tom-tom speak. With the Simmons I can get a roar. I can get a whisper *and* a roar out of a 9x13 tom-tom.

MD: The Simmons won't respond to touch?

Neil: They have a sensitivity control. You can turn it down or up. If you hit it light, it will make *the* sound; if you hit it hard, it will make *the* sound. But it's still *that* sound. With a regular tom-tom, the harder I hit it, the more that head is going to stretch, and it's going to detune itself. They have that in the Simmons. They call it "bend." But once you put that "bend" in there, it's in there.

With the regular tom-tom, there are subtle gradations of physical input depending on how much I put that stick into the head. I can see the marks on my drumheads sometimes

> "A record defines you at your absolute best. So every night I go onstage trying to play every song as good as it is on the record. That's just a totally involved commitment."

get rid of my traditional closed tom-toms because they *are* a voice. Those speak in a way that the Simmons do not. While the Simmons have a certain power and a certain dynamic quality that I like, I wasn't willing to sacrifice my acoustic drums.

So I hit on the idea of having two complete drumsets. I can turn around and I have a little 18" bass drum back there, another snare drum, another ride cymbal, and the Simmons tom-toms. It doesn't interfere with the basic relationship I have with my acoustic drums, but it gives me a new avenue of expression. And I've come to realize the limitations of the Simmons as far as expression is concerned. There are certain things they *can* do and certain things they *can't*. So when I'm playing with that little drumset, I have to play, necessarily, in a different sort of way. I can't play some of the kinds of

where literally four or five inches of that drumstick are making contact with that head. I'm hitting it so hard and stretching that head so much that the stick *literally* goes right into it. But that was the sound I was after and it's the sound that the Simmons drums try to imitate. It's that *throaty* quality of tuning the drum high and then hitting it hard so that the head stretches and detunes. You, in effect, get several notes at once. You get the initial high impact and then it descends. That's the essence of the Simmons sound. You can tune that "bend" in and you can tune sensitivity in, but you can't have it all at once. On an acoustic drum you have all of that there. I can play a triplet on an acoustic drum and have three different sounds by altering the attack. If you play a triplet on a Simmons, the three notes will all sound identical.

wanting to push himself and further his knowledge…he had such a strong passion for playing drums.

Even though he had never met my dad, Bud Bissonette, Neil showed up at his memorial service because he knew we had such a close father/son relationship. That always meant the world to me. That's the kind of guy Neil was. Neil was a wonderful human.
Gregg Bissonette (Ringo Starr & His All-Starr Band)

I did not anticipate the depth with which the news of Neil Peart's passing would affect me so

profoundly. I met Neil in 1985, when the Steve Morse Band was invited to tour with Rush during the band's *Power Windows* tour.

Throughout my life, I have met quite a few incredibly talented individuals. However, Neil—his musical prowess being a given—was of a different ilk; a breed of human being whose talents, skills, abilities, and passions spanned a vast and varied spectrum that at times, to me, appeared beyond comprehension. Drummer, lyricist, author, philosopher, bicyclist, motorcyclist, cross-country skier, sailor, mountain climber were all part of his

mantra of living life to its fullest. To choose just one of these endeavors, Neil didn't just hop on his bicycle for a thirty-minute cardio workout; on the '85/'86 *Power Windows* tour, if the next gig was within 150 miles, he would wake up at the crack of dawn and ride his bicycle for upwards of eight hours. And on a three-week break in the tour, he flew halfway around the world to ride his bike through remote parts of China for three weeks, only to return home to create one of his first literary works, chronicling this life-changing journey.

Neil Peart should be an inspiration to us all, constantly reminding us

just how precious life is, and how limitless the number of incredible experiences and challenges await us if we so choose. To know him only as the drummer and lyricist of Rush—an amazing accomplishment in and of itself—is to barely scratch the surface of this brilliant, driven, curious, multifaceted, genuine man. I am forever thankful for having had the opportunity to know Neil and to be eternally inspired by his passion and zest for life.
Rod Morgenstein (Winger, Dixie Dregs)

continues on page 30

But for me it's a positive thing. I approach the Simmons knowing that. I can tune them the way I would like them to sound and I can play them with that limitation in mind. So I play a different way, and that's healthy too. I like the idea of having two completely different drumsets, because the reverse drumset is a basic small bass drum and snare drum. I always used 18" bass drums until I joined this band. I've always loved them and the cannonlike punch that they have. An 18" bass drum is a very, very expressive instrument. I've found that, for the greatest range of expression, for me, a 24" bass drum has more voices. It can go literally, again, from a whisper to a roar, and everything in between. An 18" bass drum has one neat sound that I like—a sort of nice, real strong gut punch.

So when I turn around I have a single bass drum, hi-hat, snare, four Simmons tom-toms, and a few cymbals. It's a very simple, basic drumset. What people sometimes fail to realize about a large drumset like I use is that drumming *always* revolves around bass drum, snare drum, and hi-hat. And your fills *always* revolve around two tom-toms and your snare. For anything else, you take those patterns and transfer them to some little drums, or you translate them to some different voices. It gives you something different out of the same old patterns, or the same rudiments of set drumming.

That's basically the reason why I expanded my kit, especially being in a three-piece band. The more voices I have, the better. By the same token, I always understood the fact that all my drumming does revolve around a very small set of drums. Being able to have that little, concise set of drums behind me has proved invaluable, even in rehearsals. If we're going over a song again and again and again, instead of getting tired of it and just cranking it out, I can turn around and play the other set. It changes the whole thing and makes it fresh again. It's been a revitalizing thing for me. It's something that I think I will pursue further.

MD: What have you been using headphones onstage for?
Neil: The headphones are basically for when we use programmed sequencers or the synthesizers that are driven by arpeggiators. They're basically triggered by a drum machine with a click-track pulse. Then the arpeggiator picks that up. The song on *Signals* called "The Weapon" is based around an arpeggiator. Ironically, usually drummers are used to a band that follows them. If I tend to feel that something should be pulled back a bit or anticipated a bit, the band follows me. When you use something that's as mathematical as a sequencer or an arpeggiator, there's no way those machines are going to follow you. You have to follow them. I can use the headphones to give me that trigger with a sequencer in "Vital Signs" and with an arpeggiator in "The Weapon." I have to hear that and follow it, basically. I have to swallow my pride and be a little subservient to the machine.

Playing with headphones is not the same as playing without them. I have to use my imagination. The essence of having an imagination is that sometimes I've recorded a song all by myself, such as "YYZ" from our *Moving Pictures* album. When we did the basic track, it was just me. I went in there and played the drum track. The other guys' parts were very difficult. We figured it would make more sense if I recorded my track and then gave them a chance to work on their parts without the pressure of all of us having to do it at the same time. I had to have enough imagination to hear the song in my head and respond to all those dynamics and nuances.

With headphones on, drums do not sound like drums. Period. That's certainly a fact. But the essence of it is that I know what my drums sound like, and I know that if I play a certain pattern, it has such and such an effect on people—a certain excitement, drama, or whatever. And when I have the headphones on, yes, I have to use my imagination. It is, in a sense, a limitation, that in order to be able to follow those

---

REMEMBERING NEIL

continued from page 29

I heard *2112* or *All the World's a Stage* at a friend's house, in his basement, and I was immediately drawn to his turntable. I remember sticking my head between the speakers and being transformed to this totally different place of drumming, of music—just a different musical landscape. At the time, I was playing in bands and taking drum lessons, and at the school that I was in they would put together different bands, and I was in a band with these teenage kids,

playing Ventures and Beatles covers, nothing too challenging. But as I discovered different drumming and styles, I immediately adapted to that way. So when Neil entered my life, I started what I would call my drumming vocabulary. It expanded because of him. Things that I would call drum hooks…when Neil played "The Spirit of Radio," I remember listening to the beginning section and how he and Geddy entered the song, and thought it was the greatest thing I'd ever heard. This was drumming that I'd never heard before. And for me, on every Rush album he totally took it up again. Take

a song like "Freewill" [from *Permanent Waves*]. Man, the drumming on that, it's just beautiful the way he approaches it. Each verse, each chorus, he totally mapped it out for the drummer listening. And then you take the next album, which was *Moving Pictures*, where he totally stepped it up again, and probably created air drumming on that record with "Tom Sawyer." When that fill comes, it's like, What the hell? And he sticks in this cymbal crash in between the tom fill that was just totally unexpected. It's just beautiful. To this day I'm still inspired by Neil, by Rush. His passing hit me the hardest.

He is, to me, the greatest.
Charlie Benante (Anthrax)

Neil Peart was to my generation what Ringo Starr was to the previous one. He influenced countless people to play the drums, setting the bar incredibly high. Many of us would race home from school to learn his parts and play along with Rush records.

In addition to the incredible drumming and lyrics, I've always had great admiration and respect for his quest to improve. When Neil began studying with Freddie Gruber in the

things effectively, I have to be able to hear them well. And the most sensible way to do that is through headphones. I just decided that it's not going to make me play worse. It's just going to make me have to work harder, because when I have those headphones on, I'm going to have to think about what my playing *really* sounds like. I can't be lazy and just hear it. I have to think about it and imagine it. It is a hard thing. But at the same time, it became a whole series of progressions that we had to make, so as not to add another musician.

MD: I was going to ask if you'd ever considered adding more musicians.

Neil: Certainly we have, as a band that wants to keep improving and changing our sound. But the interpersonal chemistry among us happens to be such that we didn't want to tamper with that. We didn't want to take a chance on adding another person, because we get along well. We have a good balance of responsibilities. Also, we basically like being a trio. I think that our audience likes us being a trio, and they're proud of—as we are proud of—how much music we can create and how different we can sound being just three guys. That's something that we have to live with. We're going to have to make certain allowances for that; we're going to have to use sequencers and all kinds of interphased keyboards. We're going to have to have Alex and Geddy rooted to certain things at certain times for them to be able to cover all those bases. And anything I can do to help that along is just icing. It's the least I can do.

An example is when I added tuned percussion to my drumset. I'm by no means a classical percussionist. I can't say that I have any kind of understanding of tuned percussion. But I can learn a part and play it. It adds something to the overall texture of the band. It's been the same thing in the last few years with electronics. It would be easy for me to say, "Oh, well, I don't work with headphones on." That contradicts the whole purpose of what we are as a band. I can't take that kind of a hard line. I've said before, too, that I don't like the idea of electronics as in electronic drums. I was a bit of a purist, in a sense, saying that I like acoustic drums. But I found a way to incorporate that without compromising acoustic drums. I didn't have to throw them away or replace them. It's a balance.

It's like the old extreme of musicians wanting to be technical or emotional—saying that *only* feel is important or *only* technique is important. Well, hell, they're *both* important. Not only that, but they're both good. I want to be technical, but I also want to be really instinctive and emotional. I want to play things that are exciting, and I also want to play things that are difficult. I get a buzz and a satisfaction out of both of those.

Acoustic drums are my first love. My first relationship with things is to hit them with a stick. That still remains true. And everything that I've said about electronics in the past is still true. They *don't* replace acoustic drums. They can never hope to do so any more than an electric piano will replace an acoustic piano. Any person with a halfway open mind realizes that fact. But at the same time, it doesn't mean that it has to be one or the other. That's a mistake I fell into for a while, figuring that you had to be either going towards electronics or be a purist and stay with acoustics. Now I've found a way to have both, where I can move forward into electronics, but not have to sacrifice anything that I think is important.

That's an essential truth that people tend to wander to extremes about. A lot of people have written to me saying, "It's great that you don't want to have electronics. I'm the same way." And I'm still true to that just as I'm still true to the other thing about how headphones are a limitation. They do change your perception of what you play. It's the same thing that you have to do in the studio. Anybody who's been in the studio knows that you have to wear headphones. And that's difficult. I have to imagine a lot in the studio because I don't hear my cymbals right. I don't hear my snare drum right. I don't hear the inter-kit dynamics among snare, bass drum, tom-toms, and cymbals.

Acoustically, all those things have an interrelation that's really subtle. I can move from my snare to a certain tom-tom, and I'll know that they have a certain relation to each other. I know what I can do. But, for instance, I know that I *can't* go from my snare to my 8x12 tom and come back again. I know that acoustically it doesn't work. But I know that I can go to my 9x13 tom and come back to my snare, and that works. It's just a matter of the subtle inter-dynamics of the way I tune things and the characteristics of a particular drum of any given size. It has a certain voice about it and a certain characteristic to it. I've come to know all those things from a long familiarity—night after night of hearing what they can and will do.

---

early to mid '90s, he'd already been inducted to the *Modern Drummer* Hall of Fame and would easily go down as one of the greats, even if he never touched a stick again. He later took lessons with Peter Erskine. As an educator, what a wonderful thing for me to present this to students as inspiration. Never stop growing.

Much has been made about his privacy over the years. I never considered that as something negative. I feel it helped to provide much introspection and contemplation that led to his fantastic lyrics. He also expressed himself vehemently in his books.

I had the opportunity to sit behind his kit during the *Snakes and Arrows* tour. A buddy of mine was good friends with Rush's monitor engineer, and we were there for soundcheck, etc. There's a scene in the movie *Field of Dreams* where James Earl Jones has the opportunity to go into the field where all of the baseball players came from. He first approaches the field with giddy hesitancy because it's a sacred place. That's how I felt when climbing into Neil's space. I never felt that way sitting behind anyone else's drumset. There was mystery, greatness, history—just like him.

Resilient. Craftsman. Renaissance man. Macallan. Author. Father. These are some of the ways I will remember him. RIP, Professor.
Jeremy Hummel (Into the Spin, DrumTip)

In 1993 Neil Peart called me to play on *Burning for Buddy*, an album and video project he produced that was a tribute to Buddy Rich. We had both played with the Buddy Rich Big Band in 1991 at a concert in New York City. It is well documented how Neil decided to follow that up with a larger project based on Buddy Rich's legacy.

During the *Burning for Buddy* sessions Neil approached me and very politely asked me what I had done to improve my drumming so much since we first met in 1985, when we both played on bassist Jeff Berlin's first solo album, *Champion*. I replied, "I've been studying with Freddie Gruber," who I considered my drum guru. Neil immediately wanted to meet Freddie. Shortly after, I introduced them to each other, and they hit it off famously. Neil took his lessons with Freddie very seriously, and he and Freddie became fast friends.

continues on page 32

The drum solo is my fundamental source of research and development as far as which voices will work together. None of that has changed. I still hold to all those principles, but at the same time, I've found a way to use headphones as a tool as I've been able to use electronic drums as a tool—without negating anything else.

MD: Gary Chester wanted me to ask you if you play flat-footed on your bass drum pedals or with heels up.

Neil: I play with heels up all the time. I have a lot of equipment, and I like it all under me. I don't like things too far away. Consequently, my bass drums are very close to me. Even drummers who are smaller in stature than I am find it very uncomfortable to have things closed in that much. But I like to be able to have as much leverage as I need on any given drum. I like to be able to put my weight in the right place so that I can put whatever degree of force I want on either my left or right side, regardless. I want all my leverage there, and it's important to have everything in close. My bass drum pedal is practically right under my knee. I've noticed that drummers who sit farther back with their legs more extended tend to play flat-footed.

I use my ankle a lot. It's a not a question of playing from the thigh, although a lot of my pivoting comes from the hip. But anything fast has to come from my ankle. The same with my wrists. I play a lot with my arms, but when it comes to playing anything subtle or really quick, my wrists, my fingers, or some smaller muscles definitely have to do that. Long muscles can only take care of so much. So basically I play with my toes, but I use my ankles. Whereas with a lot of drummers who play tiptoe, a lot of their pivoting comes from the hip. I use my ankle for pivoting as well.

My two bass drums are tuned the same. But my legs aren't the same because of the long muscles, which are the easiest to get in shape and, for me, the first to go out of shape. Towards the end of a tour, I start to lose the tone of my long leg muscles. My arms and my wrists just continue to get better, and it becomes easier for me to play throughout a tour. The long muscles are the easiest to get back into shape when I start, but there's something very touchy about them. For instance, when we used to open shows I had a lot of problems with my foot because we'd only be playing forty minutes a night. There'd be no warm-up or soundcheck. The extent of my playing every day was only forty minutes, which wasn't enough for those muscles. I used to have a lot of problems with my feet and my leg muscles stiffening up and developing a kind of paralysis and a feeling that they were working against me. I've spoken to other drummers in the same circumstance who would ask me, "Are you familiar with this problem?" Or I'd ask them if they'd noticed it as a phenomenon. It's definitely true that if you're not playing enough every day, those muscles suffer the most. That's the reason why my two bass drums tend to sound different. My right leg gets a lot more exercise than my left one does.

Whether or not someone else should play either on the toes or flat-footed depends on the individual. I can't believe that some people have two feet of distance between them and their snare drum, and then another foot over to their bass drum. It's so far away. I suppose you can get just as much power from your bass drum if it's that distance from you. The same with your snare drum. You'd probably have to use your arms a lot more. But it probably does average out that you're getting as much impact into it.

It's got to be a very individual thing. I feel better if things are in close to me. I have a lot of drums and cymbals and I want them where they're usable. A good part of my drumkit is underneath me. I have pretty long arms, so a lot of it can fall within the scope of being right under my center of gravity. It's important for me to feel like I'm on top of the kit. Some people play behind their drums in a physical sense. Their kit is in front of them. I know lots of very good drummers who play that way. I don't think there's a qualitative difference there. It's just probably a matter of

REMEMBERING NEIL

continued from page 31

I saw Rush live a number of times and was always blown away by the band, the music, the presentation, and Neil's creative and compositional drumming. When Neil retired from touring in 2015, I was moved to tears when I read his *Modern Drummer* interview and how drumming had taken such a toll on his body. I'm sure it had to have been difficult to make that decision—to walk away when he did.

I knew Neil as a man of great humility, intelligence, and humor. His drumming has inspired generations and I'm sure will continue to inspire and inform drummers of the future. I am grateful to have known Neil Peart. He is already missed.

Steve Smith (Vital Information)

I bought *Moving Pictures* in 1980, after hearing "Limelight" on the radio. Neil's entrance to this song alone was worth the price of the record. The songs were like no other rock songs that I'd heard. The clean, fat sound of the recording was as appealing as the songs themselves. And Neil's playing was infused with an intoxicating combination of sophistication, impeccable execution, and a decidedly rockin' feel. Neil Peart and Rush changed rock music forever. No band that I know of, before or since, has created such sophisticated and literary yet visceral and anthemic rock music.

Dave DiCenso (independent, Josh Groban)

What can I say about Neil Peart's drumming that hasn't been said yet? A groundbreaking, massively influential, outstanding, virtuosic, contemporary, inspirational prog-rock master at the top of his work! No question, and maximum respect for that—but to me personally he was much more than that. Any time I've listened to his interviews, that incredibly intelligent, reserved appearance, the choice of words, the kindness, modesty, message, humorous storytelling, and kind personality mesmerized me. He made me feel proud to be a drummer! Through my super-intelligent late father—who was a lawyer—I've always

what you're comfortable with or used to.

MD: Your song "Losing It" seemed to be about Ernest Hemingway.

Neil: Good. Yeah. Not a lot of people have caught that.

MD: I also wonder if that is a fear you have for yourself sometime in the future.

Neil: Of course. But fortunately for me, as we covered before, I have another set of goals. When I start to feel as though I'm not improving any more as a drummer—not even getting worse, just not improving—I have another thing that I can go to work at and improve on. The two avenues that were explored in the song were, with the dancer, physical deterioration, and with the writer, mental deterioration. Actually, my original plan for that song was to carry it a little further into the area of musicians. I wanted

respond to an invitation from President Kennedy, I think, just before he died. He slaved for days just trying to write a little paragraph. The physical part of his deterioration was tragic too, because he was a very vital person. I can relate to that strongly, because I've also lived life in a very physical sense. I love physical expressions of things. And when you've depended on your brain as an instrument, and all of a sudden it doesn't respond to you.

I read a biography of John Steinbeck recently. It was the same thing. He realized that he had lost it. He knew that he couldn't do it anymore and it was a source of tremendous sadness to him and frustration. And he never stopped trying, either. That's even more sad, somehow—to see somebody trying to do something that they know they can't do.

MD: Was the dancer in "Losing It" about anyone in particular?

> "I want to be technical, but I also want to be really instinctive and emotional. I get a buzz and a satisfaction out of both of those."

to cover the idea of someone like Bob Marley, for instance, who loses it through a disease—an internal thing that you have no control over. Or in the case of Keith Moon, in a self-destructive sense, where someone loses it, but they don't really lose it. They throw it away. It's a bit too much to accomplish all in one song, but the concept I'd envisioned was all the different ways there are to lose something special. The essence was whether it was worth losing something great or whether it was worse never to have known it.

There's a pathos I feel with people who have an unrealized dream of any kind. When you talk to an older person who says, "Well, I always wanted to be such and such, but I never really gave it a shot," that's sad. But to me it's not nearly as sad as someone who was great at something and who has to watch it fade.

MD: Did Hemingway, towards the end of his life, feel like he couldn't write anymore?

Neil: It was really a sad case with him. He was trying to

Neil: Not specifically. It drew a bit from that film with Shirley MacLaine called *The Turning Point*. It was about two ballet dancers. One of them had continued on and was getting to be a bit of a has-been. The other one had given it up to get married and raise a family. I was a bit inspired from that, but it was also about the physical side of doing things as an athlete. There's a sadness to that.

Geddy's a great baseball fan. He's told me about batters, for instance, who have been beaned a couple of times and all of a sudden lose their nerve. You have to respond to that kind of tragedy compassionately. It's a horrible thing. You spend all your life learning how to do a thing and then because of something beyond your control, all of a sudden you can't do it anymore. It's very sad. There's an essential dynamic to life that you have a prime, and you have something leading up to that prime. Unfortunately, you also have to have something leading down from it.

MD: How do you feel about MTV and the effect it has on kids?

been a great fan of literature, and Neil, as the lyricist of Rush, has truly been the master of words as well as the drums—my two favorite things on planet Earth!

The other thing that greatly resonated with me over twenty years ago was the fact that someone of his caliber, career, fame, fortune, and reputation started taking drum lessons from drum guru Freddie Gruber in L.A. This kind of respect, "eagerness to learn" attitude, hunger for knowledge, modesty, and dedication to the art form of drumming is something that'll forever inspire me, and I believe this

is truly something we can all learn from. This inspiration to me personally means much more than trying to learn or copy his drumbeats, licks, and grooves. Thank you, Professor. May you rest in peace.

Gabor "Gabs" Dornyei (independent)

Just the fact that Neil Peart appeared on more covers of *Modern Drummer* than any other drummer shows his importance in the drumming community. I have never seen such commotion in the media and on social media—all musicians and bands, without exception, were in shock with

his sudden departure. He definitely set a new standard of excellence for decades to come, and all drummers, no matter what their style, respect everything he has done for our class. He will always be a unanimous favorite among us.

His work continually evolved over each of Rush's albums and has influenced at least four generations— and he will undoubtedly continue to be admired. What always caught my attention was his construction of groove patterns. Each time he repeated a part, he would add a new layer, progressing the original idea with

an added variation—this was a very strong and clear element of his style.

Countless times, he reinvented himself with new musical concepts, too. Right in the middle of a successful career, he returned to study with Freddie Gruber. This showed that everyone, even the greats, can continue to study and learn new things—a lesson in humility from one who never left the top.

All virtuous drummers, at some point in their careers, were influenced by Neil Peart. My own groove construction was based on Neil Peart's style. The best example of **continues on page 34**

Neil: It's really neat that MTV has become another avenue of exposure for some bands. It's been proven by a few different bands who wouldn't have gotten exposure on the radio, but their videos were interesting. MTV has the same flaws that radio has in terms of being too programmed and too easy to try to find a formula for.

Music is enough all by itself. Anyone who loves music knows that already. When you listen to something, you see pictures and it puts images in your mind, regardless of whether it's abstract designs or good images that good music and lyrics make you see. They make you visualize a whole cinematic thing. We have written in the past from a cinematic point of view. We have a theme in the lyrics, or sometimes even before the lyrics, we have something that we want to create. We work at it cinematically in that we create a whole background and then we put the center focus of action, or the character, in the middle of it. We work at it just like a movie.

There's no way that music means anything else. It doesn't really need a lyric sheet and it certainly doesn't need a video to express it. It's two media mixing together, just like you could put poetry into a play, or you could put a novel into a song. But it doesn't take away from either of those. Nothing's going to take the place of a good book. Nothing's going to take the place of a good record. Nothing's going to take the place of a good movie. They are each separate unto themselves. I don't have a strong relation to video or film as a medium. I don't get any satisfaction out of making a video. I get a lot more satisfaction out of writing and recording, or playing a concert.

Another thing I find frustrating as a musician and a music fan is that I really like to see people playing their instruments. If you can't get to see them live, but you see them in the *old* context of seeing a band on TV—seeing a band come on and play their song, or *pretend* to play their song at least—they have their instruments there and you can see how they look when they play. It gives you a whole new insight into the nature of that band. In a lot of modern videos, it becomes too obvious just to take a picture of the bands playing their songs.

When we've done interpretative videos where we take something *beyond* just us playing the song, we still maintain a balance of us playing the song. We'll film ourselves playing the song and then we might add some other images. The ones we did for *Signals* were "Countdown" and "Subdivisions." For "Countdown" the choices were obvious. We were there. We had friends at NASA and had access to these NASA films. Of course we're going to use those. "Subdivisions" reflects each of our upbringings. All of us were brought up in the suburbs. It reflects each of us as being a misfit and not quite fitting into the fabric of a high school society. And we wanted to express that.

But at the same time, both of those show us playing the song. We'll cut away to something like in "Subdivisions" where we had a kid representing the misfit, and we showed his life, his parents, and his school. That was the thrust of writing that song. That's important. But it's not *so* important that it should override our playing the song. It sometimes seems too facile to break things down to basics, but for me, you have to. You have to come down to the basic fact of, "What is it to be a musician?" It is to play your instrument. Therefore, when you're playing it on a stage in front of people, that is the essential reality of being a musician.

Humphrey Bogart said that the only thing he owed the public was a good performance. You can add all kinds of caveats and possible exceptions to that—which we do respond to—but fundamentally, we are there to make the best records we can make and to play the best concerts we can play. We don't always do that. But if we can do that, or at least even *try* to do that, that's our responsibility.

REMEMBERING NEIL
continued from page 33

that is my "PsychOctopus" drum solo. Immortalized on the 2011 *Modern Drummer* Festival DVD, it was totally inspired by Neil's solo "The Rhythm Method," from the album *A Show of Hands*. I have always made a point of making this clear to everyone who listened, and if this solo becomes a classic within my own repertoire, I am forever grateful to the peerless Neil Peart for the inspiration.
Aquiles Priester (Tony MacAlpine, W.A.S.P.)

Though I'd heard Rush on my local rock stations, I became convinced of the band's brilliance after the release of their *Permanent Waves* album. I couldn't put this record to the side, captivated from beginning to end by the production, mix, songs, solos, individual parts, and especially the drums. The release of their follow-up record, *Moving Pictures*, solidified the band's stamp on my musical consciousness and vocabulary. Only in my early teens at this time, I'd question myself in my approach to all things drumming based on Neil Peart's recordings and interviews.

I had always wondered how Neil got that hi-hat tone, crispness, and explosiveness. Well, in a *Modern Drummer* interview in the early '80s he mentioned what he used: a 13" Zildjiian Quick Beat top and a 13" New Beat bottom. I got that combo the first chance I got.

He mentioned his stick choice in an interview as well, Promark 747s. The same pair of sticks my father put in my hands when I began drumming. I silently felt proud that Neil preferred this stick, too. I would also later have a similar feeling about us both being DW artists.

Other things that drew me into his playing: His ride work. That playing up on the bell reminded me of the patterns Lloyd Knibb would play with the Skatalites, but applying it to some banging out and sophisticated rock music. And it was clean, articulate, and purposefully placed, like everything else he did.

He'd squeeze in full-on jazz chops in a way that was unlike anyone else at the time. He also sent me on a mission with classical/drum corps style snare work that was well constructed and executed.

continues on page 48

Neil Peart On Record

Rush came to prominence in the mid 1970s and quickly rewrote the rock music rulebook. Marrying the expansive concepts of the great British progressive-rock bands to a decidedly North American hard-rock aesthetic, Rush initially focused on complex song structures and instrumental pyrotechnics, in the process raising the performance bar for rock musicians and blowing the minds of their followers.

By the early '80s, influenced by the sounds of new wave and other contemporary styles, Rush tightened their arrangements, wrote progressively stronger hooks and melodies, and incorporated more contemporary musical elements, all the while continuing to up the rhythmic ante. This unusual recipe found a welcoming audience on FM radio with slick yet sophisticated releases like 1980's *Permanent Waves* (featuring their breakout track "The Spirit of Radio"), '81's *Moving Pictures* ("Tom Sawyer," "Limelight"), and '82's *Signals* ("Subdivisions," "New World Man").

Through a series of classic records featuring brilliant, cerebral, and yes, busy drumming, Neil Peart ascended to the throne, inarguably becoming the most popular drummer on the planet. Importantly, each new Rush album documented the creative progression of a drummer who never stopped challenging himself—and, by extension, us. Here we trace that progression by homing in on Peart's work on each of the band's studio albums. Strap yourself in: it's going to be quite a ride.

by Ilya Stemkovsky

Fly by Night (1975)

The blueprint for all future Rush albums was created here. Distancing themselves from the Zeppelin-infused riffage of their debut, and making a key line-up change with Neil Peart replacing John Rutsey behind the kit, Rush storm out of the gate with "Anthem." It was obvious these guys meant business,

with odd meters, in-your-face vocals, and virtuosic musicianship taken up a level with Peart's precision and aggression. The drummer fills every space of "By-Tor and the Snow Dog" with…well… fills—32nd-note tom rolls, hi-hat jabs, and all manners of outrageous playing set to "destroy" mode. But even early on, Peart knew how to simply lay it down for maximum effect and support, as in the chugging hi-hat 16ths on "In the End." The meticulously crafted, multilimbed drum parts and greater laser-like execution would come later as the scope of the band's writing became more complex. But it was on this record, released with little fanfare in the mid 1970s, where the bar was set, soon to be bested with regular frequency. And in Peart, a Canadian kid still in his early twenties, a star was born.

Caress of Steel (1975)

Picking up where *Fly by Night* left off less than a year later, *Caress of Steel* showcases a band more assured after constant touring. "Bastille Day" finds Peart at his most driving and propulsive, working his ride underneath a powerful guitar progression, and the much-derided "I Think I'm Going Bald" still pleases with a cool, pre-disco, offbeat hi-hat part. There's even an *almost* funky drum intro to "Lakeside Park" followed by a straight-8ths groove with Peart leaving out the backbeat of 2. But it's on the twenty-minute "The Fountain of Lamneth" where the band's creative ambitions (some would say indulgence) would mix perfectly with their growing musicianship. And though their progressive counterparts had been making multimovement compositions in England for years at that point, Rush jumped into the fray on "Lamneth" with the band's most

involved arrangement to date. In the "Didacts and Narpets" section, Peart solos in and around his toms, ripping flams and huge crashes in a burst of energy, another sign of what was to come in the form of lengthy drum showcases in concert. The side-long track intrigued, but the sections sounded thrown together, not quite a unified whole. That would come with the next album.

2112 (1976)

Rush's commercial breakthrough came with the unlikely record *2112*, after the band ignored record company pressure for something more palatable by continuing their extended-form compositional adventures with the twenty-minute, side-long title track. The road made Rush a commanding, well-oiled machine by 1976, and the different sections making up "2112" highlight all the band's strengths, from brilliant guitar and bass proficiency to the fully realized sound Peart had

cultivated by this juncture in his career. Check out the chorus of "The Temples of Syrinx" for Peart's simple, kick-heavy pattern, and the wild, 6/8 section in the "Grand Finale" section for a taste of the drummer going toe to toe with Lifeson during more guitar solo madness. But the rest of the album is equally impressive, as Peart trucks through "A Passage to Bangkok" with sloshy hats in between roundhouse fills, pseudo-shuffles his way through the verses of "The Twilight Zone," throws in some nifty kick syncopations in "Lessons," and executes the cleanest cymbal chokes in "Something for Nothing." The record would raise the band's profile and earn them an audience of devotees who would study the liner notes and come to the gigs, but Rush was only getting started.

A Farewell to Kings (1977)

The success of *2112* allowed Rush to go musically where they wished,

and where they went was into the stratosphere. The band's "middle period" begins loosely here, with an added focus on melodic songwriting that would lead to a radio hit with "Closer to the Heart" and the increased use of synthesizers rounding out the group's sound. Peart was now using an arsenal of orchestra bells, temple blocks, and chimes along with developing an even greater dexterity and technical prowess behind the kit. On the epic "Xanadu," Peart kills with a two-handed hi-hat assault, interjecting with striking snare hits, and plays the softest snare doubles on the subtler chorus of "Cinderella Man." And as "Tomorrow Never Knows" signaled a change in direction for the Fab Four, "Cygnus X-1" points the telescope towards Rush's future. The trio grooves hard together, Peart moving from one idea to the next, an odd-time splash beat here, another dark crooked waltz there, the recording more pronounced and immediate. The track's finale

includes the daring 11/8 Peart tour-de-force, before he even it out underneath the most crazed vocals of Lee's career. The band still rocked, but they were racing headlong into a new form of progressive rock.

Hemispheres (1978)

Often cited as the high-water mark for this period of the band's career, *Hemispheres* opens with another side-long masterpiece, "Cygnus X-1 Book 2: Hemispheres," and now there truly is no manual. The music is yet more complex and demanding; Peart hammers home a martial rhythm with hip, left-hand snare work, and weaves in and out of 7/8 and 6/8 passages with flair, eventually moving into yet another hard-hitting disco hi-hats section near the end of the piece. Peart is on a tear throughout, floating atop a 5/4 figure in "The Trees" with an over-the-barline quarter-note ride bell and a snare he keeps stating on the "1," then opening

up on the cymbal for tension release. On "La Villa Strangiato (An Exercise in Self-Indulgence)," the band works through several instrumental sections that allow each player to really shine. Check out the way Peart flips the beat on the atmospheric 7/8 guitar solo, the drummer building drama with each passing bar, before bringing in a "Sing Sing Sing"–style floor tom pattern and some swinging by way of Canada. Rush was having fun writing deadly serious music, and the band would quickly change direction again. Perhaps returning to the radio wasn't such a bad idea.

Permanent Waves (1980)

Released in January 1980, *Permanent Waves* not only ushered in a new decade but also solidified Rush as a commercially viable entity, with increased record sales and concert revenue. Sure, the songs were shorter, but they were no less inventive than what came before. The band just

squeezed those ideas into a tighter framework. By now, Peart had the ear of the drumming world, and his attention to detail combined with his focused power made him a major influence on many musicians. Just check out the number of different parts he whips out during "The Spirit of Radio," from that dancing ride bell thing he'd return to time and again over the next few decades, to a newfound infatuation with reggae beats. Peart is smooth as silk in the middle 6/8 guitar solo section of "Freewill," and he brings a tireless array of blazing fills and his toughest 16th-note groove yet to one of the band's last long-form, multimovement compositions, "Natural Science." These songs are still heard on FM radio today, and Peart's "more is more" approach on them continues to be studied by aspiring rock drummers serious about their craft. But what the band delivered next would make them, and Peart, legends.

fancy ride work during a wicked Lifeson guitar break. Peart leans heavy into his hats on "Red Barchetta" and lays down one of his signature spacious tom patterns in "Witch Hunt," a compositional drum approach that would be revisited often throughout the 1980s. Rush had released its most popular and arguably most accomplished record to date, but the pace, and imagination, would not stop there.

Signals (1982)
By the time of 1982's *Signals*, Rush was firing on all cylinders, existing in a brutal cycle of album/tour/album/tour that somehow still managed to yield fresh material and novel musicianship. This was the last record with longtime producer Terry Brown, and the band allowed current music to influence their sound. The Police-inspired, new-wave reggae flavors crept in for their highest-charting U.S.

Grace Under Pressure (1984)
Rush returned in 1984 with a new collection of songs featuring a bit more Lifeson guitar than was on *Signals*, as evidenced by the aggressive rock of "Afterimage" and "Between the Wheels," both with heavy offbeat cymbal work from Peart that gets the head bobbing. Some electronic drums can be heard on "Red Sector A," and the ska-like "The Enemy Within" gets a healthy dose of Peart fills that blur the "1." The drummer lays down a flam-laden snare groove on "The Body Electric," accenting with a kick-and-toms syncopation to deceive the ear, before moving to a two-handed hi-hat accompaniment underneath a guitar solo. And even though Rush was all over the airwaves at this point, they still composed using tons of different odd times, and Peart is fierce in the 5/4 verses of "Kid Gloves" and the back and forth between seven and six in "Distant Early Warning." Peart and Lee were also by now one mind,

Moving Pictures (1981)
Regarded by Rush fans and prog aficionados alike as the band's masterwork, *Moving Pictures* brilliantly combined their fully realized penchant for melodic hooks with prodigious playing leaps and bounds beyond the group's early-'70s roots. And it sounds like it was recorded yesterday.

Opener "Tom Sawyer" became a signature song, a demanding workout of shape-shifting perfection, a performance for the ages. But check out how Peart toys with time on "YYZ," navigating the Morse Code 5/4 with scalpel-like exactitude, dropping offbeat kicks in a call-and-response with his hands. On tracks like "The Camera Eye," Peart shares space with synthesizers, which grew louder in the mix, anchored the arrangements, and helped the overall sound have even more weight. But Rush was a power trio at heart, and the hard-hitting "Limelight" finds Peart balancing between start/stop verses and some

single, "New World Man," on which Peart alternates between hip, upstroke doubles and sizzling openings on the hi-hat. Though recorded at the same Toronto studio as the band's previous two records, *Signals* boasts Peart's thickest and crispiest drum tone to that point, even while synthesizers became a crucial fourth voice. Peart highlights abound, from the offbeat China pattern ending "Subdivisions," to the double-time rock urgency of "The Analog Kid," to the grooving, four-on-the-floor dotted gallop in "Digital Man." Rush was now bringing intelligent but catchy rock music to the masses, and Peart played nightly to a sea of air drummers showing him love. He also began to appear in drumming publications as *the* guy. The next, keyboard-heavy phase in the band's career begins loosely here, and *2112*, released a mere six years prior, seemed like the creation of an entirely different band.

locking in together on fills that were written out but sounded improvised. The band continued a relentless touring schedule, and their growing songbook meant that some earlier material was retired from the stage. Ten years in, and the future was still bright.

Power Windows (1985)
1985's *Power Windows*, often maligned by fans for being too slick, too synth heavy, and too poppy, is nonetheless another excellent outing for a band whose well was not running dry but simply changing flavors. This wasn't the progressive rock of the 1970s any longer, but careful listening shows inventive arrangements on complex songs that were difficult to play and not so easy on the brain. Check out one of the later verses of "The Big Money," where Peart opens his hats in and around a snare backbeat, or the song's dramatic coda containing the drummer's tasty snare rolls. Keyboard sequencing is a major

characteristic of tracks like "Grand Designs" and "Middletown Dreams," but there's no shortage of rhythmic fun coming from the drums, and no shortage of over-the-top fills. The middle section of "Marathon" is mid-'80s Peart at his best, crushing a two-chord 7/8 progression with snare injections and tension building. And "Mystic Rhythms" is all moody toms and percussive samples, with Peart sounding like he's got another limb. The old faithful might have cried "Where's the guitar?" but Rush, along with the ever-changing Peart, was already onto the next thing.

Hold Your Fire (1987)
Never ones to rest, by 1987 Rush still had settled into the comfort of more concise and palatable songwriting, but the quality of their output remained at a high level, and their albums were still automatic blind buys for musicians, especially drummers. "Force Ten," the

swing. The wild-eyed abandon of a decade past was now in the rearview mirror.

Presto (1989)
A transition period was upon Rush by 1989, as their movement away from keyboard dominance began in earnest. Maturity and discipline were also now the tools employed by Peart, the master craftsman, and his deliberate straighter rock parts in tunes like "The Pass" was the work of a thinking drummer playing for the song. But there's everything from jazzy snare ghosting in "Show Don't Tell" to hypnotic African rhythms in "Scars," which would later appear in some form during Peart's show-stopping live drum solos. Dig his four-on-the-floor kick plus offbeat splash groove in "Superconductor" and his strong, dynamic approach alternating between the softer ballad-like parts and tom-heavy sections of "Available

of pop-infused hard rock, with occasional prog tendencies. But labels never really applied to Rush, so the record contains everything from funky jams with rapping ("Roll the Bones") to kinetic, midtempo rockers ("Face Up"). Peart lays down a solid side-stick pulse in "Dreamline" and brings things down to a whisper with a softer ride cymbal in "Ghost of a Chance." Check out some of the licks Peart plays in the instrumental "Where's My Thing?" including a thunderous toms/ double bass fill and a lightning-quick accented snare roll in a measure of 6/4. On "Bravado," Peart builds the part from the ground up, starting with an insistent kick and layering toms and snare on top, until the last chorus, where he's working all the cymbals and drums, achieving a completeness that makes the track whole. There was a wind blowing from the Pacific Northwest, but Rush was anchored in, holding ground, and ready to turn up.

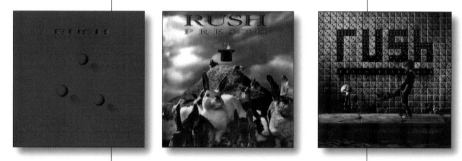

uptempo rocker opening *Hold Your Fire*, grabs your attention with Peart's chugging snare. Later he ornaments the atmospherics with simple, accented hi-hat work that eventually moves over to the snare. The sharper edges of Rush's music were being rounded off in an effort for greater accessibility, but these guys were still players, and the ping pong-like tom and cymbal pattern in the first chorus of "Time Stand Still" was still unlike anything else on the radio, or by this point, MTV. Check out the instrumental section in "Mission," with its ultra-tight Peart and Lee unison licks, and the seismic drum breaks following the guitar solo in "Turn the Page." Peart was doing his unique thing all over Rush's version of pop music, as he delved deeper into composing machine-like parts by incorporating all the random elements of his kit, filtered through his own sense of groove and

Light." With synths being tucked away subtly, more space emerged in the group's sound, but no player filled the gaps with excessive fills or licks. Peart, specifically, emerged as a grand supporter of the vocals, the bigger picture. Dated only by its digital, wet sheen, which was the norm for much rock music from this era, *Presto* did manage to chart several singles and return the band to a more pronounced power trio sound. As a new decade approached, Rush was securely in the lead pack.

Roll the Bones (1991)
As the 1990s commenced, Rush were veterans in a music business that had chewed up lesser bands unable to adapt to changing tastes. Peart, Lifeson, and Lee continued their commitment to organic music-making, and the songs making up 1991's *Roll the Bones* were Rush's usual assortment

Counterparts (1993)
By 1993, that Seattle wind had turned into a hurricane, and the unifying factor for all those West Coast "grunge" bands was their undeniable heaviness. Not to be outdone, Rush delivered the heaviest record of their career, and Peart's drums were firmly assigned with the task of bringing the weighty stuff. The tone of his kit was deeper, darker, and fuller, and this time Peart brought a fully realized "less is more" understanding to his written parts. Sure, there were drum fills, but songs like "Stick It Out" and "Cut to the Chase" came at you with a fury not heard since the band's earliest days. Still, this was Rush, and "boring" was not on the agenda. That ride bell gets a workout on "Animate," and there are slick kick drum doubles on the instrumental "Leave That Thing Alone" that are basic but perfectly placed. Check out the third chorus groove of "Nobody's Hero,"

where Peart syncopates his snare hit and ends the phrase with a floor tom backbeat, à la Steve Gadd. The band must have done something right, because *Counterparts* reached #2 on the *Billboard* Albums chart. And for Peart, a break between records would allow time for reinvention.

Test for Echo (1996)

By the mid '90s the members of Rush had families and other commitments, and they no longer needed to work at the breakneck pace of the past two decades. When the band reconvened for 1996's *Test for Echo*, it followed a period where Peart wanted to revamp his playing with help from instructional guru Freddie Gruber. And revamp they did, modifying Peart's grip, posture, drum and cymbal placement, and approach. The resulting record might not sound exactly like Peart was a new man, but the conviction with which

tragedies that sidelined the band until they returned in 2002. After having filtered their creative process through a variety of popular music trends over the previous thirty years, Rush decided to take a different approach with their newest record: post melody. It's not that there are *no* hooks in the tunes—it's just the obtuse nature of the material was yet another direction for a band always searching. Regardless, Peart comes out throwing haymakers with the pummeling double bass assault in "One Little Victory," effectively dispelling any fear that he would be rusty after a long layoff. He flips the beat with some downbeat snare trickery on the chorus of "Earthshine," and spices up the verses of "Ceiling Unlimited" with simple little tom fills, breaking up the straightness of the basic groove just enough without being overbearing. As the millennium turned, Peart's parts were still carefully orchestrated, but his

and double-bass groove opening "Armor and Sword." There are multiple instrumentals here, and Peart gives each something different, from the snares-off tom pattern in "The Main Monkey Business" to the bass and drum breaks in "Malignant Narcissism," echoing "YYZ" from *Moving Pictures*. Peart alternates between the 3/4 and 4/4 in "Workin' Them Angels" with little fuss, taking his time, letting things breathe. And if an old(er) dog could learn new tricks, this breathing space that permeated Peart's late-career drumming was a good one.

Clockwork Angels (2012)

Fans waited a half decade before another Rush studio record appeared, and longtime listeners were rewarded with one of the band's strongest efforts in years. The members of Rush were now living legends, and they had nothing to prove. Peart was now the elder statesman, the wise Zen master

he played was never greater. It was all about flow now, from the triplet feel of "Time and Motion" to the big spaces left in "Resist." Peart throws in some polyrhythmic cymbal hits in "Driven" and continues his heavy and intense drumming on the aggressive verses in "Virtuality." The recording, it should be noted, was big but clear, the mix bringing out all the nuances of Peart's kit. The instrumental "Limbo" is made up of different parts Peart experimented with in the studio, beats with no home eventually stitched together in the final product. This looseness was new for the band, but the results satisfied them internally. Little did anyone know it would be six years before Rush returned to the studio.

Vapor Trails (2002)

Following the *Test for Echo* tour in 1997, Peart endured personal

studies with jazzers and the inevitable maturity that comes to musicians who've been at it a while allowed him to become more improvisational, or at least sound that way. Of note: the negative reaction to the compressed muddiness of the original *Vapor Trails* caused Rush to release a clearer, remixed version.

Snakes & Arrows (2007)

Another five years would pass until Rush dropped original material (a covers disc, *Feedback,* came in 2004), and the results showed clearly that these guys were still not coasting. The band continued to write hard rock music with equal parts dynamic shade and riff muscle, and Peart still played with the conviction of an unknown out to prove himself. Check out the end of "Far Cry," with Peart soloing over the staccato rhythm with some rumbling toms, and the quarter-note China

who had a lifetime of innovation behind him, but whose thirst for the new still informed his approach. And, oh yeah, he was still hitting harder than metal dudes half his age.

"Caravan" is Peart bulldozing his way through everything, all lip-curling snarl and attitude, while the 6/8 title track moves from double-handed hi-hat parts to big toms. Old-school Rush heads will also notice a nod back to 1975's "Bastille Day" on "Headlong Flight," complete with unison bass and drum hits and similar guitar drive. Check out the track's cool snare intro and initial pattern. Elsewhere, Peart attacks his parts with intricacy and attention, but as always, plays the role of the anchor his bandmates can rely on.

With Peart's passing, *Clockwork Angels* became Rush's final studio statement, and with it they and Neil went out on top.

Finn Costello

The Freedom That Confidence Brings

In the summer of 1989, *MD* traveled up to Montreal to interview Neil as Rush was finishing up the recording of their thirteenth studio album, *Presto*. After a quick visit to Le Studio, where he led a tour of his drumkit and assortment of snare drums, we decamped to his lakeside retreat on the outskirts of Montreal, where the following interview took place. It quickly became clear that Neil had arrived at a new place in his view of his own playing—one where confidence had leavened the constant urge to accumulate new skills.

Interview by William F. Miller

MD: In your *Modern Drummer* cover story in '84, you said that you thought there would come a time when your playing would get as good as it could, and then not get any better. Have you reached that point?

Neil: Yes, I think I have. It's a funny kind of thing to say, because it won't read the way it's intended. It took me twenty years to reach a level of even some confidence. I'm not talking about being a virtuoso or being a master or anything like that. It took that long to reach a point where I actually thought I maybe could play, and I think the last five years have seen the cementing of that.

This has required a lot of inner evaluation and a certain amount of soul searching, too, because I had always lived on input and growth. At the end of a tour I always felt I had learned all these new things, and every record marked a significant broadening of my abilities and my choices of techniques. So now I feel I've reached my potential. To make any technical improvements in my playing would take too much time, and at this point playing a faster paradiddle doesn't mean as much to me.

I spent twenty years on technique and on learning the finer points of keeping good time, developing tempo and shadings of rhythmic feel, and keeping my mind open to other ethnic music and other drummers, and all of that was just flooding into me. When I finally became confident in my playing, all of these things finally came together. Confidence really was the key for me. I was never a confident player at all—flamboyant, overplaying, yes, but never confident. I had to step back from that twenty-year quest for knowledge and ask myself, "Do I really enjoy using all this stuff?" My consensus was that, yes, I do like being able to draw from all of these things I've worked on, but my mental approach to it has to change.

For me, the center of everything, and what I most enjoy doing, is what we—the band—have just been through, which is the process of writing new songs and arranging them. This includes working out drum patterns and trying to record the parts as well as possible and as quickly as possible. That has been the nexus of it, having to change my mental attitude toward what I do and having to re-evaluate in the true sense of values of what is important to me about it. It's not enough for me to just say, "I want to play my axe." I've spent twenty-odd years doing that, and now I have other ambitions and interests in life.

MD: So you're saying that you feel satisfied with what you are able to accomplish on a set of drums?

Neil: I think the word "satisfaction" sounds too smug. It's basically that I feel I have the raw materials to draw from to make the statement I want to make within a song. I can listen to a demo of a song and really have a wide-open mind and not have an axe to grind, which is another important thing. Through all the years of my development there were always things I was looking to use, because I learned how to do them. When I heard a song, I would look for a place to put this lovely new idea that I had. Now I listen to a song openly and try to bring to it just what it requires, finding what best satisfies the song and satisfies me. I'm not looking to impress myself or others anymore; I'm just looking to challenge myself, and to me, that's the route to satisfaction.

MD: Do you think a certain amount of your inflicting a lot of notes into Rush's music in the early days was brought on by a feeling of insecurity?

Neil: I wouldn't say it was insecurity. It was more a hunger, a desire—first to learn things and second to use them. That's what I was saying about there being a dark side to it, because I'm sure there were times when I used rhythmic ideas that maybe weren't the best for the song, but I really *had* to use them.

But they all add up to something, you know.

As a band we've grown through the same levels. We started with a total concentration on musicianship, which was for a time all we really cared about. Our songs were subject to that. We explored playing in different time signatures and odd arrangements, and stringing a whole line of disparate ideas together, somehow. So we were lucky to spend that time developing together as a band, instead of just by ourselves. We were very excited about it, and there was nothing negative about it or a question of insecurity in a negative sense.

MD: So you just wanted to see how far you could take it.

Neil: Yes. It becomes a series of experimentations, and like all experimentations, there are failures and there are successes, and looking back, I can judge them objectively. But all of them went somewhere. Even the failures taught us something as far as what not to do, in terms of the band anyway. It wasn't like we were sidemen trying to please someone else. I wasn't working in the studios doing jingles. I didn't have to conform. All of us were wide open to do what we wanted. We had, and still have, a different set of parameters than a lot of other musicians have to work in.

MD: Do you think yours is the best position to be in, as far as being a musician?

Neil: No question. I don't think many people would argue with that. It is pleasant sometimes to be a sideman, though. All of us in this band have done it to varying degrees. I have a friend who writes TV and film music, for instance. He's doing music for a soap at the moment, and it's set in Chicago. So he was writing a lot of slide guitar stuff with old blues patterns, and he called me to play on it. I had to play a lot of brushes, and all I did was what he told me. It was great. There was no weight on my shoulders, no responsibility, easy. There's a real joy to that when you're used to having the responsibility of everything. The three of us are very democratic in a musical sense as well as a responsibility sense, and we share the responsibilities amongst ourselves according to what we most prefer to do. However, stepping outside of that is a pleasure. But I have to think that the ideal is being in a band where you're allowed to do exactly what you want. It's hard to argue with that.

MD: Getting back to what I was asking before, are you sure there aren't *any* techniques you'd like to get into on the drums?

Neil: I really don't think so. Like I said, after twenty years of playing, I've developed a lot of things that have proven valuable to me—even the rudiments. There's a track on the new album where I play a pattern that involves eight different ethnic drums, which I assigned to pads. I played the bass drum and snare drum parts with my feet, using my own sampled sounds triggered with foot triggers. The pattern I play with my hands couldn't be played without paradiddles, because I have to have my hands accenting in certain places. Without knowing how to do a paradiddle, I couldn't have done that.

Double-stroke rolls pop up in my playing all the time, and since I spent days and weeks banging on a pillow, "Mama Dada Mama Dada," I can do a double-stroke roll. It is still a valuable thing to me, and time well spent. And that's true for any time that I've spent woodshedding a particular approach or listening to a style of music enough to understand it, like reggae or fusion. A lot of it I'll listen to as a drummer, just listening to it to understand. It's the same reason for reading *Modern Drummer*—to read what other drummers have to say about things, and either get inspired or angry. But all of that input is really important, and the time spent practicing is very valuable.

I do get really annoyed with musicians who are proud of the fact that they don't practice and never took a lesson. I just think that is such a cheat to say, "I just play simple; I don't need that." It's not really true. You can listen to some simple drummers and tell they know everything. It's implicit. They have a certain confidence and agility

on the drumset. There was a drummer featured in *MD* a while back, Manu Katché, and most of his drumming is very simple, but it is so elegant. His work on the Robbie Robertson album or his work with Joni Mitchell or Peter Gabriel is a joy to listen to. The Robbie Robertson album is my favorite of Manu's playing, and I think there may be three fills on the songs he played on the album. His rhythms are such a hybrid between West African music and Western music.

There's an English pop band called

China Crisis, and the drummer plays very simple patterns with very few fills, but again, what he plays is so elegant, and right for the music, and you can tell he has confidence. When he plays difficult patterns, he plays them with such authority that they just flow by you smoothly. Many drummers try to pull off a more difficult pattern or fill, and it comes off slightly less than smooth. I've been guilty of that myself certainly! The really good drummers make what they're playing sound effortless—not labored.

When you have drummers who've spent a lot of time learning, and a lot of time practicing and playing different styles of music, when they

do set themselves to play simply, they have a certain authority and a uniqueness to what they're doing that sets them apart. They're not just playing the only beat they know. And that's what a lot of so-called simple drummers are guilty of. They're playing simply because that's all they know. That's sad in one sense because it's so limiting. They're victims to the "less is more" approach because they don't understand exactly what it means. You have to know what you want to play and what you want to leave out—not

just play the only beat you know. A lot of times, less is less.

There are songs on the new album where originally I heard the demo that Alex and Geddy had made with a drum machine. Parts of it might have been recorded to a purely off-the-cuff, moronic drumbeat. When I came to work out my own parts for the song, I tried everything. My basic way to work on a song is to try everything I know and then eliminate all of the stuff that doesn't work, until I pare it down to something that satisfies me. But there were some parts of some songs that demanded to be simple. And it's a reality that you just have to face. If it works best that way, it's incumbent

upon you not to mess it up. [laughs]

I have to find other ways to musically satisfy myself, and I've experimented a lot, particularly in the '80s, trying to find ways to make things interesting to me. Playing a four-on-the-floor bass drum pattern has been a real challenge for me, because I like it. I've always liked dance music, but I could not sit there for five minutes and play only that; I would shoot myself. So I have to find ways to somehow make it work for me, because I want to do it, but in a way that's going to be technically and mentally challenging. So I'll take a song that demands that simple part and say, "Okay, if I have to play that simple part here, then I'll find a spot elsewhere in the song to try to get away with more." If I have to play a simple pattern, I'll try to find ways to make variations in that pattern so that it's really long, like a sixteen- or twenty-four-bar pattern of repeating things so that I have to remember the simple pattern stretched over a long period of time.

Then you get into the question of delivering that pattern perfectly, too. Again, anyone who has spent time learning and practicing drums knows what you can do with a simple 2 and 4 beat, and how many different ways you can learn that, even with metronomic time. You can push the beat, land dead on the beat, or pull it back as far as you can. Working with a click track in the studio, as I have done for the last several years, I learned to play games with that, too. I don't use a conventional click, by the way. I use a quarter-note bass drum sound. So if I'm playing along with it and I can't hear it, I know I'm in time. That's great because then I don't have to listen to the stupid thing. It's almost become a subliminal relationship with this bass drum pounding away, and I just sit in with it. As you get more confident with a click, you start fooling around with how much latitude you can get away with. It's like, "Just how far back can I pull this thing?" So being able to experiment within the framework of the click is something I like to do.

A good drummer that I like who plays simply is Phil Gould, who used to be with Level 42. He plays very simple, R&B-influenced drumming, but when he pulls a fill out it'll be a beautiful fill. And his feel is great. If you try to tap along with their downbeat-on-the-3 type of songs, you'll just about break your hand trying to come down behind the beat as much as he does. He has that feel down so well. It's very satisfying for me to listen to from a drummer's point of view or from a music fan's point of view. It feels great, has tremendous authority, and has the spice of a great little fill leaping out of it.

The three drummers I mentioned I can count among my favorite drummers, although they don't play the kind of drumming that I like playing. They're playing the kind of stuff that I like to listen to. Music that I like to listen to is not always what I would like to be playing. For instance, I could never be a reggae drummer; I would go nuts. But I love to listen to it; it's so infectious and I love the rhythm. But I couldn't discipline myself enough to shut off my ideas.

MD: Would you say that overall you prefer to listen to a simple drummer more than a busier player?

Neil: For me it's more the style of music rather than the style of drummer. I do enjoy organized music, and it's one of the things that keeps me from getting emotional about jazz. I can listen to it, be inspired by it live, and appreciate it, certainly. But when it comes to music for pleasure, I like music that is constructed and organized, and that time has been spent on the craft of it.

Technique, though, is important to me. I'm really impressed by it when I hear it done well. But there is just so little of it around on display, and what there is tends to be devoted to jazz. I guess that's just an unfortunate void that is in modern music.

MD: You mentioned earlier that you get the most enjoyment out of arranging new songs and coming up with new drum patterns for songs. How do you go about coming up with your drum parts?

Neil: I usually work out my parts by myself now. Geddy and Alex will put down a rough demo tape of the song in a basic arrangement form with a drum machine. Then I go up to the demo studio alone and go over it and try what works and what doesn't. Gradually I'll refine the drum part down to something that will work.

MD: How much time does that process take?

Neil: It depends on the song. It's probably about a day for each song. That's the best way for me to do it—just immerse myself in one song. But that's not to say I work out every single note that I'm going to be playing. I'll decide where I may want a special fill, or where a specific time pattern is to be played, but I leave plenty of freedom in the parts for some creativity in the studio. I said before that I liked organized music, but I also like spontaneity in its appropriate place. The studio is the perfect place for that because you're allowed to keep being spontaneous until you're spontaneously good!

MD: You mentioned that you don't feel you can improve much beyond where you are now. How important is practicing to you now?

Neil: I read a great quote recently by a young classical violinist. She was asked if she ever practiced, and her response was, "I never practice, I only play." And that was not to say that she didn't pick up her instrument and play, but she never picked it up to practice without playing music. That's basically the way it is for me. If I sit down at my drums informally, I just sit down and play. I don't worry about practicing a pattern or something. I'm a bit worried about the smugness of having arrived at a certain point. Not by a longshot have

I learned everything there is to know, but I've learned enough to satisfy me.

I have a little set of drums set up in my basement at home, and I like to sit down and play with brushes—just playing around. I have a marimba that I get on and play. During a break in the preparations for the new album, I recorded some basic tracks that I can play marimba along to. I just picked out some chords and keys that I liked and recorded them. I have them on cassette so I can play along any time I want to. I enjoy that because it allows

I was wondering just how far back I was going to have to go to get it back. But I found that after so many years of playing, and especially so many years of touring, the muscle memory is intense. All I really had to do was get some calluses back on my hands. I hadn't forgotten how to do a thing; I hadn't lost any fluidity or agility. The smaller fast-twitch muscles in the wrists and fingers had to be developed a little bit, but it was nowhere near as difficult as I thought it was going to be.

It surprised me. I was never that

full strength all of the time.

I also feel a tremendous amount of responsibility about playing live. You're up there to deliver, and there are no excuses. It doesn't matter how you're feeling or how things are going technologically or whatever. That attitude is sort of inbred in me in a puritanical way, that if it's worth doing, it's worth doing well. My father used to hammer that into me, but it's become kind of a credo of my own.

MD: When you've been on a long tour, do you notice that you're thinking less

me the chance to play the instrument instead of playing scales or technical things alone.

MD: Do you have to practice a certain amount of time just to maintain your abilities? Does it go away?

Neil: Ironically, no. I traveled a great deal last year, and there was a period of several months where I was continents away from any drums to play. When I started to work on getting back in shape playing-wise for the new album,

confident to think that I could lay off and still be able to play. I always thought that you had to maintain this thing. Before tours, I would always start weeks in advance preparing by myself, putting on headphones and playing along with our records. I think that was more a matter of getting into shape for touring physically, and not mentally. After hundreds and hundreds of shows of very intensive drumming, you can't avoid playing a lot. You're putting out

about every note that you're playing and more about just the spices, as you say?

Neil: Yes, I'd say that's definitely true. Ideally, you shouldn't have to think about what you're doing, but you should always be thinking about what you're *going* to do. You always have to be well ahead of yourself. And by being able to think ahead, your drumming has so much more confidence and authority because

you know what's coming. Mistakes are made in moments of indecision. The more playing you do, like during a tour, for example, the better that "automatic pilot" becomes. You're not turning your mind off. On the contrary, you're turning it on in a much broader sense.

MD: *Presto* is on a new record label for Rush. How did that come about?

Neil: Well, we had been with Phonogram since day one, so that's fourteen years. We had signed several contracts over the years with them, and we'd had good relations with them. The band had talked about making a change in the past but never did it, and then when our last contract with Phonogram expired, we decided not to renew. We started to feel a little taken for granted. We are

whole machinery rested on us—that if we stopped doing interviews, if we stopped touring for any reason, nobody else would be doing anything.

That had a good side to it as well. In the early days we were left alone too. We were allowed to take four albums before we even broke even. Most bands at that time, or especially this time, would not get that kind of latitude. We were kind of overlooked. It was a small company at the time, and they were a little bit disorganized. Rush has outlived, it would seem, countless hierarchies of management at the label. We just went along through all of that. And we also weathered through the "hot new band" syndrome, where the label would get excited about some new band that would last a year

ourselves, which is serious enough.

When you go in with the blank slate and begin the whole process of coming up with a record, it's a fearsome thing. In fact, it's something I avoid. If we have decided to go to work on some new material, I always try to get away and work on lyrics to have something ready. For the most part, when we begin working on a new project we all have ideas to get things rolling. Sometimes we do start from scratch, though. I think that can be a very positive approach. We have gone into a record situation and been one song short for an album, due to whatever reason, and sometimes good things come from that. We've even gone so far as to plan for it, where we'll write all the material except for

> ## "An important dividing point for any drummer is when you find out that the way your hero plays is not the way you should play."

not a record company's dream. We go along from album to album and sell a respectable amount, but we never have blockbuster hits and we don't go quadruple platinum. We just go along at our own speed, and it works out great.

We've never had any really strong radio-play support, so touring has always been our only mode of exposure. As far as we could see, we were out there selling our own records, which is fine, but we thought that maybe another record company could help us out a bit more, and not make it always incumbent upon us to sell our goods. We felt that the

or two and then be gone, but we're still there. That was the problem: We were just there.

MD: Do you have any added pressure on you with this album since this is a new situation with a new label?

Neil: No, to the contrary, I think it's up to them to prove it. We've had a lot of albums that have done pretty well. Atlantic, our new label, is convinced that they can do better for us. We're not saying, "Sign us because we'll sell more records with you." They're saying, "Sign with us because we'll sell more records." It's a pretty simple thing. It doesn't put any pressure on us at all, any more than we already place on

one song, and then have to come up with something on the spot. On our album *Hold Your Fire*, we'd written the entire album, and at the last minute we decided that we wanted a different kind of song. So on our very last day of pre-production, we wrote what became the opening song on the album, "Force Ten." So it was done on a self-imposed kind of pressure.

MD: How do you feel that song turned out?

Neil: Oh, great! It's one of my enduring favorites from that album. Another song that we did this same way was "Vital Signs" from *Moving Pictures*. That song was last minute in the studio!

We'd finished everything else for the record, so we felt free to try something. It could be anything we wanted it to be, so that was a refreshing feeling. So it can be a very beneficial thing.

MD: Now that the band seems to be

Andrew MacNaughtan

starting fresh, with a new label and all, how would you describe the music on this new album?

Neil: For one thing, I think we've stretched the parameters a little further. As records become less and less a part of the modern media, that's given us a certain freedom time-wise. We're no longer regimented to twenty minutes a side for an album. Records are less than 10 percent of what people purchase now. We looked at the cassette and the CD as the definitive versions, so we thought in terms of roughly an hour of music. We gave ourselves the option for more songs, and more room to poke into the corners stylistically. That extra latitude

makes quite a bit of difference in how we would normally do things.

We ended up with eleven songs, and they're all quite different. With this album, we started out with a couple of basic underlying ideas to work from.

We discussed the idea of letting the music grow from our basic unit, which is guitar, bass, and drums. On past albums we tended to write a lot with keyboards and then apply the other instruments afterwards. We thought it would be more interesting to be a bit more linear and do the writing around the guitar framework, and thinking of it as an ensemble as guitar, bass, and drums. Not to be reactionary—we won't omit keyboards as a point of principle. To the contrary, we will probably use keyboards as much as ever, but the focus will be different.

MD: Were there any moments on the new album when you found yourself being challenged by a drum part?

Neil: I mentioned before the dichotomy of balancing simple and complex, which is something that is always difficult. I find simple parts challenging for me. The most challenging aspect of new music is coming up with the right part or the right pattern. Some things just seem to fall together, where I hear the piece and immediately have an idea, and luckily it works. However, that's the exception.

There's a song on the album called "Show Don't Tell," which begins with a syncopated guitar riff that appears two or three times throughout the song. That was about the hardest thing for me to find the right pattern for. I wanted to maintain a groove and yet follow the bizarre syncopations that the guitar riff was leading into. It was demanding technically, but at the same time, because of that, we were determined that it should have a rhythmic groove under it.

It's not enough for us to produce a part that's technically demanding; it has to have an overwhelming significance musically. So it had to groove into the rest of the song and it had to have a pulse to it that was apart from what we were playing.

There's another song on the album, called "Scars." On this song I was playing eight different pads with my hands in a pattern, while I played snare and bass drum parts with my feet. I was using paradiddles with my hands to get the accents in the right place and on the right pads. Then I had to organize the different sounds on the pads correctly so they would fall in the order I wanted them to. Then I had to arrange all of that into a series of rhythmic patterns, not just one. It was more than a day's work before I even played a note.

That was a challenge of a different sort, but it came about in an interesting way. When Geddy and Alex did the demo for the song, they put all kinds of percussion on the track, including congas, timbales, and bongos. We talked about bringing in a percussionist to play in addition to the drum pattern that I might play. I wanted to bring in Alex Acuña, someone who is tremendously facile in that area, who could make the track exciting as well as interesting. I figured he could assign me the simple parts

and we could do it together. But then they thought, "What if Neil did it all himself using pads?" So it happened as I described, with me playing the percussion parts with my hands and holding down the snare and bass parts with my feet. It was very satisfying to me to come up with a part that worked by myself.

MD: Is that something you'll be able to pull off live?

Neil: Oh, absolutely! That's the thing, there isn't an overdub on it. When we first played the tape for our producer, he thought I overdubbed the whole thing. Most listeners will probably think that when they hear the song.

Sampling has been a godsend to me, to be able to include sounds in my playing without having to overdub anything. I have little triggers placed around my kit so I can always get to one if I have a special sound that I want to use on a given song. Sampling brings the world of percussion to a place the size of a coin. Around an acoustic drumset there are plenty of places to stick a little trigger, and of course there's always room for a footswitch. You can always slip a foot off of the hi-hat and send off another sound. I feel it really adds a lot to the character of what I'm doing.

MD: On the last few albums you experimented a great deal with sampling and coming up with your own unique sounds to trigger. Did you continue with this on the new album?

Neil: Yes, I did a little bit. I really did resist getting into electronics for a long time—long after just about everyone else took it up. It got to the point where I couldn't resist it. But even then I didn't want to replace my acoustic set. That's when I came up with the idea of the back-to-front satellite kit. Anybody who saw my kit in the late '70s knows I tried to put everything up there, including all types of percussion instruments. It just got to the point where I could not get any more around me. I wanted more keyboard-percussion items on my kit because at the time I was really pushing myself to play more parts on mallet instruments. I never expected to become a virtuoso on keyboard percussion, but I thought I could contribute to the band sonically.

All of those instruments are big. You know, when you start wanting to have a marimba, glockenspiel, timpani, and chimes, it's just an impossibility to get it around you. So when sampling came along, that's when electronics just won me over completely. When the KAT MIDI mallet controller came along, that was what I'd been hoping for. All of the keyboard percussion stuff that I'd been trying to fit in physically and also get reproduced in a live setting, I was finally able to do. I used to have a glockenspiel where the KAT is now

in my kit. We would mike those bells, and that mic would pick up only part of the instrument, but it would pick up half the drumkit and most of the bass sound! So using the KAT completely avoids those types of problems.

I sample all of my own sounds. If I happen to need a timbale sample because I want a timbale on my right-hand side—my acoustic timbale is on my left—I sample my own timbale. On the song I mentioned earlier, "Scars," I sampled my own snare drum and played it with my foot. On the last studio album, we had a song called "Mission," which had a syncopated marimba, bass guitar, and snare drum solo. When it was originally recorded, I recorded the snare drum and overdubbed the marimba to it. Live, I assigned both the snare drum sound and the marimba sound to the same *pad*, so I can have both sounds! On the song "Time Stand Still" I used temple block sounds. Through the wonder of electronics, I was able to manipulate the pitches of the temple blocks, so I got the sound I heard in my head for that part. I have an antique Chinese drum at home that's too fragile to do anything with, but by sampling, I was able to use it on the record.

MD: Were there any new drum products that you used on the new album, other than electronics?

Neil: Snare drums have been my main

REMEMBERING NEIL

continued from page 34

Some of the funkiest drummers I know went in on "Tom Sawyer" because the groove was undeniable. "YYZ" was on everybody's list, too. His fills were so tasty that everybody had to learn them all, along with their sequence.

The way he'd play odd time signatures gave me grief, but he made them feel as normal as 4/4.

The fact that he also played the marimba, bells, and other percussion but also wrote mind-expanding lyrics blew my mind.

My brother Norwood Fisher (bassist), Kendall Jones (original guitar player for Fishbone), and I even started our own progressive-rock band. We were super influenced by Rush, and I got to try all of that "what would Neil do?" stuff. Those four-stroke rolls are still one of my go-to licks, among other great things I got from listening so attentively to the work of the great Neil Peart.

Highlight: Standing behind him off stage but with a clear view at a festival in Canada. Educational to say the least. Truly,

Phillip Fisher (Fishbone)

I've long thought that Neil Peart was the Escoffier of the drums. One of the most famous chefs of all time, Auguste Escoffier's approach to French haute cuisine was shaped by his time spent in the military. In Escoffier's "brigade de cuisine" approach, every member of the kitchen staff had a highly curated role and was expected to execute their contribution to each dish with militaristic precision. As a result, when we dine at a high-caliber restaurant in 2020, dishes arrive with consistency and precision, crafted thoughtfully, executed with impeccably high standards.

So too with Neil's drumming. Those larger-than-life, highly air-drummable fills at the end of the guitar solo of "Tom Sawyer"? He played them in London in 1983 exactly the same way that he played them in Concord, New Hampshire, in 1990. That syncopated 16th-note ride cymbal pattern in "Red Barchetta"? Same in Flagstaff, Arizona, in 1987 as in Brazil in 2002. The intro fill in "Limelight" after Alex Lifeson's opening guitar arpeggio? Same in… okay, you get the point.

Consistency. Intentionality. Night. After. Night. Sticking the landings. Landing the stickings. Serving the

area of research lately. I tend to go through periods of examination of the drums that I use, the heads that I use, and so on. I'm constantly re-evaluating what I use, and I try not to take any of it for granted. As I went through the rehearsal process, I had time to experiment. I was going over the songs on my own, not wasting anyone else's time, so I recorded what I was doing and really listened to the snare drum. I tried each of the tracks with different ones.

I really got to know my little snare family. I had a rough idea what each of the drums could do, but I never had the time to really experiment and find out what I like about each of them. I have my old faithful Slingerland snare that has been my number-one snare for years. I've always kept my ears open over the years for different drums, but that one always sounded best. But this time I really wanted to experiment. I tried a few piccolo snares, some of the custom-made snares, just trying whatever I could get my hands on. I had an old Camco snare drum that was given to me by Tama in Japan, and suddenly it sounded great to me. I liked it for years, but all of a sudden it started sounding real good to me. I ended up using it on four songs on the album. It's a very bright-sounding drum.

Solid Percussion has a drum that I really like. It's a piccolo drum that has a solid note in a useable range. Most piccolos have tremendous definition and a great high-end crack, but they don't have much in the way of a bottom end. The Solid drum that I have is made of cocobolo wood, which gives it a resonance that carries into lower frequencies. That must be the fundamental difference, because I tried another piccolo of theirs made of ply maple, and it sounded like a good-sounding piccolo, but not as versatile as the solid-shell cocobolo. It's a joyous drum to play. I used that drum for most of the record.

MD: When you showed us your kit and all of your snare drums in the studio, you didn't have any snare drum deeper than a 5" shell. You're not interested in deep-shelled snare drums?

Neil: Well, I've tried them, but I just don't like the sound. The distance between the heads gives the drum an odd response, at least to me. They feel

Andrew MacNaughtan

funny to me. I know they have their uses, but they don't fall into what I'm doing.

I'm the same way with tom-toms. I practically had to special-order a set that didn't have deep-shelled toms. Everyone thinks that depth equals volume or resonance, or something. It's

something that I've experimented with and have found no basis in fact. I use the standard tom sizes and get a sound that I'm most happy with.

MD: Which snare drum are you going to take out with you on the road?

Neil: Now, that's a tough one! Number one [the Slingerland] has been number one for a long time. It really does it all live, but at this point I'm not sure. I would think that the cocobolo drum is a strong contender because it really does everything well.

MD: Talking about drums, besides your snare drum sound, you've always had an excellent bass drum sound. You're probably going to tell me that you changed your bass drum setup on every album and tour, but how do you have them tuned and muffled?

Neil: Actually, you're right, I haven't changed what I do with them over the last few years. In the studio, I generally take off the front heads and use quite heavy damping. I'll use those quilted

---

audience with the highest of quality. The deliberate similitude in Neil's execution was a feature, not a bug. Thank you, Neil.
Mark Stepro (Butch Walker, Brett Dennen)

Neil compared the physicality of drumming to that of an athlete. I think the best athletes are students of the game—constantly observing details and subtleties in order to continue to grow, excel, and stand above the rest. As a drummer and former athlete, I consider Neil a superior student of the game.

He pulled inspiration from those musicians he admired and took ideas and execution to levels most of us only dream of achieving. Supremely technical, musical, and creative, his mark on the community is immeasurable.
Dena Tauriello (independent, Broadway's *Little Shop of Horrors*)

Never have I been aware of someone with such a dedication to their craft that, even in his forties, while already considered by many for decades to be one of the absolute best to ever pick up two sticks, he

took drum lessons again to expand that craft. For me, that's huge. Not as huge, though, as hearing "Tom Sawyer" on the radio for the first time at age seven and being drawn into the world of Rush and, as a drummer, Neil Peart in particular. I would have to count him more as an inspiration than an influence, because his level was so far beyond anything I have thus far been able to approach. But many, many hours of my life have been spent trying to learn his licks and fills. Every once in a while, someone comes along who changes the game completely, and Neil Peart was one of

the few that unquestionably changed the way the instrument that we all love was perceived and approached going forward. Rest in power, Professor!
Kliph Scurlock (Gruff Rhys)

As a young drummer I was in awe of Neil Peart's technical prowess and the amount of drums he played—wow! But what resonates most with me is that he was not just the drummer for Rush; he wrote the lyrics and was the driving force of the band. And from what I've heard, he was also an extremely kind person.

continues on page 50

packing blankets placed right against the head.

It's a funny thing with damping. I wonder if I'll get to the point where I'll be able to get the sound I want without any damping. Years ago I muffled everything on the kit—the toms and the snare. Then as I became better at tuning drums, I stopped using muffling completely on toms and snare drums in the studio. But with the bass drums, I don't know; it's one hell of a big barrel with too much out-of-control transient stuff going on.

For live work, I use both heads on the drum. The front head has a hole just large enough to get a mic inside. For muffling I use a product I saw advertised in your very pages. It's a crescent-shaped muffling device that just sits inside the drum and rests against both heads.

MD: Does that muffle the drums a lot?
Neil: No. It's a very light foam that lets a lot of the air pass through it, so the drum isn't completely dead. The thing I've always liked about double-headed bass drums is that they have a liveliness that feels great, and they're much more dynamic. It's just like the difference between a double-headed tom and an open tom. The open tom has one sound, whereas the double-headed drum has an infinite variety of sounds.

As for heads on the bass drums, I like the clear dots for their durability. And I just use your typical felt beater. It's mundane, I know. [laughs]

MD: Speaking of toms, for the longest time you had both double- and single-headed drums in your setup, and you mentioned in previous interviews that you liked that setup. However, now you're only using double-headed drums.

Neil: That's right. During the last album I recorded a song with the open toms and then re-recorded it with double-headed toms, and the effects were surprising for me. The only open toms I had on my kit were the four highest drums, the 6", 8", 10", and 12". With two heads, the drums just came alive.

I ended up changing my setup a little bit because I was duplicating a drum size. My toms used to range from left to right, 6", 8", 10", 12", all open toms, and then 12", 13", 15", and 18" double-headed toms. When I completely switched over to double-headed toms, I got rid of one of the 12" toms.

MD: With the upcoming tour, are you planning on using the revolving riser with the two drumkits?

Neil: Yes, because it gives me the flexibility to use both electronics and acoustics. I don't have to compromise one for the other.

MD: How did you come up with the arrangement of the instruments on the electronic kit? I mean, the ride cymbal is practically on top of the snare drum!

Neil: Yes, that's a bit different. It just becomes inevitabilities. It reminds me of Sherlock Holmes: "Eliminate the impossible, and whatever's left must be the truth." It kind of comes down to that with putting together a drumset.

A lot of times people think you start with all this equipment and figure out a place to put it. For drummers, I think as your kit changes and grows, it does so by one little unit at a time. When my kit started growing from a small drumkit into a big one, it was literally one cowbell, one cymbal, one whatever, found its spot. Other things would then have to work around that. You find little ideas that will help you economize on space and let you squeeze something in. Putting one cymbal on top of another is a time-honored one, and getting the right angle of playability on your toms and getting things in close enough to you so that you can play them with conviction. Things have to be in reach and controllable.

When it came to adding the back kit, once I had thought of getting an acoustic bass drum and snare drum, cymbals, and then placing the electronic pads around that, it all sort of fell into place. As far as having a ride cymbal above a snare drum, I think it's great. It makes me do different things. And because of where I have that

---

REMEMBERING NEIL
continued from page 49

He elevated drummers as people and demonstrated that they do more than just play amazing fills. They are also intellectual, and he made that cool. What an inspiration for other drummers and musicians. He strived to always be the best he could possibly be and was constantly learning more about drumming.
Kevin March (Guided by Voices)

There's something about Rush that drummers tend to gravitate towards. For me it was a way to test and expand my own skills against one of the greats. At some point my taste in music changed considerably, but I was always drawn back to listen to Neil's remarkable drumming. Precise, well-considered, and executed with ferocious intensity, which is clearly a mirror of the kind of person he was. Thank you, Neil.
Ira Elliot (Nada Surf)

Ritualistically playing through *Moving Pictures* as an eleven-year-old boy introduced me to the musical excitement I'd chase for the rest of my life. Neil invented me. Hitting the last third of "Red Barchetta," feeling like I was in a speeding car, seeing the landscape rush by, it converted me—made me want to be a musician. Thanks, Neil! Much love to you on your way.
Matt Johnson (Jade Bird, St. Vincent, Rufus Wainwright)

I grew up playing jazz music around my grandfather. At the age of ten, I was introduced to Rush. Neil's drumming captivated me. I didn't realize it at the time, but Neil was the bridge for me between rock drumming and fusion/jazz, where drums are more deeply involved in the song presentation. Many aspects of Neil's playing permeated my musical development: his creation of "contra" melodic ride crown patterns made a second melody to the music; the use of orchestra and electronic tones added to the kit; and Neil's use of crashes in the middle of tom fills. He used these stabbing kick/cymbal punches in a new and deliberate way. After many years of playing, I can still hear where his influence shows up in a way that makes me think about the composition with more reverence. His

cymbal positioned, as well as the ride cymbal from my acoustic kit, I have two ride cymbals that I can reach. I've been playing patterns lately involving 16th notes between two ride cymbals that I could never do on a normal kit.

MD: At every Rush concert there are drummers in the audience playing along with you, air-drumming. Do you try to exactly reproduce your recorded parts live?

Neil: It depends if it's hard enough. I mentioned before about difficulty being an underrated quality, because

drumming along at shows, I take that as a compliment that they like the fills. I spend a lot of time trying to be able to come up with the right fills, so if they're enjoyed by the audience that way, terrific.

MD: In performance, you always have an expression on your face of sheer concentration.

Neil: I'd call it desperate concentration. [laughs]

MD: But your expression is not too extreme when you compare it to other rock drummers. And yet, you

he was probably the most flamboyant drummer there has been. So I think in the hands of someone who can already play, showmanship is great.

For me, to toss a stick up in the air is a really dangerous thing. Who knows where it's going to come down? So it adds a certain amount of risk to the performance, and a certain amount of excitement. And I like to toss them high, so it's a challenge. It's not something you can take for granted; it's a little moment of tension for me.

That's an interesting point you

> ## "I was never a confident player at all— flamboyant, overplaying, yes, but never confident."

it's the difficulty of a song that keeps it fresh. If we've gone to the trouble of making a song a challenge to us, then we really don't get tired of playing it.

Our song "Tom Sawyer" is a perfect example of a song that is a complete challenge for me to play years after the record came out, because it's difficult physically and mentally. So to me, there's no sense messing with it. I'm just trying to make it as accurate and as musical as possible. But there are other songs that do get tired or we become disenchanted with, so we certainly change them. If some songs just are past the point of interest for us, we retire them. As far as people air-

do things like stick tosses and twirls. How do you feel about drumming and showmanship?

Neil: I think it's great, as long as it's both; the drumming has to be as important as the showmanship. When drumming and showmanship are talked about, they tend to be like technique and feel, as if they were mutually exclusive of each other. Obviously they need not be.

Gene Krupa was probably my first seed of wanting to be a drummer. There's no question that he was very flamboyant. To me he was the first rock drummer. Keith Moon was another early drummer that I admired a lot, and

mentioned about facial expression, though. It seems that when I'm performing there's so much chaos going on inside of me, and yet when I see a film or a still photograph of myself, it doesn't seem to reflect the reality as I know it. I feel like I'm literally a storm. My mind and my body are just frantic, completely over the top. I never feel like it's ever totally under control.

MD: With all of the years of loud playing that you've done, have you noticed any problems with your hearing?

Neil: No, I haven't. I think it's an ill-understood thing, the effects of loud sounds on the ears. I've read a lot

poetic and lyrical mastery played a huge role in his drumming, connecting drumming with the composition, similar to how jazz drumming uses melody parts. I barely knew the lyrics to the songs I was playing with bands, while Neil was writing all of his!

I met Neil through Freddie Gruber. We were studying with him at the same time. He was a man of precision and diligence, in everything he did. Rush's shows were displays of how to give back to fans, always providing more than what was expected. I was at Neil's second-to-last show on the R40 tour in Irvine, California. It was the best

concert I've ever seen and a fitting finale to an amazing career. Neil will rest alongside the greatest to play this instrument. His memory will live on for many reasons, none the least of which is best described as: Excellence. Bravo, Neil! Thank you. RIP.
Russ Miller (Andrea Bocelli, *American Idol*)

It's no secret that Neil Peart is one of the most influential drummers and lyricists of all time. You cannot listen to a Rush song and not break a sweat air-drumming to his perfectly calculated parts.

Neil made lead singers want to be drummers, made guitarists want to trade picks for sticks, and inspired everyone to learn his beats note for note. He elevated the game to make drummers strive to get better and be more creative behind the kit. He showed us all how to step outside the box and make the most complicated licks seem so musical and perfect— you can't imagine them played any other way.

We've lost a legend, an innovator, a hero, and an icon. His imagination and creativity brought out the drummer in all of us. Neil's musicianship will

continue to inspire generations to come, and his legacy will be untouchable for the rest of time.
RIP Neal Peart
Tucker Rule (Thursday, Frank Iero and the Future Violents)

I was just a wee one when I first heard of Neil Peart.

I didn't know up or down regarding music, but what stands out to me now is that I knew of him before I knew of Rush.

While I flailed around trying to be the next Tony Hawk, I had some friends

continues on page 52

about it, and most of the information is conflicting. The band has a serious ear check every year before we begin recording an album, because in the studio you're talking about increments of equalization that are so tiny that we think it's very important, aside from the obvious reasons. It may be the case that I'll go deaf when I'm sixty—as long as I don't go blind.

By the way, I really object to ear protection. When I see bands that play ridiculously loud and wear ear plugs, I think it's a stupid thing. If *you're* not going to accept it, why should you bludgeon your audience with it? I love loud music and always have, and I think there's a certain forcefulness about it that's irreplaceable and part of the energy of rock that I like. However, I think you're losing touch with your instrument with ear plugs, and if you need them to get through a performance, then maybe the music is too loud.

MD: Do you find that a long tour affects you emotionally?

Neil: Touring alone does, just because you're isolated away from everything. We were lucky to have come up through the ranks slowly. We saw a lot of other bands headlining and saw how they handled fame with all its temptations. I certainly got to see how dangerous it is for an unstable person to deal with the whole situation.

I've seen many of them just crumble underneath it. So strong character is pretty much an irreplaceable quality to have in this business. That is something that doesn't always go with a very creative personality.

MD: Does the band have a lot of input into all of the elaborate production "events" that happen in a Rush performance?

Neil: As I mentioned earlier, each of us in the band has different areas that interest us, so we specialize in them. Geddy, for instance, is very interested in visual arts, and he's a big film buff. He was very influential with our live concert video, *A Show of Hands*, because it was a way for him to apply an interest. I've always had a secondary interest in both words and visual images, so art direction falls into my job description, as well as being the stenographer for the band, collecting up all of the credits and lyrics for album covers, submitting them, and making sure they're all organized. It's a way for us to help each other and the band so that all of us don't have to do everything.

MD: You just mentioned your concert video, *A Show of Hands*. Watching it, it's clear that you have to play along with a lot of sequenced parts. Do you have any suggestions on working with a sequencer in a live setting?

Neil: It's very similar to working with

a click in the studio. It's really just a matter of practice. It's a barrier that drummers need to get over. Once you get over it, working with sequencers really becomes a second-nature type of thing. One difficult thing about sequencers live is being able to hear them. I still use headphones a lot for that reason.

MD: There still seemed to be some sequenced parts where you weren't wearing headphones, though.

Neil: Oh, yeah, a lot of them. I just have them through my monitors. In fact, a lot of them I trigger myself. The challenge to it really is that many of our sequenced parts aren't entire songs in length. Of course, the sequence is the exact tempo that the record was made to, and playing live, that is not always a realistic proposition. But in this case, I have to set myself up through the whole song so that maybe in the second chorus, when the sequencer comes in, I'm going to lock in with it and it's not going to sound as if suddenly the whole song slowed down or got faster. That takes a lot of practice, and it's just a matter of time.

Speaking of sequencers, each of us triggers these things live onstage. The line we draw is that all of those things have to be triggered manually. It's not like using tapes. Sequencers, especially in the context that we use them, are coming in all over the place

REMEMBERING NEIL

continued from page 51

come by with tapes to put in the boom box. At the same time a kid down the road that did the BMX thing, not the skating thing, got a sweet drumkit from his folks. He was hell bent on learning everything Rush.

"Dude…like…seriously, dude…you gotta check this out."

I didn't start out wanting to play drums. I wanted to play guitar like Dave Mustaine: off the rails and seemingly seconds from death.

At the time good music elicited

flight or fight.

Kill or be killed.

Rush didn't quite fit in, but Neil did.

Details sketch a quick picture, but Neil did not.

What the hell are they talking about in their songs? Temples?

That was a bit odd to my skater brain, but it was—and is, and will always be—absolutely impossible to not appreciate the musicianship on all parts.

I never had the pleasure of meeting Neil, and to some extent I'm glad I didn't. I've met many of my heroes, and I cherish those experiences, but

there is something to be said about maintaining a hero.

To have not known the band at the time, Neil will always be the man before the band.

Alone he defined and continues to define the drummer's role. His outreach, as described above, is second to none and indefinable. In many ways he challenged me, and in many ways he showed me how.

Thank you, Neil.

Chris Adler

I was not prepared for this. Not for how suddenly the news hit—a

short bulletin out of the blue on a Friday afternoon. How could this have happened? We were just getting used to the idea of him being retired, adjusting to the fact that there wouldn't be another tour next year. It was trouble enough trying to figure how the drum universe was going to manage without that dependable benchmark against which all else could be measured.

No, I was not prepared for this. Instead, I had been wondering, what's next for him? What will he morph into…as a creative force, as a writer, as a husband, as a father? I was not

in our performances. They have to be triggered obviously to the millisecond, or they'll be off from what we're playing. The dangers that can happen musically are nerve-racking. We don't feel as if we're cheating because of the way it's all put together by us, as opposed to if we were up there playing along to tapes. We'd never be comfortable with that.

MD: Over the years you've been known for your long and well-executed drum

fit it in with all of the songs we wanted to include, so I went in and killed a lot of the things in the solo that had appeared on earlier recorded solos of mine, so that the listener would have something fresh to hear. For the video, I had even less time for the solo. But I was still very happy with what was presented there, and since I got to decide where to edit it, it was no imposition.

MD: Were you triggering the horn kicks

have a Synclavier, which is a super-deluxe synthesizer. We analyzed the chording of the Basie samples and reproduced them synthetically. So I got all of the intervals I wanted, and it ended up sounding beautiful. I could then wipe the guilt off my brow, because I'd gone to the trouble and expense of creating those samples.

MD: During that section, how did you go about triggering those horn hits?

Neil: With Simmons pads. I assigned

> "You shouldn't have to think about what you're doing, but you should always be thinking about what you're *going* to do. By being able to think ahead, your drumming has so much more confidence and authority."

solos. The solo on *A Show of Hands* seems to have been edited.

Neil: It was truncated quite a bit. It had to be in order for it to fit within a certain amount of time. When we were coming down to deciding what to put on the tape, whether it be my drum solo or another song, I told them that I would prefer another song. And then I went on a bike trip of the Rockies. When I came back, I got a call from the office asking me if I'd like to include the drum solo after all. We only had a certain amount of time on the CD to

at the end?

Neil: Yes, I was. There was an interesting story behind that section of the solo. I took the idea from a Count Basie CD that I have. I sampled the horn hits off the CD and triggered them live, but I didn't feel right about using someone else's sounds on our record. I have strict morality about sampling, and it's one reason why I use mostly my own samples. I don't like to think that they've been robbed off of someone else's record.

So I went into the studio, where they

each one to a different pad, and to a foot switch. I struck the pad and crash cymbal at the same time, so the hits came off exactly together. I worked it out so that things were in the right place so that I could do that kind of drum construction I wanted and be in the right place for the brass accents.

MD: Over the years, many times you've arranged drum fills in particular songs from simpler in the beginning to much more complex by the end. Is this something you make a conscious decision about, or has this just

prepared for the second act to be cut short.

Most of all, I wasn't prepared for how deeply the news would impact me. I can't say I was always the biggest fan. Since I first became aware of him in 1979, there had been periods of infatuation, periods of obsession, and periods where my focus was elsewhere. Over the years and decades, he had come and gone from the forefront of my "drummer's mind." And yet, since 1979 he had always been there—a consistent, continuous, creative force in drumming and music. Saying something important with each

record, each book, each DVD. And whether we considered ourselves fans or not, we could all agree that he stood for something—always presenting his art with an integrity as strong as his talent. We could all agree on that, and so we were not prepared when he was suddenly taken from us.

In my book *The Ultimate History of Rock 'n' Roll Drumming*, I made the case that with the death of John Bonham in 1980, Neil Peart picked up the mantle of "world's greatest" and never really put it down. Like Bonham, Peart's life was the stuff of legend—complete with epic triumphs and

horrific tragedies. At the center of it all, however, remained the most normal of men. An intensely private person, one who never cared for spectacle.

And so, as he had handled all that life presented him (both the glorious and the tragic), so he handled the "event" of his passing—out of the spotlight and with great humility. And yet no one can deny that Neil Peart was a towering presence. A teacher to us all, in one way or another.

I was not prepared for any of this, and now I feel a very big void in my heart. Rest in peace, good sir. You truly made a difference in the world.

Daniel Glass (Royal Crown Revue, Brian Setzer)

Neil is gone, but not really. His influence spreads far and wide as the Ghost Rider lives on in the hearts and minds of drummers and air-drummers now and well into the future. RIP, buddy. Thanks for endless inspiration.

Pat Mastelotto (King Crimson, ORk, Stick Men)

Neil was the finest-tuned human being on earth and vibrated at a

continues on page 54

happened naturally?

Neil: It's a conscious decision. I do it because I hate doing the same fill twice in the same song. As I expressed before, I do like simple fills. But if I do one once in a song, then I feel compelled to do something different the next time. Usually there's a relationship between the fills I play within a given song. They're either variations on each other, or they're progressions towards a certain thing. Let's say the first fill I play in a song will intimate a triplet feel. The next fill will state it a bit more clearly, and on the last fill, it will be no-holds-barred. Ride-outs in songs that have fades are always the time when Geddy and I stretch a bit. At that point the main statement of the song has been made, and we've been good boys throughout, and then the ride-out comes and we feel we can let loose.

A lot of drummers think that playing busy is as simple as playing everything you know all the time. But there really is a broader significance of those things and the application of things. I know that in a lot of people's minds I probably overplay, but in my own aesthetic I don't. And I don't intrude upon other people. Just as I am sure other people have a firm rationale for doing what they do, I have very well–thought out parameters for approaching things the way I do.

When I was younger, Keith Moon was my idol, and because of this I always wanted to be in a band that played Who songs. But when I finally got in a band that was playing Who songs, it was all so crazy that it didn't suit my character. My personality demanded structure and organization, and within the context of trying to play like Keith Moon in Who songs, it wasn't me. That's an important dividing point for any drummer—when you find out that the way your hero plays is not the way you should play. That was a significant turning point for me, when I found out that the way I thought I wanted to play really wasn't the way I wanted to play.

MD: Throughout this interview you've mentioned drummers who've inspired you. But there are a lot of drummers who *you've* inspired. In fact, you're probably the most popular drummer…

Neil: …in this room! [laughs]

MD: Seriously, you may be the most popular drummer to emerge in the last twenty years. What do you think it is about your playing that has interested so many drummers?

Neil: I guess it's that I play a lot within the context of the band. We've had a lot of good fortune being in a band that plays the kind of music we want to play, and that stretches out all over the place. I suppose my appeal would be to primarily younger drummers, who would be more impressed by a lot of playing. It's also that the band I'm in has a certain amount of success and has given me a great deal of visibility.

That's really a tough question. There are so many things involved. As a band we went to the trouble of learning all those technical things that take a long time to learn. And just as I can't help admiring any drummer I hear who learned how to play all of the rudiments, learned how to apply them, learned how to keep good time—those things carry a lot of weight with me and will win the respect of most any drummer.

MD: Watching *A Show of Hands*, one is struck by the amount of fun that you and the rest of the band seem to be having.

Neil: Again, on another night it would show so much more because, on that night, we were concentrating so much on trying to be good. But I'm glad it shows in that context.

MD: You've been in Rush now a long time.

Neil: It's fifteen years this year.

MD: Do you really still enjoy it?

Neil: Oh, yeah. I mean, there are nights, and there are *nights*; any musician knows that. But after all of these years, there are still really magical, wonderful performances that we have where there's no other place I'd rather be.

REMEMBERING NEIL

continued from page 53

higher level than us mortals. Perfect drum parts with ever-evolving musical patterns. His lyrics were thoughtful and danced with the phrasing of a hand percussionist. Fitting altogether like an MC Escher mystifying masterpiece. Albert Einstein + Bruce Lee + Shakespeare = Neil Peart.

We miss you.

Stephen Perkins

I don't think there's a single drummer, me included, whose life has not been touched and influenced by the unbounded creativity and positive musical energy of Neil Peart. Besides his massive contribution to the world of rock drumming, it is beyond admirable that he felt humble and human enough to continue studying with some of the jazz icons of the time. We have so much to learn from drumming legends like this. To continue through decades with a love and passion for the instrument is a true testament to greatness. His vision will be sorely missed across our whole planet.

Pete Lockett (independent)

"How many drummers does it take to change a light bulb? Three—one to do it and two to talk about how much better Neil Peart would have done it." These jokes exist for a reason. We lost a deep thinker and the world's favorite drummer. Rest easy, Neil.

Navene Koperweis (Entheos)

My world changed the day I heard Neil for the first time. My cousin played *Exit…Stage Left* for me when I was twelve or so, and when I heard the drum solo on "YYZ" my wheels turned so hard that it felt like my brain melted on the spot. I wanted to sound like Neil. I wanted to play the same drumset like Neil. I wanted to be Neil. I know I'm the norm rather than the exception, as Rush left their indelible mark on so many fans and musicians through the years—especially drummers—because of their talent, originality, and world-class musicianship.

It was hard for me to get out of my Rush/Neil phase. I couldn't get enough of the music and the drumming. My playing has changed and evolved a lot through the years, but I still find myself channeling his wit, smarts, and compositional skills on the kit. He left me a huge gift, and I will forever be

Neil Peart, Writer

by Ilya Stemkovsky

It would make sense that Neil Peart's forays into prose writing would be of a remarkably high standard, not only because he was such a brilliant lyricist, but because he was such an able craftsman. Like his meticulously constructed drum parts, Peart's books are the work of an artist paying close attention to detail while he composes something to make you think and also feel.

That word, "compositional," which is so often used to describe Neil Peart the drummer, also applies to his written word outside of the songs he wrote for Rush. A quick internet image search of the band in the 1970s will yield multiple photos of Peart's face buried in a book of some sort, and aside from his own pure enjoyment, it was years of study of countless writers that led the drummer/lyricist to eventually try his hand at becoming an author.

And if Peart's songs tackled everything from fantasy to technology to religion to relationships, and everything in between, his seven books, inspired mostly by his adventurous excursions by bicycle and motorcycle between Rush tours, paint the picture of a more or less independent inland traveler, all-too-human, dealing with life's mysteries and tragedies and beauty. For those looking to go beyond the lyric sheet, what follows is a quick guide to the Professor's excellent output of books.

continues on page 56

---

thankful for it. He might be gone, but he's surely not forgotten.
Antonio Sánchez (Migration/Bad Hombre)

I can't think of a drummer that had a bigger influence on me than Neil Peart. As a kid I was fascinated by his equipment and setup onstage. Of course my first drumset had to be red as well; that was the color that Neil's drums were. I strived to make my kit bigger and bigger, until I actually had to routinely schlep my drums to rehearsals and shows. At that point my kit got smaller and smaller.

If I think about the thing that I learned the most from Neil, it was that the drums were a compositional element. The drum part mattered as much as any of the other instruments. But it didn't hold that weight automatically; you had to make it count. There was a heavy responsibility on the player to hear that call and then meet the challenge of making your part worthy of the music you were contributing to. Neil reminded us that we are not the "timekeepers," we are songwriters. We just happen to be sitting in back, behind the drums, when we compose.
Chris Prescott (Pinback)

Like so many other preteen, misfit drummers "living on the fringes of the city" during the 1970s and '80s, I idolized Neil Peart. Every other kid like me felt the same way, and we constantly compared notes: "Can you play 'Tom Sawyer' yet?"…"Which is your favorite Neil solo, 'Working Man' or 'YYZ'?"…etc.

But he meant so much more than that in retrospect. Our fascination with Rush music and Neil's unique drumming kept us out of trouble and focused on emulating him in every way, trying to nail his fills, and even analyzing his lyrics. He brought so much joy, diligence, ambition, motivation, and musical/rhythmic curiosity to young, aspiring drummers. When I think about it now, copying his parts perfectly was never the most important, impossible goal that I made it out to be then. The process of trying sparked my own ideas and was of even greater value. I became my own drummer while trying to become him!

I know I'm not alone with that sentiment, and that's a beautiful legacy. Rest in peace, Master Neil.
Bob D'Amico (Sebadoh, the Fiery Furnaces)

continues on page 62

Neil Peart, Writer continued from page 55

The Masked Rider: Cycling in West Africa (1996)

Peart on a 1988 bicycle tour through Cameroon. This travel memoir describes the journey and his experiences, from contracting dysentery to a confrontation with an armed soldier to navigating dirt roads off the beaten path. Peart explores his own emotions along the way, the different "masks" that he discovers he wears. And though he always had a reputation of being fiercely private, it's in his books where you get to see what he was like in his personal life.

An excerpt from The Masked Rider: "I am sometimes overly concerned about people who don't really *matter* to me emotionally. For example, I would rather be early for an appointment and have to wait myself than inconvenience anyone else (though I naively expect the same consideration in return). But at the other extreme, I am jealous of my time and work, and am sometimes short even with friends when a phone call interrupts me in the middle of something 'important'—when it's not *convenient* to speak with them."

There's history, culture, interesting people, all told in a likeable first-person narrative style that puts you in that sub-Saharan country you've only seen in National Geographic, but now your favorite drummer was there and reporting back.

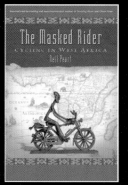

Ghost Rider: Travels on the Healing Road (2002)

In a ten-month period spanning 1997 and 1998, Peart lost both his nineteen-year-old daughter in a car accident and his wife to cancer. Faced with overwhelming sadness and isolated from the world in his Canadian home on the lake, he was left without direction. Neil told his Rush bandmates that he was "retired." Early in the book, Peart writes, "I was going. I still didn't know where (Alaska? Mexico? Patagonia?), or for how long (two months? four months? a year?), but I knew I had to go. My life depended on it."

This memoir tells of the sense of devastation that led Peart on a year-long, 55,000-mile journey by motorcycle across much of North America, down through Mexico to Belize, and back again to Quebec. It's personal, heartbreaking, funny, and tragic at the same time, a journey from grief to healing during which our hero is constantly reminded about his losses, but where he triumphs in the end. Like with his previous book, if you didn't know Peart personally, you will feel like you did after reading this one.

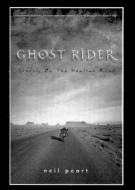

Traveling Music: Playing Back the Soundtrack to My Life and Times (2004)

This time Peart's vehicle of choice is a car, as he drives his BMW from Los Angeles to Big Bend National Park in Southwest Texas while acting as his own DJ. Traveling Music is nicely autobiographical, as Peart reminisces about his upbringing and inspirations before joining Rush and shares his thoughts about everything from Frank Sinatra to Linkin Park to Radiohead. You get the sense of being in the passenger seat with Neil, and lines in Rush's "Red Barchetta" come to mind: "Wind in my hair, shifting and drifting, mechanical music, adrenaline surge." Ever wanted to know what Peart thought about Manu Katché's drumming or Jeff Buckley's Grace? Look no further.

Roadshow: Landscape with Drums: A Concert Tour by Motorcycle (2006)

In 2004 Rush embarked on its 30th-anniversary R30 tour, and Peart traveled between shows by motorcycle, chronicling his journey and delivering with a sharp eye and great care almost everything you'd want to know as a fan of the band. Roadshow acts as a behind-the-scenes memoir, and as a travelogue, and it details the challenges of big-time rock touring. No, Peart didn't like touring. No, he didn't really love meeting fans. He certainly didn't want to see us air-drum to "Tom Sawyer" if we met him at a diner. But his reflections are always touching and poignant, and we get an inside look at Peart's constant strive for perfection. It might sound perfect to you, out there in section 300, but it's interesting to read how critical the man behind the kit is of himself.

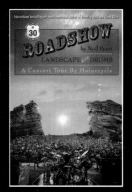

Far and Away: A Prize Every Time (2011)

Following in the tradition of Ghost Rider and Traveling Music, the twenty-two "open letter"–format stories making up Far and Away originally appeared as blog posts on Peart's website, NeilPeart.net. He shares his experiences as he travels along the back roads of North America, Europe, and South America, in journeys that span almost four years. There are observations about nature, the birth of his daughter, and learning from Freddie Gruber and Peter Erskine.

Far and Near: On Days Like These (2014)

More stories gathered from Peart's website. In this second volume of a trilogy of books, the voice in Far and Near "still aims at the feeling that someone you know took the time and care to write the best letter he could—to share his life, work, and travels." Peart writes of outdoor life, receiving honors, and drumming, drumming, drumming. Another look into the inner workings of Peart's ever-inquisitive mind.

Far and Wide: Bring That Horizon to Me! (2016)

The third and final book in the trilogy follows the R40 tour, Rush's last, and Peart reflects on five decades of drumming with an eye on the finish line. There's more insightfulness and humor sprinkled throughout, and even before Peart's retirement from touring and subsequent untimely death in 2020, there was a definitive sense of closure to the book. The last chapter ends with the band's final bow after their final song of their final show. Collectively, all of Peart's travel books are really an Odyssey. He's our Ulysses, and we were along for the ride.

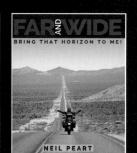

The Fearlessness Of Experience

Peter Erskine's musical path has been very different from that of Neil Peart. Nonetheless, the Rush drummer's influence on him was profound.

Shortly after I began my association with DW (which lasted from 2006 to 2015), Don Lombardi—the founder of DW as well as the Drum Channel—put me in touch with Neil Peart. Neil, who had been studying with Freddie Gruber, was looking for a jazz drumming mentor who could help him with some specific things related to an upcoming Buddy Rich Memorial Concert performance (which took place in 2008). Neil was not the first rock drummer to come knocking on my door by way of Oxnard (the home of DW), but he was certainly the most serious as well as the most famous. He was ready to get to work.

I treated Neil in pretty much the same way I would treat any student, allowing for his schedule to determine the frequency of our get-togethers but not allowing anything about his fame to get in the way of his learning. And he brought only humility plus keen attention to our first and every subsequent lesson. He wanted me to show him some things and I happily obliged.

Neil was very self-aware and knew that the relatively limited instruction he received during his formative years (limited in the sense that he began working well before he'd had an opportunity to do something like study at a conservatory…then again, how many rock drummers study at a conservatory? Quiet down and that will be enough from you for now, Mr. Aronoff) did not provide him with the same set of tools that his drumming heroes Gene Krupa and Buddy Rich enjoyed. As I understood it, Neil was self-taught for the most part, and he did not spend much time in the jazz universe.

Neil's homework consisted primarily of listening to recordings I had chosen for him and then practicing the hi-hat. As he was getting ready to go out on tour with Rush, I asked him what his backstage warm-up set consisted of: Was it an entire drumset? ("Yes.") A big drumset? ("Yes.") "Well," I said, "your crew's gonna love me…I'm suggesting that you get rid of all of that and just have a drum throne and a hi-hat so you can really focus on this. Okay, a practice pad, too." I'm not sure that he followed my advice on that, but he did spend a lot of time working on his hi-hat technique… not for anything fancy, just to get better-acquainted with the art and feel of opening the hat a bit just before the swung 8th note would be played. His years of not playing jazz pretty much solidified his habit of opening up the hat for beats 1 and 3, a kind of binary rock thing, I guess. To be honest, I am not certain that Neil ever fully "got" the jazz hi-hat thing. What he got, I hope, was the confidence to go out there and have fun playing it. Note: the trial by fire of playing a Buddy Rich chart can be anything but fun. Now, maybe I'm a lousy teacher. But I do know that these lessons (which touched on things other than/in addition to the hi-hat) did manage to open him up to being more in the moment with his drumming. He told me so, and I believe him.

We wrote to each other in bursts of inspired communication, always followed by silence. I so enjoyed our correspondence. I don't want to betray anything that he confided or wrote to me, but the following will reflect the genial tone of our missives to one another:

> **November 5, 2009, 3:43 a.m.**
>
> **Hello Peter,**
>
> **I hope all's well with you and Mutsy.**
>
> **I have just posted a new story on neilpeart.net with some thoughts on drumming I hope you might appreciate.**
>
> **Hope to see you sometime soon!**
>
> **NEP**

(The link to the piece is not active now, but I recall that he recounted our lessons in some detail and was very generous with his kind mention and praise of me. It was titled "Autumn Serenade.")

I replied:

> **You're a good man, Neil.**
>
> **Thank you for that Autumn Serenade.**
>
> **(in return, a haiku for you, being sent from the delightful city of Helsinki)**
>
> **Went for a walk here.**
> **The calendar says Autumn.**
> **My ears say "Winter."**
>
> **Peter**

Much has and will be written about Neil. Many drummers will talk about the influence he had upon their drumming. Neil had a very big influence on me, but it was not so much related to my drumming. It was more of a life thing. I'm improvising here, kindly bear with me….

Neil enjoyed great fame and adulation. He worked tremendously hard to achieve all of that. Neil reveled in the work process and did not take a moment of it for granted. How many of us can play an extended solo piece—in the midst of a mind-bendingly complex series of songs where intricacies abound, most of them at full throttle—and not only hold the attention of a stadium full of people but thrill them as well? I know that I can't. Yet, he filled his days with the reading of books and devouring thousands of miles on the open road with his motorcycle. I guess that, in the process of testing himself, he wanted to learn how much a man can explore and endure. He experienced and he lived life, and he knew that the only meaningful way to do that was to do it. To put in the work. To set out.

And, thanks to meeting him, he indirectly encouraged me to emulate his fearlessness of experience. For me, it was with a word processor and a camera, not a hi-hat or a Harley-Davidson. He encouraged me to express myself on the page. I'm enjoying the journey. I wrote a book (No Beethoven), and he penned a gracious quote for the back of the book. Thanks for that and more, Neil.

As you might imagine, I think of him often.

His death came far too soon. His work and his inspiration will live on.

Peter Erskine

February 1994

In Search Of The Right Feel

After twenty years with Rush, Neil was still finding ways to challenge himself—and his fans. In his *MD* interview following the release of the band's *Counterparts* album, the drummer revealed how a desire to incorporate improvisation—and even chance—into their process led to positive results.

Interview by William F. Miller

World Inspiration

Neil's love of bicycling and travel is well known—it's almost the stuff of legend. While on tour with Rush he's been known to avoid the tour bus and bike to the next town and venue. When not on the road with Rush, he's taken his bike to the four corners of the globe, including Europe, mainland China, and Africa.

Upon entering Peart's Toronto home, one is immediately struck by the fact that this man has seen and experienced locales most people can't imagine. "Here's a prized possession of mine," he says proudly, showing a raw-metal sculpture standing about ten inches high and resembling a tribal version of Rodin's "The Thinker". "It's from Africa. It weighs about twenty pounds, and I had to carry it a hundred miles on my bike. But it was worth it."

Neil's passion for authentic African art is obvious. Unique drums, with their rich, hand-carved elegance, are displayed in his home with reverence. Original Chinese gongs decorate a few of the walls. The decor hints at the fact that a drummer lives in the house, shouts the fact that a world traveler resides there.

Peart's love of travel is obvious, but does actually going to other parts of the world inspire him musically? "First of all, I think travel is very important for any person," he insists. "It's affected me enormously, and I'm sure it filters down to my work. Africa is not an abstraction to me anymore—neither is China. They're places I've experienced, places where I've met people, made friends—and just broadened my thinking.

"I've written lyrics that were directly influenced by my travels abroad. In a drumming sense, I've had some interesting experiences in different countries, experiences that may not *directly* affect the way I play drums, but that certainly inspire my feelings about drumming. And I've gotten very interested in hand drumming. Lately I've been working on playing the djembe."

One way Peart's wanderlust has directly affected the sound of his drums is through sampling. "One of the small drums I brought from China is an antique that's too fragile to play. So I took it and a few of the other delicate instruments that I own and sampled them—along with many of my other instruments like my temple blocks and glockenspiel. I've built up a huge library of sounds, and they've made their way onto our albums in many of the different patterns I play."

A particular pattern Neil has recorded that demonstrates the value of "world inspiration" comes from Rush's 1991 studio album, *Roll the Bones*. "On that record we had a song called

Andrew MacNaughtan

'Heresy' that had a drum pattern I heard when I was in Togo. I was laying on a rooftop one night and heard two drummers playing in the next valley, and the rhythm stuck in my head. When we started working on the song, I realized that beat would complement it well."

Premature Obituary

August 24, 1993, a day that will live in infamy—well, at least at the offices of *Modern Drummer*. It seems a radio station in Cleveland, Ohio, made the announcement that Neil Peart was dying of colon cancer. For the rest of the day the telephones at *MD* rang off the hook from distressed Rush fans. How is Neil's health?

"You don't know how many times I've heard that rumor," Peart says, angrily. "Strangers have come up to me and asked, 'Is it true? Are you dying of cancer?' If it were true, imagine the insensitivity of someone asking you point-blank if you're dying. Be that as it may, let me put an end to all of these rumors. I'm absolutely fine, and as far as I know I plan on living a long and happy life."

But why the rumors? It seems that, when Neil prepares for his trips abroad, he practically shaves his head for ease of maintenance. This presumably leads people to think he's having chemotherapy. "I think what also convinced people was that on our last tour I was wearing bandannas on my head," he says. "Even my daughter said I looked like a chemotherapy patient! But those bandannas did an excellent job keeping the sweat out of my eyes.

"It doesn't even take that, though," Neil continues. "I've been hearing these rumors for at least eight years. I came back from a bike tour of Europe, and my manager called me up and said, 'I just heard you were killed in an accident in Switzerland. I guess that isn't accurate.' There's no basis for any of this—it's absurd."

A Little Raw

For anyone who's heard the latest Rush release, *Counterparts*, it's obvious that Neil, along with the rest of the band, is feeling very healthy. *Counterparts* is the heaviest Rush album in years. While there are moments of vintage Rush on the record, there's also a sense of further development by a band that prides itself on improving. According to Neil, "We try to stretch in several directions at once now. On our earlier records our learning curve was much steeper—we were changing and growing a lot. We seemed to concentrate on one thing at a time. We started with musicianship, then concentrated on songwriting, then on arranging, all as almost separate courses of study. That evolution is very easy to trace. By the time we got to our last album, *Roll the Bones*, we felt we really had a full toolbox."

For *Counterparts*, the decision was made to sharpen the tools, as it were, to add an edge to the overall sound of the band. "This time we made the conscious decision to go for a more organic, raw sound, and yet still have it be something

that we would want to listen to," Neil explains. "It had to have a certain amount of refinement. By organic, we wanted to stress the nucleus of the band—guitar, bass, drums—and downplay the digital stuff, the sound processing and that sort of thing. As long-time listeners of music, I think we have pretty sophisticated tastes, so we weren't about to go in and make a thrash record. But we did want elements of that in our music."

According to Neil, the band had a carefully formulated plan. "We decided to use two different engineers, something we'd never done before. Normally we'd use an engineer for the entire process, right down to the final mixing. I always wondered why certain artists would bring in someone new, but we found that changing engineers really helped us get what we were after.

"We listened to literally dozens of engineers, knowing that we had to find the right guys if this plan of ours was going to work. To record the tracks, we chose Kevin 'Caveman' Shirley, whose work we enjoyed. He's known for raw guitar sounds as well as getting some very good drum sounds. When we interviewed him, he had some very intriguing concepts, like putting bottom end on cymbals. And he was very concerned with mic placement, as far as how it affects the drum sound, rather than just changing EQs or other board effects. He was determined to capture the natural sound of my drumset as accurately as possible. He didn't use any reverb. He wanted a purity of real sound, which was a unique way of working for us.

"The other engineer we used, Michael Letho, was brought in to mix the tracks," Neil continues. "His forte is mixing, and he constructed some beautiful mixes with instruments coming in and out, perfectly complementing each other. He brought a certain amount of refinement to the proceedings. If we had just used Michael, the record might have been too refined. Had we just used the Caveman, it would have been too raw. So we had the best combination of influences."

As well as their plan worked, there were some difficulties for the band with this new approach. "Using a minimal amount of reverb was hard for us," Neil says. "If the drums sounded a bit raw, we'd always just lay on that reverb and smooth everything out. Holding back on the reverb made this record a bit more difficult because the flaws were so apparent. If there was a 'bark' on the snare drum or a 'grunch' in a guitar note, it was obvious. But we kept them in right up to the final mixing stages.

"I also tended to listen to this record throughout the making of it much less than I normally would. With previous records we refined them as we went along. We would use one engineer and he would do rough mixes as the recording went along. When we'd hear those rough mixes along the way, they'd sound really good—almost like a record. Well, this time it *didn't*."

The Prize Drum

As for the drum sound on *Counterparts*, Neil made the decision not to vary it as radically as on prior albums. On 1989's *Presto*, for instance, Neil used a wide array of snare drums. "I didn't alter things as much for this record," he says. "I was quite satisfied with the up-front sound we were getting." Upon listening to the record, however, one will immediately notice that Neil's snare sound is a bit lower-pitched than on the last several Rush releases. "I used some different snare drums, but for the majority of the record I used my Solid Percussion deep-shelled drum. In the past I used their piccolo drum, and of course my old standard Slingerland.

"I still have my arsenal of snare drums, but I didn't feel the need to use them all," Neil continues. "My prize drum is an old Rogers Dyna-Sonic. It was my dream drum when I was a kid, so I *had* to have one! When I was fourteen or fifteen years old, a drummer using a Rogers Dyna-Sonic snare had more impact on me than if he had two Rolls-Royces! Every time I look at that drum it gives me a spark of joy—but I just never use it. My favorite 'working' drum is still my old Slingerland. I've had it for years, and it's never let me down. I thought when I got the Solid drum it would replace the Slingerland, but the Slingerland drum is just so versatile. That drum is a wonder—it's sensitive *and* aggressive.

"My main attitude for this record was, I want the drums to sound like *my* drums," Neil says. "I didn't want the engineer to process them into something else. What I like them to do is take my sound and change the atmosphere *around* my drums to better help the sound work within a given composition. On a less aggressive song the engineer may smooth out the edges of my sound, adding a bit of 'air' to the track. On an aggressive number, the engineer will leave it raw. It's still my sound—my signature—yet it works within the given song more effectively. I like that approach because the differences are subtle."

Dangerous Waters

If you've ever attended a Rush concert, you've undoubtedly seen many audience members air-drumming along with Neil. It can be an odd sight, especially when it's apparent that these fans know his playing note-for-note, right down to the fills. Neil's thoughts on his highly scripted drum parts may be changing. "I'm always listening to tapes of shows on the road, so I know what's working and what sections might need attention," he says. "I noticed on the last tour that, for the first time, the tapes were really a pleasure to listen to. I don't

want you to think the tapes were flawless, but the quality of the performance seemed to be on a very listenable level. Our goal has always been to be able to accurately reproduce our studio work live. After so many years we finally started to realize that we *can* do it. It sounds small, but for us it was a big achievement.

"That realization gave us a lot of confidence to change arrangements live—stretching out songs and being more spontaneous in our performances. We were excited to be at a point where we felt we could have the best of both worlds: to be able to control our organized sections as well as have the confidence to stretch. There's no sense saying that music should be only orchestrated or only spontaneous. The only thing with spontaneity is that it tends to be less reliable!

"I remember talking to Mickey Hart during our last tour," Neil continues. "I had written to him after having read his excellent book *Drumming on the Edge of Magic*. So he gave me a call, and that's how we hooked up. Seeing the Grateful Dead was impressive, realizing just how much improvisation goes on at their shows. Mickey told me that some nights a Dead show is dull; the improvisational thing just won't get going. Yet on other nights it's just magical. It's a risk that the band takes every night, and their audience takes that chance too. I respect the band for having the courage to do that.

"I've been pushing myself into those more dangerous, improvisational waters," says Neil. "It's both a quality and a flaw in my character that I prepare to death! I love rehearsing and getting better and better. I enjoy the process. Before we record an album, I learn the new songs inside out, refining every little detail. And that's why I continued to play the exact same parts live as I recorded, because I spent so much time getting every element right. In Tim Alexander's *Modern Drummer* cover story [September '93 issue] he mentioned that he had never noticed that about me until Primus went on the road with us and he could see me perform every night. I'm *glad* to be able to play a song like 'Tom Sawyer' the same night after night, because it's so damned hard to play!

"With our newer material, though, I recognize that I don't like it sounding over-rehearsed. So in preparing to record the songs, I started leaving gaps in certain transitions or sections. I wouldn't let myself finalize a part, even up to the point when I would be recording the song. And that certainly added to the pressure for me. Then when I actually recorded

Andrew MacNaughtan

a part and played what may have even been a mistake, with closer examination that mistake may have ended up bringing something magical to the track. Then I have to learn the mistake so I'll be able to play it live! But little by little that attitude of opening things up is coming into our music."

Finding the Right Feel

Counterparts is another solid showing for Neil's drumming. His drum parts consistently balance more standard beats with totally original patterns. Neil has a general approach: "When constructing drum parts, I have to be sensitive to the songs, of course. I don't just play what satisfies me. You'll never hear me making noise under a vocal part. There's a certain level of respect you have to have. But on the other hand, when it comes to a guitar solo section, for example, to us that section isn't a guitar solo, it's a *band* solo. So all of us construct it as our own part. From an arrangement perspective, those sections are free game. As long as what we're doing works and helps make the track more exciting, it's acceptable.

"Finding the right feel for different parts of a song is always a challenge for me, because I hate to repeat things," Neil explains. "There are certain fundamental rock rhythms that at times work and need to be played and repeated, and I don't mind playing them. The same is true for a standard approach to playing a fill—going from snare to tom, for instance. To me they're like using the words 'so' and 'and': They're the articles of the language, and to me there's no shame in using them. On the other hand, I do want to explore fresh areas. I like to weld influences together to come up with something new. I don't pretend to think I'm inventing originality, but I'm hoping to create something original by combining previously disparate influences.

"For the opening track, 'Animate,' for instance, I used a basic R&B rhythm that I played back in my early days, coupled with that hypnotic effect that a lot of the British bands of the turn of the '90s had—bands like Curve and Lush. The middle section of the tune is a result of the impact African music has had on me, although it wasn't a specific African rhythm. I hear a section of a tune, and immediately I have to make choices, and many times those world influences I talked about earlier will come in to play and contribute to my parts.

"Other songs on the record required me to find fresh ways to approach familiar, time-honored drum parts," Neil continues. "I think the nature of the songs on this album brought out a lot of my R&B background, and I don't think that's an area I'm known for. But all the first bands I played in were blue-eyed soul bands. I played a lot of James Brown and Wilson Pickett tunes, because in the Toronto area that's what was popular at the time. All of us grew up playing 'In the Midnight Hour.'

"R&B is a part of my roots, and as a band I think we all played it and enjoyed it. But as we developed, we drifted off into the other styles of the '60s, and when the British progressive bands came along we went in that direction.

"The instrumental track on this record, 'Leave that Thing Alone,' is built around R&B bass/drum interplay. But to make it original I change up parts. In the second verse I go into a Nigerian beat, like something you'd hear on a King Sunny Ade record. Later in the song I go into a quasi-jazz pattern, and all these things are introduced for our own entertainment as well as to make the piece more interesting.

"When I hear Geddy and Alex's demos, the influences are sometimes very clear to me," Neil says. "And I think we're secure enough to directly use those influences. If Geddy and Alex bring in a tune that has a section that sounds like the Who's *Live at Leeds*, I'm definitely going to put on my Keith Moon hat and go with it. If there's a song with a '90s grunge-rock section, we're secure enough to go in that direction. All of these things are amusing to us, but they're also available to us to try and create something fresh from their inspiration."

A song like "Stick It Out" proved difficult for Neil because it is fairly simple. "How could I approach that song properly," he muses, "and yet give it a touch of elegance that I would want a riff-rock song to have? I don't want it to be the same type of thing you'd hear on rock radio. So I started bringing in

REMEMBERING NEIL
continued from page 55

Today, in the YouTube era, chops are pretty ubiquitous. But in 1981 chops were more elusive, especially outside of jazz/fusion. One didn't really hear a lot of chops on mainstream rock radio—until *Moving Pictures* came out. Like all my young drummer friends, I was blown away when I heard "Tom Sawyer" on the radio for the first time, and Neil Peart became one of my first drum heroes. As I grew up, my musical tastes changed, and my drumming influences changed, but my respect for Neil Peart never diminished. If anything, it's grown over the years. There are a handful of revolutionary drummers, in various genres, who've changed everything, and Neil Peart is absolutely one of them. His passing is a profound loss to the drumming world.
Steven Wolf (independent)

In 1986, someone played me Neil Peart's legendary drum solo on *Exit… Stage Left*. I was instantly captivated by the energy, musicality, sound, and technique I heard in that solo, and it helped set me on my lifelong drumming journey. I spent much of my time from the age of twelve to seventeen listening to Rush and learning to play Neil's drum parts. This turned out to be a fruitful course of study, helping me in particular to develop a strong sense of four-limb independence, which continues to serve me well as a jazz drummer.

I saw Rush live thirty-three times between 1987 and their final tour in 2015. In concert, Neil had a nearly unparalleled ability to not only play all of his carefully composed parts accurately, but with incredible clarity and projection—every note was crystal clear, even at the back of a giant arena.

I continue to listen to Rush regularly to this day, and I'm always discovering new things in their music. Although I make my living playing music quite different from Rush's, Neil Peart remains my biggest influence and favorite drummer—my number one. Thank you, Neil.
Paul Wells (Curtis Stigers, Vince Giordano)

Although I was shocked and deeply saddened to hear of Neil's passing, it was also truly heartening to see the immense impact he had on so many musicians and listeners. The things he did for drumming, for the drumming

Latin and fusion influences. There's a verse where I went for a Weather Report–type effect. I used some tricky turnarounds in the ride cymbal pattern, where it goes from downbeat to upbeat accents—anything I could think of to make it my own. That song verges on parody for us, so we had to walk a careful line. We responded to the power of the riff, yet still found some ways to twist it to make it something more.

Andrew MacNaughtan

"'The Speed of Love' is kind of a mid-tempo, more sensitive rock song," Neil continues. "That song probably took me the longest to find just the right elements I wanted to have in the drum part. What made it a challenge is that I wanted the feel and the transitions between sections to be just right. I played

that song over and over, refining it until I was satisfied. I don't think a listener will hear all the work that went into that track."

Accident by Design

While Peart may turn to many outside influences to help him create within Rush, there are some elements in his playing that are definitely his own. Neil concurs. "I think I do have certain signature licks that I play. And I don't mind a certain amount of repetition if it is indeed something that is my own. I suppose it takes a bit of repetition to *make* it my own! It does become hard to pick these things up, though, because they tend to be subtle, at least to me.

"I think what happens is, you'll hear a certain drummer play a great beat or fill, and then you'll practice what you *think* you're hearing. Many times the result of that effort ends up being something that is completely your own. Even if you can duplicate the exact notes, in a different drummer's hands it just won't sound the same."

Neil feels that a lot of what he plays is a reflection of his personality. "I do like things to be organized," he admits. "If something is well organized, it has the potential to be something special. I tend to approach life that same way. If I'm going on a trip somewhere, like the bush in Africa, you'd better believe I've spent a lot of time figuring out what to take so I'll be prepared. I might be organized, but at the same time that's hardly a safe circumstance. Organization is not necessarily a conservative thing."

Neil's approach to music is certainly similar. "When we go in to record, I spare no self-flagellation of playing the songs over and over again until I've got them. And it's the same thing before a tour: I spend weeks just rehearsing on my own before we start as a band. But I know it's time well spent, because that work gives me the confidence to step off into the unknown with some foundation.

"When I went into the studio to record my parts for *Counterparts*, I was prepared," Neil insists. "That's why I could record all of my tracks in first and second takes. We put together and learned the material, we worked with [co-producer] Peter Collins refining the material, and then I practiced for another week to get totally comfortable with the songs and the changes to those songs. I recorded all of the drum tracks on this record in one day and two afternoons—that's all it took because I was prepared.

"My whole approach to life is accident by design," Neil says. "Everything I do has to be that well organized, or I'm not

community, and for the style of music he was known for, were invaluable lifelong contributions that helped advance an art form we all love, and that's the kind of legacy only a select group of musicians ever attain.
Paul Wertico (Wertico, Cain and Gray, educator, author)

As a budding young drummer in the '70s, I vividly remember the first time I dropped the needle on *All the World's a Stage*. A high school classmate loaned me the LP and urged me, "Check this drummer out!" Hearing Neil Peart for the first time was nothing short

of a revelation. The precision of his meticulously arranged and executed parts, the signature cascading tom fills, and a seemingly effortless navigation of odd times—all within a new, heavier, guitar-based paradigm of progressive rock. And he wrote the lyrics! This was unlike anything or anyone I had heard before. In an instant, a seismic shift occurred in what I thought I knew about rock drumming and what a drummer could do.

Shortly thereafter, like many drummers of my generation, my kit suddenly grew another kick drum and multiple toms. The mission

was laid out plain and simple: try to play like Neil! Easier said than done, I soon came to find out. But we all tried—oh, how we tried. His books were a window into his life of music, travel, and adventure. Even after living through unimaginable tragedy, his message to us seemed to be, "Be the best you can be and live your best life." For that, and all the drumming inspiration, I thank you, Professor!
Billy Orrico (Angel)

Neil was a generational talent. He was my Buddy Rich. A legend. He influenced the world of music, not

just one genre. To say he's left a lasting legacy is a huge understatement.
Keio Stroud (Big and Rich, Nashville sessions)

Not only was Neil Peart your favorite drummer's favorite drummer, but he was the favorite drummer of your mechanic, math teacher, and uncle. He elevated the role of the drummer far beyond being just a timekeeper.
Gunnar Olsen (Bruce Springsteen, Mother Feather, Big Data)

Neil Peart was and still is an inspiration for me to live more
continues on page 64

comfortable with it. But at the same time, within that frame of organization, I'm really comfortable with contingencies, because I'm prepared. It's an interesting thing because a lot of people say it's better to be spontaneous, to breeze through and let whatever happens happen. What I find with those people is that they're not prepared to take advantage of the opportunities when they occur."

The Ultimate Involvement

With so many years of intense drumming behind him, you might think that a certain amount of burnout would have set in on Neil. Quite the contrary. He still seems earnest about his deep feelings for drumming. "There are certain things about my playing that are just an honest reflection of me. I couldn't stop playing hard physically, because I love physical exertion in so many other areas of my life. And that actually *came* from drumming, because it was my first physical endeavor—my first sport, if you like. Before it I had never been involved in anything athletic. Drumming gave me the stamina to get interested in cycling, cross-country skiing, and long-distance swimming. So that comes out of my drumming naturally.

"I've had this fleeting thought over the last year or so, trying to think of any other human activity that so much uses everything you've got physically *and* mentally. For me, playing drums is the ultimate involvement. It's as involving to an athletic degree as a marathon run is, but at the same time your mind is as busy as an engineer's is, with all the calculations a drummer has to make.

"I have a quote from a NASA director who was a friend of ours," Neil continues. "He came to see us play, and afterwards he made the comment that I'm obviously using a great deal of mental energy. He thought it was funny that I would expend so much mental energy on playing *drums*. He said it with a certain amount of disdain—but that's what it takes! When you apply the standards I've described to drumming, it does become the ultimate expression both mentally and physically."

Peart on Congas?

If you've followed Neil's career, you've seen his kit evolve. Over the last few years he's done away with his second bass drum (opting for a double pedal), added a floor tom on the left side, and changed his overall tom positioning. For the new album, though, Neil didn't alter his kit. "By adding the floor tom on the left and shifting my tom sizes down, which is what I did for the last record, that gave me a lot of possibilities. I think that change gave me a whole new starting point and made a lot of my fills just sound different. It drove me to change a lot of preconceptions about the fills and patterns that I play. I think I'm still exploring it."

Neil did have a specific idea he wanted to try: "I thought of a radical idea for a kit that came about due to the interest I've developed in hand drums, which I really began exploring during our last tour. After staring at a computer keyboard for long periods of time, there's nothing better than sitting down and playing congas. It's a great release. So I came up with a setup where I could play congas and bongos with my hands, yet still trigger bass drum and snare drum sounds with my feet. I've been using my feet to trigger kick and snare sounds for a few years now on certain songs in our set. So I thought the concept was a little radical, but still very interesting and very possible. But there was one problem: The songs didn't really call for any bongo or conga parts! I was set up for a stylistic shift and prepared and interested to make it, but in fact didn't have a place for it. Maybe I'll be able to apply it next time."

What inspired him to get into hand drumming? According to Neil, "During our last tour, Primus was opening for us, and Herb Alexander and I would have jams in the tune-up room before the show. He had a PureCussion drumset in there, and I had some hand drums. We'd be jamming, and members of their band and our band would drift in and out of the room and join us in making some impromptu music. For the most part people would be using instruments that they don't normally play. Someone would pick up an accordion, and someone else

REMEMBERING NEIL
continued from page 63

fully, think more freely, and practice more creativity. Thank you, Neil Peart.
Jeff Sipe (independent)

Neil taught me how to create musical parts, develop musical fills, play in odd times, and explore sound palettes and rhythm. What an incredible foundation his style laid out for young drummers, even beyond his incredible chops. I was able to spend about twenty minutes with him one time up at the DW factory. It was an amazing experience to speak

to him as a peer and be treated with such respect by one of my biggest childhood heroes.
Blair Sinta (Alanis Morissette, Chris Cornell, Melissa Etheridge)

Neil Peart's contribution to the drumming industry remains unparalleled.
Horacio Hernandez (independent)

Neil was a legend! Not just in the drummer world, but for all musicians. Who didn't want to be like Neil—a pillar of the rock community, whose incredible talent has influenced so many others. His work will continue

to inspire for generations. Rest well, Neil!
Jerry Pentecost (Old Crow Medicine Show, Brent Cobb)

Peart's fully blossomed creativity in his drum parts and lyrics was so fully supported by his work ethic. This generous approach shared his passionate voice with us all.
Billy Ward (Chris Shinn)

When it came to millions of music enthusiasts, Neil was a household name. It's no small feat to create a sonic signature that was instantly recognizable the world over

for generations of musicians and fans. Thank you, Neil, for your contributions to drumming and the world of music for many years to come.
Rich Redmond (Jason Aldean, sessions, educator)

My drumming path was forever changed after hearing my first Rush song—"Tom Sawyer," naturally. That inherent eight-bar drum break is practically a right of passage for a drummer to learn. This was also probably the first time I ever tried to play an odd meter. I was hooked and went out and accrued every album (on cassette or vinyl) I could find. Moreover,

would pick up a flute—that was primo! Somebody would be playing bass, and somebody would be playing on anything we could find to hit.

"We had some great jams with just found sounds," Neil continues. "I remember one in particular where I was playing a beautiful pattern on a bicycle frame against Herb's drumming on a garbage can, and it was happening! In Berlin we had dressing rooms that were just little outdoor trailers. There were all sorts of metal grids from the arena stacked outside. We set up in this little shed—it was raining outside—and both bands were just jamming on found percussion and a few other instruments. It was a great escape from the day, and a good musical exploration."

Neil Also Waltzes

The backstage jam sessions also led Neil to new areas in his drumming. "At a later point during the tour, Primus were gone and we were out with Mr. Big. So I went out and got a

to get my other limbs to work over the top of it. It was an ideal activity for me to be doing before a show. It kept my drumming alive for me during the last part of the tour, when I'm normally feeling like I've been out for too long."

Rich Vs. Peart

The drumming community witnessed a rare event a couple of years ago when Neil Peart agreed to headline the Buddy Rich Memorial Concert, held in New York. Neil, who avoids performing clinics, made the exception due to the fact that his involvement would help provide a college scholarship for a needy drummer. But what was it like to go from a three-piece rock group to a sixteen-piece big band? According to Neil, "It was a major, major challenge. I vacillated a lot about accepting it, and I wished I had an excuse not to! I wished I could have said, 'Sorry, I'm going to be in Finland that day.' All kidding aside, I realized that year that I had been playing drums for twenty-five years, so I felt I should do it for myself to mark

> "I've been pushing myself into more dangerous, improvisational waters. It's both a quality and a flaw in my character that I prepare to death."

PureCussion set for myself, because I really enjoyed Herb's. I set myself a course of study. It was getting near the end of the tour; you'd think I'd not want to even be *thinking* about playing drums. In fact, I found that playing something different was the cure for the usual boredom that sets in. I'd go into the tune-up room and play Max Roach's 'The Drum Also Waltzes.' It was such a good exercise for me, and it was so different from what I was playing onstage."

Neil also received some tips from Pat Torpey, the drummer with Mr. Big. "Pat's an accomplished drummer with a background in some areas of drumming that I'm not familiar with—Latin, for instance. He showed me some great patterns to practice. And I was just exploring any possibility I could come up with. I'd play an ostinato pattern and then try

the occasion.

"I got the video of the first Buddy Rich Memorial Concert, and I was just so impressed at how well everyone played—I had enormous self-doubt after seeing it," Neil admits. "But then I got inspired and thought, I'll do it like Buddy would have done it! I realized that all the other drummers essentially just 'did themselves,' as opposed to trying to play in a similar style to Buddy. I tried to learn what Buddy played on the songs I was going to be performing, exactly as he played them. I wanted to honor him by trying to play as much like him as I could. I even tried to figure out the stickings he used, as much as possible. I felt safe, in a way, following his example into what were unknown musical waters for me. It was such a challenge because I had to try and get into his mind. Wandering around

my mind was blown when I found out that the drummer wrote all the lyrics. I remember going as far as to pick up a copy of Ayn Rand's *The Fountainhead* because Peart attributed some of his lyrical content to her philosophical ideas.

The first time I saw Rush play, I couldn't believe that every person as far as I could see was air-drumming along the entire night. Neil's drum parts were always creative, memorable, and melodic. He was always pushing the envelope, from augmenting the timbres of his kit with tubular bells, crotales, woodblocks, and a glockenspiel, to adding a full electronic kit, which would sometimes rotate mid-song at

a live show. After an already successful thirty-year career, Neil completely changed the way he physically and mentally approached the drums after taking lessons with Freddie Gruber. His constant search for knowledge, experience, and growth was quite inspiring.

Thank you, Neil.
Joe Tomino (Dub Trio, Birth, Yellowstone Apocalypse)

Air-drumming to "Subdivisions" as I type...the first time I read about Neil Peart was in an interview with hero Brad Wilk from the November 1996 issue of *Modern Drummer*—the year I started

playing. Peart's drumming blew me away, with equal parts precision, power, fearlessness, and finesse, and it still had room to deliver joy. Thank you, King Neil. Your compositions, lyrics, discipline, and curiosity will forever inspire my drumming, writing, and productions.
Elliot Jacobson (Ingrid Michaelson, Elle King, sessions)

Neil was an icon who influenced so many people to push boundaries and be different. His work on the drums went beyond the music, and his mark will always be remembered by generations. He was truly legendary.
Anup Sastry (independent)

Sometimes you don't choose your influences. Sometimes they choose you. When I was younger, I would name Billy Cobham, Terry Bozzio, Art Blakey, Buddy Rich, and maybe Tony Williams as my influences, but as an autodidact, I could only pretend to play like them. I almost never cited Neil, even though if I were to be honest with myself, I probably sounded more like him than the other gentlemen.

The fact is, for what I was doing at the time, my playing was probably far more informed by Neil than any of my proclaimed heroes. I never owned any Rush albums, but they were in heavy

continues on page 73

inside Buddy's conception of things was amazing. To see how he would set up a fill and execute it, and even how he would view an entire arrangement, was very rewarding research for me."

Unfortunately for Neil, the evening wasn't as successful as he had hoped. "I did have a few problems with the event. I was the last drummer to rehearse with the band on the rehearsal day, and since it was late in the day a few of the guys in the band had to leave to play gigs. Steve Marcus, Buddy's long-time tenor sax player, had to leave. The pianist had to leave early, so that was a drag. The Basie and Ellington songs I performed were both founded on piano/bass/drums trio, and to not be able to fully rehearse with the piano made it difficult. The setup on the day of the concert wasn't well planned, either. I was far away from the band, and it was very tough for me to hear them. The horns were inaudible to me! When I watch the video of my performance, I can see myself *straining* to hear them. It's hard to play under those conditions.

"The performance came off okay," says Neil, "but I just didn't enjoy it. The next day I had a long drive from New York back to Toronto, and the drive was the perfect therapy for my disappointment. I really got to think about it, and I got re-inspired to try it again. I want to be able to enjoy it and do the kind of job I know I can do. I hope to perform with the band again."

The performance helped to inspire Neil in other ways. "When I got back to Toronto, Rush was in the midst of working on *Roll the Bones*, and I was writing the lyrics for a song called 'Bravado.' It has a line, 'We burn our wings flying too close to the sun.' Well, I'd aimed for this incredibly high goal, to play like Buddy Rich in *his* band—to play like the greatest drummer who has ever played. If I burned my wings a little, big deal!"

The Future of Drumming

Rush has been around a long time. They've influenced a host of bands, some of which are almost direct descendants—groups like Primus, Queensrÿche, Dream Theater, and Fates Warning. They all name Rush as a major influence. But does Neil feel as if he's passing the torch to these new bands? "On reflection, yes, I do think that passing the torch is an accurate metaphor. I had a lot of reflections over the last couple of years about the nature of heroism, what a 'role model' is supposed to be, and the differences between the two. That thought manifested itself in a song on the new album called 'Nobody's Hero.' A role

model is obviously a very positive example of what can be accomplished, and it's what I think, with all humility and pride, Rush has been—a good role model for other bands. We've done things the way we think they should be done: on our terms, making all of our decisions based on that and not on the market or what the record company told us we should do."

As for his own place in drumming history, Neil is quite humble. "I suppose I've set an example as a busy drummer: a guy who has played a lot of different parts over the years—and has *still* been able to make a living," Neil says jokingly. "But this brings me to an interesting point. A few years back drummers were being shoved down further and further in the creative process. I was really wondering what was happening to all of the young drummers. At that point most everything you heard on the radio had drum machines. The drummers you heard were just keeping a beat. It was considered very uncool to play drum fills—and God help you if you did a drum solo! In the '80s there was no place for a drummer to *play*. I was very concerned about the future of drumming.

"We got to the '90s," Neil continues, "and suddenly all sorts of bands came up with drummers who are *playing*. The recent bands coming out of Seattle and from across the States are revealing some fantastic drummers. Somehow, the torch was passed. These drummers were practicing and improving throughout the '80s, preparing for the time when they'd get the chance. I honestly feel this is a very exciting time for drumming. It's so gratifying to hear it come back, and come back with such a *vengeance*. Just a few of the newer guys I've been enjoying include Dave Abbruzzese of Pearl Jam, Matt Cameron from Soundgarden and Temple of the Dog—I love his playing—and Chad Gracey from the band Live, who plays just what you want to hear."

It would seem that Neil Peart is now secure with the state of drumming. At this point no one can deny his contribution. "If nothing else, I did consider myself a champion of drumming as an art form. The people who I held up and admired from the past had always approached it that way, right from the first players I ever heard—Gene Krupa and Buddy Rich. I always championed the values of musicianship and of drummers who could actually *play*. All of that mattered to me and always will. A few years back it seemed as if those things didn't matter anymore, and I felt undercut and genuinely worried. But with this new generation of drummers coming up, I can breathe a huge sigh of relief. Everything's all right!"

> "My main attitude for this record was, I want the drums to sound like my drums. I didn't want the engineer to process them into something else."

February 1995

Walking In Big Shoes: Neil Peart On The Making Of Burning For Buddy

The previous May, at Manhattan's famous Power Station recording studio, Neil had orchestrated one of the most historic meetings of drumming talent of the modern era, in tribute to the music of Buddy Rich, the greatest drummer of the previous generation. Neil did his usual "homework," taking months studying Buddy and his music. *MD* was there during the recording, and followed up with him about this most ambitious of projects.

Interview by William F. Miller

MD: Over the past six months you've listened to more Buddy Rich music than probably anybody *ever* has. Do you like Buddy's playing now more or less than when you started this whole thing?

Neil: Good question. I have to say I enjoy his playing *infinitely* more, and certainly, as you say, I've studied it in such depth. To prepare for this project I studied his playing, his arrangements, and more importantly how he approached the arrangements. I've listened to all sorts of tapes and watched literally hundreds of film and video clips of him.

MD: With all of this study, was there anything about Buddy's music that surprised you when you actually sat down with the band and started going over the material?

Neil: Nearly *everything*. [laughs] In the larger sense I was surprised at how good the music was and how good the arrangements were when I got to know them better. In some cases, if the arrangements were more intricate, more complicated, they demanded more listening.

When I was in the studio with the band and they were doing a first run-through with a new drummer, I made a point to always go out into the room. There was a little corner where I could sit and hear all of the horns, feel the bass and piano from the rhythm section booth behind me, and be right in front of the drummer. I would close my eyes and it was all *right there* the way you're supposed to hear it. The power and the interplay was so nice.

MD: Being in a room with all those musicians must have been a bit different from your "usual" trio.

Neil: But there was a similarity in that the big band had just as much power as a rock band—maybe *more* power. I think it was that power that largely attracted me to big band playing, and that's another thing that sounds so good when you're actually in the room. There's such a great feeling

Andrew MacNaughtan

when you're hitting the shots with the band, pulling that trigger. It's a really powerful gun, the brass section. Buddy used to compare playing with a big band to driving a Ferrari and hitting the accelerator—just so much power. The music has that.

Another thing I really enjoy about Buddy's music is that it's very modern. As I mentioned in the liner notes, Buddy was not about nostalgia. He was always changing his repertoire, always wanting new arrangements, always getting new guys in the band.

Consequently, his music changed so much. From the late '40s right up until he died, he kept changing and growing.

MD: Were you a big fan of Buddy's early on in your development?

Neil: I have to admit I hadn't been

continues on page 71

Andrew MacNaughtan

The Participants

As the main instigator and producer of *Burning for Buddy*, Neil
Peart had the unique position of being "behind the glass"
while several of today's finest drummers recorded for *him*.
Here are his thoughts on their musical contributions.

Simon Phillips

Simon was incredibly meticulous, very professional, and prepared. He came in with his own charts, and he had his own ideas of how the songs should be performed. He introduced dynamics into the arrangements that weren't there previously, which was also a nice touch.

I requested that he do "Dancing Men" because I knew he'd do a great job with it, and it was the track I wanted to open the album with. He nailed it almost immediately—and that arrangement is challenging. Simon wanted to record "Goodbye Yesterday," so he did that, too.

Simon had also prepared "Norwegian Wood," so even though it was late in the day, we thought we'd try to get a take. I was concerned because most of the guys in the band had gigs at night— doing Broadway shows like *Damn Yankees, Crazy for You,* and *Kiss of the Spider Woman*. So at the very last point of a very tiring day, Simon and the whole band did a beautiful job on "Norwegian Wood." Simon played brilliantly. He's known for his tremendous technique, but he actually impressed me even more with his musicality. I can understand why he's achieved the high status he has.

Dave Weckl

Dave has a very methodical way of working, and he's *very* self-critical. He knew when he had to pull back the tempo or push it a bit. He had beautiful-sounding drums and cymbals and a very musical approach to his instrument.

Dave told me a good story about one of the tunes he recorded, "Time Check." When he was sixteen years old, he used to play along with that song. He used to take his parents' stereo and slow the turntable down to learn the part, so the song had a special emotional appeal for him. He gave a knockout performance on it. Although it isn't on the first release, it will be on the next. But "Time Check" was the song that had a special place in his heart, and that's such a common image for any drummer—to take a turntable or tape player and slow down the tune to figure out what's being played. I think everybody's been through that.

Steve Gadd

A lot of people might be surprised to hear that he was nervous about the session. I greeted him and asked how he was, and he said, "I'll be so glad when this is over." I thought to myself, why should *you* be nervous? You're Steve Gadd! His version of "Love for Sale" has become my favorite of everything we recorded. I just loved the feel he created. Plus, the solos that the different musicians played on it were superb.

Steve was self-critical in the same way that Dave was. He was very critical of what he was doing and how it should be, and he wanted to go back and do it again I had to stop him and say, "Look, it's beautiful. Stop now." He was someone who exemplifies the quote I once heard, "No art is ever finished, it's only abandoned." He demands so much of himself, and consequently was tending to sense flaws when there were none, where the time was perfect and his execution flawless.

Steve Smith

Steve was one of the few guys who I had met before. I've known him for a few years now, and it's been a thrill to see how he's developed as a player. He just knocked all of us over with his musicality, his precision, and just how far he has taken his craft over the years. He is a master drummer. It's a beautiful thing to see someone in possession of such a high level of mastery that he is enjoying right now. He's earned it. It's just inspirational to see what he has done.

I think what is really astounding about Steve is that his abilities go a lot deeper than sheer technique. He has a musical sense to his playing that really elevates the music. You can certainly hear it on the track on the first release, "Nutville." Steve played great with the band, and he certainly inspired me!

Matt Sorum

Matt was just a total joy to work with. As far as I'm concerned, he's a prince among men. Matt was so excited to be there, and he seemed so thrilled to hear himself with that band—he really kicked them. After one of the takes, one of the horn players called out, "Hey, who is this guy?" And Matt stood up, struck a pose, and said, "I'm the heavy metal guy." He had a great sense of humor.

The following day he sent over three big trays of fruit and cheese, two cases of Heineken for the band, a bottle of scotch for me, and a bottle of champagne for Cathy Rich, plus he sent notes to everybody. He was just so grateful, and he expressed his gratefulness so beautifully. It was a really nice thing to do.

Manu Katché

Manu surprised me. I've always loved his playing, and he was somebody I really wanted to have for this project. I think he's a real groundbreaker. I thought I had a pretty good idea of how he played, but I was wrong! You should hear the drum solo that he played on "No Jive"—it's insane. I couldn't believe it. It's weird, and yet it's perfect. When he's playing for someone else, he plays in a supportive and very fluid way. So when he played this solo, he surprised me.

Manu played on the session with percussionist Mino Cinelu. They knew each other and had worked together before; they did a lot of their conversing in the softest French. They were both just so personable and so soulful as people and as players. Everybody remarked that there seemed to be a warm glow in the room while those two were working. In both of their cases their playing is certainly very warm, and their hearts are too.

continues on page 73

a fanatic about Buddy at all. That's perhaps another irony. I never got the chance to meet him, and what's even odder is that I never saw him play live. As a teenager I saw him play on television several times, but I wasn't a fanatic. I was an *admirer*—I guess that would be the right term. I always knew he was the best and I respected that. Unfortunately at that time my tastes seemed to lay elsewhere.

MD: So is this love of big band music a more recent development for you?

Neil: Actually, no. The big band thing was born through my father. Big band was his favorite music, so I heard a lot of it. When I got interested in drumming, I heard his music and what the drummers were doing, so I was aware of it.

MD: I remember you telling me that since that music was what your father listened to, you seemed to rebel against it.

Neil: I did that in so far as what I wanted to play, but I did enjoy listening to it. I got interested in Duke Ellington's music and Count Basie's music. I started buying those records in my teens. I started buying Sinatra records then, too. When I lived in England, I went to see Tony Bennett at the London Palladium when I was eighteen, by *choice,* and loved the man. Kenny Clare was playing drums for him then. That was a case where age and generation

didn't matter. Kenny Clare was one of the most exciting drummers I ever saw. Many of the big band drummers were like that. Sonny Payne had that quality. And obviously, Gene Krupa too. You couldn't help but be excited by them if you were a young drummer, regardless of style or preference. So I think it came around full circle for me, when, in 1991, Buddy's daughter, Cathy, asked me to perform with the big band for the scholarship show. While I was very intimidated by it, it sounded like an enormous challenge and an opportunity to actually play some of this music I loved. I went into that experience for that reason, basically as a good way to challenge myself. I hate

Neil: Honestly, no. There was just so much learning to do, and I did a lot of it along the way. I couldn't sit down with the band on day one and give them a speech and say, "This is how it's going to be. Here's how we're going to work. Here's what I expect from you. Here's what you can expect from me." All of that had to be felt out step-by-step.

While this was my first official project as a producer, I have worked with many good producers over the years, and I do have some experience! [laughs] I think I've learned what a musician wants to have from a producer. I decided on my basic role in my own mind: I had to be a facilitator and make it easy for people to work, and I had

producer he's just listening to the song and the total picture of what's going on. I decided that's the right way to go for this project.
MD: So you didn't have comments for drummers after they made a take?
Neil: I did, but only in so far as how what they played affected the arrangement—did it help to get the song across? Unfortunately, what that meant was that I couldn't take advantage of all those free drum lessons and tips I could have picked up had I just focused on what the drummers were playing!

Basically all of the musicians were producing themselves. I expected them to critique their own parts and

> ## "I think it was that power that largely attracted me to big band playing. There's such a great feeling when you're hitting the shots with the band, pulling that trigger."

when things get too safe.
MD: But what led you from that point to getting so involved in a much larger project like *Burning*?
Neil: Actually, to be perfectly honest, all I wanted was a very selfish thing— the chance to play big band music again! In my darkest little mean heart of hearts all I wanted was to feel the excitement of kicking a big band. I wished somebody would make a record so I could have the opportunity to play with Buddy's band again under more controlled circumstances than a live concert, and I guess I realized I was the one to do it! That truly was the germ of the whole thing.
MD: And you felt equipped to take on the project?

to be a motivator—get them working, that sort of thing.
MD: Was there any particular producer you modeled yourself after?
Neil: I've learned from many of the producers that Rush has worked with over the years. I think an important lesson I learned from Peter Collins—a producer we've worked with on three of our records—is that a producer doesn't need to be overly concerned with certain things. Peter always stays away from the technical side of making records. He leaves the sound to the engineer and to the musicians. He even leaves the details of the performance to the musicians—*they* can worry about it and quibble about it with the engineer and the other musicians. As a

know if they could live with it or not. I couldn't sit there and listen to the whole piece of music plus fifteen separate parts in every nuance and detail. So it quickly became apparent that that couldn't be part of the job.

The first thing I would do after a take was to ask everybody, "How did you feel about it?" Then if someone said, "I made a mistake in bar 43," "Good, let's listen to the take and see if the rest of it is acceptable and if we can fix that one part." I counted on everybody there to critique themselves, and I was told that the musicians were not used to being worked with in that way. Some of them said that after all these years it's nice that somebody is asking their opinion of their work. The byproduct of

THE PARTICIPANTS
continued from page 71

Billy Cobham

Bill is such a consummate professional, and I have to say I'm indebted to him. He recorded on one of the last days of the session. At that point there were a few tunes that I really wanted to have recorded, and without even knowing the arrangements he came in and did them. In Buddy's band, as you know, there were no drum charts, so Bill used the lead trumpet part as his guide, and he sight-read the tracks. Everyone thinks of him as a great technician, but he's also a skilled reader. I joked with him that I really appreciated his "taking requests."

Bill was very interpretive in his style, which really interests me. His style is so seemingly unstructured. It's so contrary to the way that I think. He's happy to try any number of different ways of approaching a tune. I found that to be very interesting.

Rod Morgenstein

I've known Rod for years, and he's a favorite of mine as a player and as a person. He was nervous about doing it, like the rest of us were, but he came in and did a good job very quickly. He was really well prepared.

The tune we originally sent him, "Good News," is a really long piece. After he received it, he called me up and said, "This piece is eleven minutes long. Are you sure you want me to do this one?" I got worried, but I had the record of Buddy's version, so I listened to it. I felt it was such a great piece of music that I had to say to Rod, "Go ahead, but we'll have to record something shorter too." I got him to do "Machine" as well, which is another tune that I really liked. And as expected, he did a great job.

Max Roach

Max didn't want to record with the band, so we thought that we'd have him play some of his solo pieces. I told him the story about "The Drum Also Waltzes," that it had been passed on to me by another drummer. I was doing it in my current solo, and Steve Smith was using it as a clinic exercise to teach people. It seemed to please Max that an idea of his had survived and continued to instruct new generations of drummers.

When he recorded, he was the only one there; the band wasn't around. We had the lights softened. Before he began his piece, he would wait for our cue. He'd have his sticks raised, and after we gave him the go-ahead, he'd take a few more seconds and then begin. It was a beautiful moment, and Max approached his playing with so much dignity. I was very impressed with his respect for the drums.

The hard thing for me was choosing how to present these solo pieces on the album. I didn't want this to be a totally drum-focused record with lots of solos, because I didn't want to alienate any listeners. But I actually got the idea for the solution from a Brazilian record I have that has a little percussion interlude that just weaves in and out from time to time. I always thought that was a nice idea.

The piece creates a very hypnotic feel—just a quiet, repetitive pattern. It's almost like a heartbeat. And due to a slight accident that happened during the mixing stages—where a lengthy delay was applied to the solo—the hypnotic effect is even enhanced. The effect worked so well, we ended up keeping it. I was very happy with the way it turned out.

Kenny Aronoff

Kenny is such an energetic person, and he came in and just delivered on his two tunes. He and I had a bit in common because we're both known as rock drummers, and while he has training in other areas of percussion, he makes his living playing rock 'n' roll drums. We both challenged ourselves by playing tunes that were more jazz-leaning, and I was really thrilled to hear how Kenny interpreted his tunes.

I love the job he did on "Straight, No Chaser." It is so powerful and punchy. To me it's obviously a rock drummer playing in terms of its weight and even some of the figures he used, but it worked. We kidded each other when we were listening back to the tracks, pointing and shouting "Rock! Rock!" when we heard a fill or figure that was more like something a rock drummer would play.

Kenny also helped me add percussion to one of the other tracks, "Pick Up the Pieces." That happened when I was mixing the track in Montreal and Kenny just happened to be in town doing some session work. He called to say he was in the area, so I invited him over. We had a lot of fun overdubbing the percussion parts during the drum break in "Pieces." It was actually a great opportunity for the two of us to work together as drummers with nobody else there. That was a particularly enjoyable experience for me. We called ourselves the Bald Bongo Brothers.

Omar Hakim

Omar and I first met at the Buddy Rich scholarship concert in '91. He is one of those people who I felt an immediate affinity for. I love his playing—the fluidity of it. It's smooth and yet it has a snappy excitement to it, and he plays with such a good feel.

"Slo-Funk" was the tune that I think he had done at the scholarship concert and the one so well suited to his style. He came in and did an excellent job on it. Unfortunately, he was very uncomfortable with the rented drumkit he had sent to the session—he never seemed satisfied with it. He ended up deciding not to record the other track he had prepared, but I was very happy to have him do the one tune.

Joe Morello

I always tried to go out into the room when a drummer first played through a tune with the

continues on page 75

that was that everybody started to feel a certain responsibility to the project, everybody wanted it to be as good as they could make it.

MD: I understand the pace of recording was very fast.

Neil: Yes. We had two weeks to record a lot of music. We were recording two drummers a day, and I jokingly told everybody that they had a four-take maximum. Most of the drummers nailed the parts fast. I think working that way added a certain spark to the music. Every track is alive and full of energy.

Everything had its adventure. Every song started new and every drummer that came through the door was a new starting point. We had to set up the drummer's gear, get sounds quickly, and *go*. Everything happened so fast. That was the astonishing part. The day we recorded Simon Phillips, we did three songs with him, and that was after doing two with somebody else. We recorded five tunes that day, and at the end of the day I couldn't remember

REMEMBERING NEIL
continued from page 65

rotation in the record store I worked in as a teen. I also saw them in concert back then, and I knew I was there to see and hear something exceptional.

I remember conversing with Greg Ginn from Black Flag back in the day about Neil. We both dug how he played a terrific chunky groove and gave each note its full value.

I felt for Neil as he dealt with a great deal of adversity and tragedy later in his life. It really hit home for me when his health issues became too much for him to continue. As a drummer, the most athletic of instrumentalists, it has forced me to examine my own limitations and fears as I get older.

Neil Peart did more than affect the way I play; he changed the face of modern rock drumming and bucked the stereotype of the "dumb drummer." I will always be grateful.
Sim Cain (Rollins Band, John Zorn, Dean Ween Group)

Neil Peart was such a monumental figure. His knowledge of the instrument was invaluable, and his willingness to share spoke greatly of the kind of individual he was. He will live forever through his musical contributions.
Chaun Horton (Alice Smith/Nate Mercereau)

As an exponent of reggae music, I have always been paying close attention to the pioneers of the genre. However, after in-depth research, Neil Peart made me realize that I had to think out of the box, and that there is much more to learn. His approach was not just a mere, "set up, play for a few hours, get paid, leave, and repeat the routine tomorrow." No! It was in fact a lifestyle for him.

Neil viewed the drums as much more than an instrument. He had a dream kit, a setup that blew everyone's mind. That's where I'd say the term "office" was derived. His methodology of drumming was conversational rather than a monologue. He engaged his audience and gave them an experience. By himself he was a complete band; however, this does not take away from the fact that he complements the band immaculately and his fellow musicians are just as present. He took the risk of reinventing himself after thirty years, when many

continues on page 74

who we started with that morning. I think that happened because we had to pour all of our concentration so totally into each song. The world began and ended at that point.

MD: I would imagine that the level of stress you were going through during those two weeks was incredible.

Neil: It was intensely stressful. It really was. The level of concentration that it took, the level of focus that it took, the discipline.... We were invited out every night to check out other players in New York. All the musicians working in town would say, "Come on down and see us tonight." But I couldn't because we were starting 9 every morning and I had to be my absolute sharpest.

MD: How did you decide on the drummers you wanted to include?

Neil: I had a list in mind of players who are my favorite drummers. And Cathy recommended people she had worked with on other Buddy Rich Memorial concerts. Obviously, we also wanted some of the legendary figures, some of Buddy's peers, like Joe Morello and Ed Shaughnessy.

Neil and Bill Bruford

Neil and Ed Shaughnessy

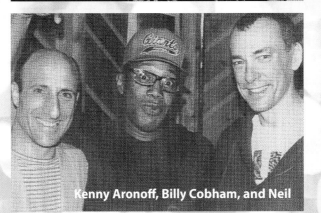
Kenny Aronoff, Billy Cobham, and Neil

I was disappointed that Louie Bellson couldn't make it, but unfortunately he was in Europe at the time. Vinnie Colaiuta was another drummer I really wanted to include because he had been so good with the band on one of the previous scholarship concerts. Unfortunately, he was in Europe at the time. There were a couple of schedule conflicts that kept a few people from participating.

We had a two-week window we had to record in—if people couldn't come through that window, then we had to miss them. Even at that, in those two weeks we recorded over three hours of music! That's why the first CD has seventy-six minutes crammed on it. I wanted to get as much on as I could, not only for its own sake, but also because I have all this other great material still waiting to be released.

MD: How did you decide on the tunes to be recorded and which drummers would record them?

Neil: Actually, Cathy and her husband, Steve Arnold, had a great deal to do with that. They both know Buddy's music very well. Cathy and Steve's intimacy with the repertoire was invaluable. In some cases we chose a tune based on the availability of the music,

REMEMBERING NEIL

continued from page 73

would have gotten complacent. It was an indication that no matter your level, you should never stop learning, and that there are endless opportunities to become a better you.

Certainly he has impacted the lives of drummers with confidence around the kit. Additionally as drummers we are not shadows; we represent the backbone. Another lesson is that there is an area for all, from the simplest of drummers to the "beasts."

Neil, I will continue to engage my

audience and value them for turning up for the experience. I will not be confined by the rules but rather think out of the proverbial box. I will continue to reinvent myself. Thanks for sharing your gift with the world. You have certainly left an indelible mark.
Courtney "Bam" Diedrick (Damian Marley, Playing for Change, I-Taweh)

Neil Peart was a force on the drumkit. As a kid growing up in Baltimore, Rush was played faithfully on the local hard-rock radio station. How did he play like that? I still don't know the answer, but it certainly

sounds cool.
Tim Kuhl (solo artist, Margaret Glaspy)

Neil showed us how to make the drums work on every level. His tweaking of sounds, toms, and combining the pads with the drumheads and forming a unique style—he kept always changing with time and being the best drummer he could be at each moment. Today we study his recordings, we watch his videos, and we still learn with every lesson he left behind. To that you add his skills as a writer, and you get a master at his craft. We drummers now

are left with this huge library of ideas, styles, and motivation from one of the greats.
Frank Amente (iLe, Baterisma, Calle 13)

Neil Peart's passing creates a vacuum in the drumming community. We have lost one of the greatest minds of our instrument; a genius that inspired so many to go forward, to push the limits of one's creativity, to not settle for average.

I can safely say that if it weren't for Neil, I would not have even begun to play drums. He was my very first inspiration, the type of inspiration that

band, just so I could get an idea what their drums sounded like acoustically. It was very interesting to hear the fire in Joe's playing in the room. When he booted that bass drum, boy, it was *booted*. His touch and control are such that there is tremendous restraint to his playing—a very refined approach—and the dynamic range of it is generally low, physically low off the head and also low in terms of volume. But when he does give a little snap of the wrist or a little extra "oomph" on the cymbal, you're aware of it.

When he first came in, I didn't expect a very energetic performance from him; he was kind of stooped and slow-moving, and he kept saying, "It's too early in the day to play." But when he was behind his drums he was committed to his performance. There was so much fire in his playing, and that was inspirational to see a guy just sit down and deliver the goods. We captured a bit of history with him.

Bill Bruford

Bill brought in an original piece, "Lingo," which was a real challenge for the band. It was a very polyrhythmic piece, quite different from what we'd been doing, but I was happy to see the commitment the band put into learning the song quickly. Bill made the remark, "They could have ruined this for me."

Everyone poured themselves into that piece and made it happen. It's a special piece because it has the flavor of the band, yet it's rhythmically and structurally more adventurous, which goes to Bill's compositional roots. That was an interesting piece to see go down.

Bill also came in very well prepared for "Willow Crest," a piece from Buddy's book. He had written out a basic chart of it for himself. Again, like so many of us, he was nervous about it but at the same time very concerned. He came in with a total commitment to make his time there the most valuable it could be for the whole project as well as for himself.

Marvin "Smitty" Smith

"Smitty" is a born master drummer—it's unbelievable how good he is. But he's also a great personality—really cheery, sprightly, and happy. He's happy behind his drums, he's happy when he's not behind his drums. He's a good influence and he was actually around for a few of the other days when he wasn't recording; he was always a ray of sunshine to be around.

To give you an idea how impressive his playing was, he recorded both of his songs on first takes. He was obviously very easy for the band to play with because his playing was so smooth, so consistent, so rooted in that style of music—it made it easy for everybody to lock in. So all respect to his ability as a drummer *and* as a person.

Steve Ferrone

Steve is a real character. I've admired his work for a long time. I actually met him almost twenty years ago when he was with Brian Auger's group. Rush's tour manager had previously worked with Brian Auger, so we met somewhere socially all that time ago. I followed his work, especially the work he did on the Bryan Ferry record last year, and I've really admired what he's done.

I wanted him to come in and play "Keep the Customer Satisfied," which he did, but he also brought in an arrangement of "Pick Up the Pieces," obviously a tune he's known for from his Average White Band days. It was an arrangement written for full big band by Arif Mardin for a jazz festival Steve played years ago. It really shows Steve's ability to play with a great feel.

Steve's another one of those drummers who is so casual and so comfortable with what he does—no tension, no self-consciousness—just walks in, sits down, and delivers.

Ed Shaughnessy

Ed was kind of a guru figure for me. He's a master at this style of music, and I was very excited to have him play with the band. I learned a lot from watching him work.

Ed's such a comfortable man—comfortable with himself, comfortable with the world—very easygoing. But when he got down to work, he took on a whole different focus—way more serious, more resilient, less humorous, and more demanding. He actually was the first drummer to record for the session, which was fortunate for us because he took control of the band and got things off to an excellent start.

Ed recorded "Shawnee" and "Mr. Humble." "Mr. Humble" was a tune I guess he had written for Buddy. Whenever Buddy appeared on *The Tonight Show* they'd do this thing called "Mr. Humble," because Ed always said that whenever Buddy came in, Johnny Carson would say, "Here's Mr. Humble." And Buddy would say, "Hey, when you're the greatest, what do you have to be humble about?"

---

the style, and how it would work with a certain drummer. And if a drummer requested a particular piece, we tried to accommodate him.

For instance, when I was asked to do the scholarship show, I was looking for a fast and a slow swing tune. They sent me eight or ten different tunes from which I picked "Cotton Tail" and "One O'clock Jump," because they were the type of traditional things I really wanted to try myself on. Other drummers took the same route, where they just asked for some suggestions based on style and then chose from there.

MD: Were there any specific things you picked up from some of the other drummers who participated?

Neil: Being exposed to so much great playing over the two weeks was extremely inspiring. So much was played that I'm sure some of it stuck with me. But I do remember specifically trying to find out more about playing big band drumming. I tried to speak with the drummers who had that experience. Ed Shaughnessy and I had dinner one night, and I picked his brains about the music and about how a lot of the older guys played.

It was very interesting to me to watch the way Ed played, actually. I liked it. He took a looser approach because of his confidence with the music. He was so comfortable with the

---

makes a fifteen-year-old kid in Brazil who just listened to *Moving Pictures* for the very first time go crazy imagining what can be done on this incredible instrument we are lucky to play. So many musicians nowadays have him to thank for.

Neil also gifted us with a different, fascinating side of his personality when writing lyrics for Rush, and in his books, where we get a view into his motorcycle adventures. If that weren't enough, one can also draw endless inspiration from his resilient personality while going through some of life's most traumatic moments, such as the loss of a wife and daughter.

I perfectly remember being in the first row at Maracanã Stadium in Rio de Janeiro, watching their Rush in Rio performance in the early 2000s. That moment marked me forever, and I never looked back. A few years later, I made a move to the U.S. to pursue music full time, a lot of it fueled by Neil and how humble and hardworking he was. Thank you, Neil, for all that you did. Heaven is much richer now. Rest in peace.

Bruno Esrubilsky (Mitski, independent)

I sadly never got to meet Neil. In the late '80s, early '90s Neil would fly out Freddie Gruber from California to New York City and pay him crazy money to spend a week with him to work on drum things. During a few of those one-week visits Freddie would call me and ask if I was playing in town because he wanted to bring Neil down. The timing never worked. Sadly, I was either on the road or not working in New York that week.

Freddie and Neil loved each other. He would always talk about how much Neil loved jazz. That wasn't hard to believe, because while Neil played mostly rock language, it was obvious that he thought like a jazz musician, because he spent so much time going beyond just playing a beat with typical fills. Neil was always taking every section of a tune and arranging the concept and musical decisions and choosing atypical grooves and fills for the constantly moving and changing sections of Rush's music. I know from talking to many of Neil's friends, like Freddie, Terry Bozzio, Don Lombardi, and others, that he was, with all his success and status, a completely humble and sweet guy who loved everybody and had so much respect

continues on page 76

style that he had a more relaxed feel than I think a lot of us less-experienced big band guys hoped to have. I liked the way he was able to be very precise and very considerate about what he played and where.

We talked about timekeeping in a big band sense. In the middle of "Shawnee," one of the tunes he recorded, there is a little fanfare section where he pulled the time way back. If he had continued the time through that section, it would have sounded awful. It proved that metronomes and drum machines *don't*

of the music. That's where the sheer level of skill can be astonishing, and I learned that from certain drummers on this project.

MD: You mentioned that there were minimal edits made to the tracks, although you would pull a solo section from one take and stick it in another take if that one was superior. When you're actually lifting sections and the drummers are not playing to a click, how can the sections from different takes be in time with each other?

Neil: Believe it or not, it wasn't a

different takes is amazing.

Neil: That's a testament to the quality of these players. Any time we needed to repair a take, for any reason, to get a better solo, a different drum break, or a major chunk of the tune, we were surprised at how in time everything was. These guys were *that* in control of the time; they were all that good.

It's like Buddy always said: If you're a good drummer you should be able to play all styles, that if you're a good jazz drummer you should be able to play rock and vice versa. It's true, as Kenny Aronoff and I both found. We both had little experience playing jazz. We both put a lot of time and research into finding out how to go about it, getting people to help us, rehearsing it, preparing for it, and—I think I can say, at least in his case—turning in a really credible job of it. It's proof of what Buddy said.

MD: How do you think Buddy would have felt about this whole project?

Neil: Well, not knowing the man, it's hard to say. But everyone's telling me he'd be beaming. We did a good job on his music, everybody played well, and the spirit of the whole occasion was great. So many of his friends and colleagues came together to honor him for what he did for music and for our instrument. Attention is being paid.

> "We recorded five tunes that day, and at the end of the day I couldn't remember who we started with that morning. We had to pour all of our concentration so totally into each song. The world began and ended at that point."

apply to this kind of music. It has to be felt by the drummer, controlled by the drummer. The time can't be allowed to speed up or slow down. The drummer has to be in full control of the time. But there are instances when you have to "shade the edges" of time for the sake

problem with any of these drummers. Any of the edits we made involved whole sections. We couldn't just take a solo, for example, because of all the background spilling.

MD: But for the drummers to be so accurate with the time among a few

REMEMBERING NEIL

continued from page 75

and love for music and musicians of every style. I will always wish that the timing had worked out, because I am sure it would have been a time I would have always remembered.

Much love, Neil.
Gerry Gibbs (independent)

The loss of Neil Peart was devastating on two levels—as a friend and as a drumming icon. The more you got to know Neil, the more you felt he was truly a regular guy

whose passion and work ethic left an unforgettable mark on drummers of today and the future. He spent weeks at the Drum Channel studio preparing before each tour and would always ask me who might be coming around. He was as excited to meet other drummers as they were to meet him. Going from stadium to stadium on his motorcycle, often staying at a local motel along the way and working out at the local YMCA, was Neil. He would always tell me an important thing for him was to always be prepared. The last thing he said to me as we hugged goodbye was, "Don, we did it and we

did it the right way." When you were with Neil, that was the only way it would be.

Don Lombardi (founder, Drum Workshop)

One of my earliest memories is drumming to "Tom Sawyer" on the seats of my mom's car on the way to daycare. Even as an eight-year-old, it was apparent to me that Neil's drumming was something special, powerful. He was the spark that lit a lifelong fire for the drums and music. I'm not alone in this realization. That young boy from Iowa could never have

imagined the friendship to come with Neil Peart. He shared his adventures motorcycling, sailing, touring, and drumming. Every day ended with a Macallan and lots of laughter. More than all this, Bubba was there for me when my own dad died of cancer. He brought me In-n-Out after I got creamed on my motorcycle. He'd meet with Make-a-Wish kids in secret, play drums with them, and take them for milkshakes. He was that kind of dude. Extraordinarily kind, even after the universe took everything from him. He left our world a better place than he found it.

continues on page 86

The Evolution Of A Live Rig

Neil Peart played a number of different kits during his forty years of touring with Rush. Here we discuss the major evolutionary changes his kit went through by focusing on the setups he sported during the first three, classic Rush live albums plus the unique approach he took during their *R40* tour.

by Ilya Stemkovsky

Paul Natkin

All the World's a Stage (1976)

The *2112* album gave Rush their first taste of success, and their newfound fans were willing to go wherever the band took them. Recorded in their hometown of Toronto in 1976, *All the World's a Stage* is maximum rock 'n' roll; Rush is running their involved tunes with an accuracy and ferocity many veteran acts couldn't approach. Peart's parts aren't yet written in stone,

and he's able to really rock out on tracks like "In the End" and "Something for Nothing," whipping out tidal wave tom rolls and go-for-broke cymbal crashes. Geddy Lee introduces Peart as "the Professor" before the drum solo inside "Working Man/Finding My Way," and all the flavors he'd return to time and time again are already present, from the sprightly rudimental snare work to those melodic cowbell phrases. This earliest live document proved Rush were a force to be reckoned with in the concert arena, and it capped off the first phase in what would be a long career. By the time they released another live set, Rush would be internationally championed rock royalty, and their stage work would achieve a new level of authority.

The kit Neil used during the concerts documented on *All the World's a Stage* was a maple-shell Slingerland with a chrome finish, lovingly referred to as "Chromey." Prominently displayed on the album cover, this seven-up, one-down layout had certain unique characteristics that would not carry over to later setups.

The four concert-tom sizes lasted through several subsequent tours, but the three main toms in front of Neil were a bit smaller than ones he eventually would employ. For a drummer who played lots of long and involved fills, it's interesting that Neil only used one floor tom during this era, and would do so until later adding a timpani to his right for color.

Of note was Neil's reliance on his Slingerland Artist snare drum, referred to as "Old Faithful," which would grace many future studio recordings and live shows. Neil played Zildjian cymbals for a long time, and the basic setup here would remain the same for years, with 13" hi-hats, two crashes to his left, a splash in front, and a crash, splash, and ride configuration to his right side. China cymbals were not yet present during this time, and Neil's percussion was minimal, including a small array of orchestra bells, cowbells, and wind chimes. Promark 747 Rock model sticks and Ludwig Speed King pedals rounded out the equipment.

Exit…Stage Left (1981)

Recorded during tours supporting 1980's *Permanent Waves* and 1981's *Moving Pictures*, *Exit…Stage Left* presents Rush at the height of its powers, at the crucial intersection where their most ambitious material meets their newfound superstardom. All three musicians play with an increased level of assuredness—check Rush's touring itinerary from this era for an eye-popping amount of road work—and Peart's drumming in particular has developed a razor-sharp edge honed over time. Where the raw *All the World's a Stage* clobbered the listener with a hard rock approach that owed much to Peart influences like the Who's Keith Moon and King Crimson's Michael Giles, here the drummer further shows off the refinements featured in his recent studio work. Peart weaves in and out of the twisting "Jacob's Ladder" with confidence, while album gems like "A Passage to Bangkok"

truly crackle with life on an airtight recording with very little crowd noise. Epic studio showcases like "Xanadu" are imbued with the taut quality of the band's current work, as was Peart's solo in "YYZ," which underwent fine-tuning and became a real Rush concert highlight. If their first live album was an opening salvo of energy and chops, *Exit…* was Rush finding its concert sound, with Peart leading the way.

Exit…Stage Left saw Neil's switch to Tama drums, with the 1980 and 1981 tours featured on the album presenting a few significant changes to the equipment. The Tama Superstar kit in custom Rosewood finish was "vibra-fibed," with the inside of the shells treated with a thin coat of fiberglass, and the bass drums went up a size to 24". Neil would also add timpani, brass timbales, and, later, Tama gong bass drums. The "Old Faithful" 5.5x14 Slingerland snare was retained, however. In the April/May 1980 issue of *Modern Drummer*, Neil says of the drum, "Every other snare I've had chokes somewhere, either very quietly or if you hit it too hard. This one never chokes. You can play it very delicately or you can pound it to death. It always produces a very clean, very crisp sound. It has a lot of power, which I didn't expect from a wooden drum."

Neil used head models made by a variety of manufacturers, including Remo Clear Dots on his snare and bass drums, Ludwig Silver Dots on his concert toms, and Evans heads on his rack and floor toms. As Rush's music grew more expansive, so did Neil's percussion setup, by now including crotales, tubular bells, and temple blocks in addition to what was already present earlier. Brass-plated Tama hardware was a final detail.

A Show of Hands (1989)

The last of Rush's "classic era" live offerings was assembled using shows mostly from the *Hold Your Fire* tour of 1988, and while the resulting sound and setlist varies greatly from their first two concert discs, this is still Rush bringing their A game to fans who couldn't get enough. Featuring Peart's self-actualized mastery of combining his acoustic drums with an electronic kit and percussion, the noise Rush made with three guys onstage was huge. The drummer's verve on dynamic tracks like "Marathon" and "Manhattan Project" is a marvel to hear, his parts formulated as if by a machine to be performed by a machine, and the mix has an almost too-perfect, antiseptic studio quality. Peart, though, is very human, and here he combines flawlessness with a bead of sweat. Peart's drum solo, "The Rhythm

Andrew MacNaughtan

Method," further advances on previously developed accented snare work with the addition of electronic marimba and triggered horn hits. There would be many more tours yielding more live recordings, but none more essential than these first three.

For the 1988 *Hold Your Fire* tour that provided the majority of performances on *A Show of Hands*, Neil once again chose to make a change in drum manufacturer, this time settling on a set of Ludwig Super Classics in a white/pink sparkle finish. The "Vibra-fibing" process returned, and most of the concert toms were replaced with double-headed drums for uniformity. The big leap from the *Exit…Stage Left* setup was the prominent addition of electronics. A MalletKAT controller, which now allowed Neil to recreate many of the percussion sounds like temple blocks, was added to the Simmons electronic modules he'd introduced a few years earlier. Also present were Yamaha MIDI controllers, Akai samplers, and a swanky rotating drum riser.

"The song 'Mission' had a syncopated marimba, bass guitar, and snare drum solo," Neil told *MD* in his December 1989 cover story. "I originally recorded the snare and overdubbed the marimba. Live, I assigned both the snare and marimba sound to the same pad—so I can have both sounds! Through the wonder of electronics, I was able to manipulate the pitches of the temple blocks on 'Time Stand Still,' so I got the sound I heard in my head." Neil was now surrounded 360 degrees by toys of all sorts, and he was able to reproduce the band's increasingly electronic-oriented sounds faithfully in the concert space.

R40 Live (2015)

Rush embarked on their final tour knowing full well that it would be a summation of all the group had achieved and then some. Documenting the Peart/Lifeson/Lee trio's fortieth year together, *R40 Live*, recorded in 2015, again in their hometown

of Toronto, boasted a unique setlist that worked backwards chronologically. Beginning with Peart's hammering tom work on "The Anarchist" and double kick flourishes in "Far Cry," this was the band proving that their latest material was as strong as the stuff they put out during their classic period, and that Peart was still up to the challenge of creating imaginative drum parts. For the second set, Peart switched from his modern kit to a replica drumset he'd played

in the late 1970s, and he rips on deep fan wish list numbers like "Natural Science" and "Hemispheres" with still-brilliant technical prowess and trademark power. Before the show concludes with the band's early riff songs like "What You're Doing," we hear Peart swim in the odd-time sea of rarities like "Losing It" with the maturity of a player with years at the game. Not merely a nostalgia cash-grab, *R40 Live* showcases a still-able band, and puts an exclamation point on an incredible career.

For the *R40* tour, Neil pulled out all the stops, adopting a more-is-more attitude by featuring not one but two full kits used throughout the course of the unique, "backwards in time" performance. The set list would begin with Rush's recent repertoire, as Neil would play the "modern kit," a beautiful DW Black Pearl–finish monster made from a 1,500-year-old Romanian River Oak tree.

"The first kit in the first set is evolved as an instrument of perfect comfort," Neil said in the January 2016 issue of *MD*. "I can play it with my eyes closed. The musicality through the cymbals and the toms. Everything is carefully chosen and put where it should be. I tell people, don't look at those 47 drums. It's a four-drum setup. Look at the middle, everything spins off from there."

Rounding things out were assorted Sabian Paragon cymbals, various electronics including Roland V-Drums and MalletKATs, and Ableton Live running on a MacBook Pro. The hardware was even gold-plated. But the great surprise was a totally separate second kit, nicknamed "El Darko," used later in the show for all the material from *Moving Pictures* and before. This was a DW replica of Peart's classic Slingerland kit from the late 1970s, and it featured two bass drums as well as four "open" concert toms used for the first time since the mid-'80s *Power Windows* Tama kit. This black chrome-finish beast, also made from that 1,500-year-old tree, sounded great, but was tougher to tame for the older, wiser Peart.

In the 2016 *MD* piece, Neil shared, "I had the notion that, wouldn't it be great if instead of having the rotating set I've had for years that kind of contrasts the acoustic and electronic drums, I went to a whole second drumset. I always say this about old cars and old motorcycles, I love them, and old drums, I love them, but new ones are better. The ergonomics of it all [were tough]. I used to make everything so close and under me. But it was counterintuitive thinking. I used to think the closer it is, the more power I can get on it, but that's not true. You have to get it the right distance. Close or near doesn't matter. And the way the set list works out, I had to solo on that set.

"I'd much rather solo on my modern set in every sense," Peart went on, "musically and physically. But there are cool things as well. I used to have timbales on my left side and I got those again, and playing two bass drums again was fun."

Neil and Rush went out on the highest of notes, giving fans a concert experience filled with music spanning the band's entire career, still played at peak level. Peart would hang up the sticks and put down the pen with no regrets.

Sayre Berman

The Story of Chromey

In 1987, *Modern Drummer* held a contest where entrants were instructed to send in a two-minute, unaccompanied drum solo on cassette, to be judged by none other than Neil Peart himself. The 1,776 entries received were whittled down by *MD*'s editors to 46, from which Peart chose the winners. And the prize? It sounds too good to be true, but the three top winners would each receive a kit that Peart had recorded with and used in live performances throughout Rush's career. (Unable to keep his winners to three, Neil asked his cymbal company at the time, Zildjian, to put together a fourth prize package, a set of new cymbals.)

Perhaps Neil's most famous kit, the Slingerland Chrome set he used on the recordings and tours for *Fly by Night*, *Caress of Steel*, *2112*, and *All the World's a Stage*—yes, the drums on the cover of that seminal live album—were won by a drummer named Mark Feldman. Now cut to sometime in 2009, and *MD* photographer John Fell, who at the time was a partner in Brooklyn music store Main Drag Music, was visited by Feldman, who wanted to sell the kit on consignment. Fell, who'd worked in museums prior to entering drum retail and repair, discussed with his colleagues what to do with the kit and how to sell it. "The enemy of conservation is restoration," says Fell. "But since we were selling it, we decided to keep it as is—not even conserve it, let alone restore it. It was even in

Neil's tuning."

There was a long, intense eBay auction, which resulted in some Rush fans asking to see and touch the kit, and the store decided that it needed to be put on display. In one particularly odd wrinkle to the story, Fell received multiple phone calls from an anonymous shadow figure calling himself "the High Priest from the Temple of Syrinx," who insisted that the kit wasn't authentic. The bidding price froze at $2,112 (of course), and then $21,012, and the drums eventually sold for around $25,000.

And who showed up to pick up the kit? A collector named Dean Bobisud, who drove all the way from Chicago. "He owned a pizzeria, and he sold a Corvette to do this," says Fell. "He was a serious Rush fanatic, with a shrine of Peart's sticks and guitar picks. He arrived in a van with a bunch of matching drum bags, and was very excited. He even put a chicken suit on for the photo—the actual chicken suit that Rush's crew used onstage during their tours. They'd have rotisserie chickens turning onstage, and techs wearing these suits would come out and baste them." The kit was eventually restored and has since made the showcase rounds, as documented on the internet.

It seems that, indeed, all the world's a stage, and some of us are merely players…wearing chicken suits.

Courtesy John Fell

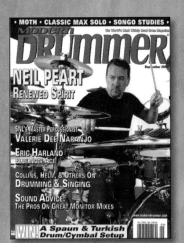

September 2002

The Fire Returns

It had been six years since his last *Modern Drummer* interview. It had been a time of unimaginable setbacks— and, somehow, profound personal growth.

Interview by William F. Miller

MD: I just want to start off by saying thanks for granting us the interview. I know this is tough for you.

Neil: I haven't done one of these in a long time. I don't know how good it will be.

MD: Let's start with something easy. Your drumming sounds good on *Vapor Trails*. In fact, it's one of your most grooving performances.

Neil: Well, that's a wonderful comment. I'm sure glad to hear it, because I was trying my best to achieve that. The whole way we went about making this record was so different from any we've done in the past that it might have permitted a more grooving approach to come through.

A lot of the songs were just jams, where Geddy and Alex got together in front of a recorder, set up a groove on a rhythm machine, and started playing. And then later, Geddy would go back and sift through those jams and say, "This eight bars is good," "This four bars is good," or, "If we took that two bars and repeated it, that would be good." So they stitched together these things into a structure.

At the same time, I was feeding Geddy lyrics so he could sing over the ideas they were coming up with. And then we did what we call leapfrogging, where we individually work on the songs ourselves—the drum parts, guitar parts, and vocal/bass parts—without holding up each other and without getting caught up in too much editorial commentary from each other.

MD: Can you elaborate on the idea of leapfrogging?

Neil: We start off with that rough tape Geddy will have created, and then Alex will add guitar parts more to the vision he has for the song. Then I'll take that tape and come up with drum parts that I think will work. Then Geddy will respond to *my* drum parts and say, "Well, the bass part would be better if it went like this." Then I'll hear that and it'll give me ideas. So we're constantly improvising and developing the ideas, even though we're never really playing the song together.

MD: It sounds as if you don't like each other.

Neil: [laughs] That's not the case *at all*. We've played together for twenty-seven years. I was actually thinking today about how many times we've played together. It's something like

tens of thousands of times. We really know each other well as players and as people. So it isn't necessary for us to sit in a room and hash it out all at the same time. Our current thinking goes on to that work tape. My current thinking on the drum part goes on there, and then it's talked about, of course, in between each of those takes: "Well, I like what you're doing, but it might be cool if you did this."

A good example of this process is "One Little Victory." I'd been working on that tune and came up with that double bass part. I thought it worked perfectly for the end of the song. But Geddy said, "That's a great part. You ought to open the song with it. That would just kill." Frankly, I wouldn't have done it that way—I don't think I would have been so assertive—but Geddy suggested it and I said, "Okay, I'll try it."

MD: One thing I'm not clear about is, how did this method of developing parts help you to create a more grooving performance?

Neil: For this record we moved straight into the recording studio, where in the past we'd always go through that process of refinement—arranging the

song, working on our parts, and then all being satisfied with them—before we'd go into the studio. I would then go in and record all of the drum parts in two days. I would be focused on producing *that* performance, the one that we had come up with during our refining process.

That method has good qualities, in that it would sometimes drive me to a level that I hadn't reached before, just putting that pressure on me to push a little further. So I like that in a way. But for *Vapor Trails* we decided to stay in the same studio where we were doing the writing and pre-production and just gradually start recording songs that we thought were ready. It was a much more gradual process.

Andrew MacNaughtan

If I went in to work on a drum part, I could just play around with it and not be so stressed about it. There was never any pressure that it *had* to be the final take. A lot of the drum tracks were spontaneous in the sense that things had never been played that way before. It was an easier way to work.

MD: I can see how that attitude would help you groove. But you also mentioned earlier that the feel was something you were very concerned about.

Neil: The pulse was a big factor in my thinking. In the past, I would focus on the technical parts. That was the challenge, pulling off some little bit that I liked. That's what I was listening for. This time I was thinking about smoothing out my parts, making them less jarring for the listener.

MD: So would you say this is one way you've grown musically during the long break away from the band?

Neil: I suppose so. Not only should your approach to the instrument grow with time, but so should your understanding of what you're trying to achieve. I found that for this record I was thinking on different levels, trying to satisfy what I wanted to hear in any given song. My critical faculties have refined and developed to where I'm listening for a whole musical effect to come out of the technique, not the technique itself.

MD: Besides the focus on the groove, the other thing that jumps out about *Vapor Trails* is the aggressive nature of the material and the production. This is one of the heaviest records you guys have ever done.

Neil: Yeah, it is, and that's another thing that grew organically. A distinct thing about the way the three of us work together is that we never sit down on day one and lay out a format and say, "Okay, here's what we want to do. We want to shape it like this. I want this kind of feel. And I want a certain number of songs with these themes."

MD: I assumed you did that.

Neil: No, not at all. To the total contrary, we let things grow. We took our time. It had been five years since we worked together on a creative level, so we deliberately made it gradual and relaxed. We paced it in a way that would be organic. We didn't set any deadlines. We didn't say, "By four weeks we want all the songs to be written, and three weeks later we'll be ready for demos."

We didn't lay it out that way at all. We just started working: "Let's see what happens."

I described the way that Geddy and Alex worked together just playing, basically stitching ideas together. But that was a process that took weeks. I was working on lyrics at the same time, but there were no songs coming out. So I was on hold at that point. I actually started writing a book to fill the time, which is called *Ghost Rider*, about my motorcycling travels over the past few years. But I was in kind of a waiting mode.

MD: I guess at that point you weren't drumming a lot. What was going on with your playing?

Neil: Actually, besides writing, I was practicing every day. I was playing all of the time, which was great because it helped me fine-tune my skills. I'd go in there every day and work on something and record it myself as a demo for my own reference.

MD: The three of you were all in the same location?

Neil: Right. We stayed in a small studio here in Toronto, with me at one end of the building writing lyrics and playing drums and Geddy and Alex at the other end working on ideas. We actually refined the studio, because we didn't want to be forced into another facility to make the record. We completely changed the room to make it sound good for drums. And we did it inexpensively. We put up sheets of wallboard where required and livened the room.

We didn't feel any pressure regarding how much time we were taking, partly because we weren't working in some expensive studio environment. It was our space, our own little music factory that we would go to every day to do our work.

MD: In that setting, I would think it might be hard to know when a record was finished. You could just keep working on parts.

Neil: We didn't even add up the number of songs, to give you an example of how casual we were about it. We just kept writing. We didn't time them out to see if we had enough for a finished CD. Once we had ten songs we started to think, "Well, maybe that's enough." But then Geddy and Alex said, "No, we're not done writing yet." They felt they needed more pieces of music to

completely contain all they wanted to express.

I think that Geddy and Alex had certain inner musical agendas of their own for what they wanted to accomplish. For instance, I know that Alex was determined not to have any keyboards on the record. He wanted to cover that role texturally and harmonically on the guitar.

MD: Did you have an individual agenda? The reason I ask is, there's a certain amount of swagger coming from the drum chair. It wasn't just volume….

Neil: No, I understand. I think I know what you're getting at, and it intrigues me. I think what *was* going on in the drum parts was an adrenaline factor, which really pumped up the performance. While I'd like to think I was playing with a bit of swagger, as you say, I think it was more a case of my being very excited about the material and about being back together making music I love with my friends.

MD: You can hear that in the music.

Neil: Yeah, I think there's also a new level of freshness for me, coming back to the instrument with a new sense of rededication. During my time away I really was repelled by anything that was so central to my life, like drumming and music. I didn't play for two years. I didn't *touch* a drumstick for two years. Everything that had been the center of my life before was obviously not good for me emotionally, so I wanted nothing to do with it.

When I did come back and play, it was when I was at the very lowest point. I was so desperate. It was like, what can I do now? But the answer came to me: I'll play the drums.

I rented a little rehearsal studio, took a drumset in there, and played every day. I started surrendering to drumming and exploring it in an organic way. At a certain point I realized I was telling my story on the drums. I was playing through every emotion the past two years had put me through. There were

the angry parts, the sorrowful parts, the traveling parts: "Okay, this is me on the road," "This is me really mad." The drums were helping me express my feelings, my story. It showed me that the drums were still an instrument I could communicate through and that I could surrender to.

That all happened during a two-week period, where I poured myself into the drums and nourished myself with them. And then I realized, okay, I'm ready to play, but I'm not ready to work. I knew I couldn't face the pressure of collaboration and the ambition of creating and being responsible to other people. I knew I didn't have the strength for any of that. But I knew I *could* play if I wanted to, that I *could* tell my story, and that I had something to communicate. That was a really important turning point for me. And even though it was almost another two years before that bore fruit, it still took seed in my mind as something to hold on to.

MD: Was there ever a point during those bleak years where you felt like you just wouldn't come back to music and drumming at all?

Neil: There was a period of time when I was *certain* that I would never play drums or write lyrics or a book again. Because who cares? What does it matter? It didn't matter. Nothing mattered very much.

The only thing I was motivated to do was travel, to just go down the road every day to see what was over the next hill or around the next corner. Hope was the only muscle at work then, the hope that maybe something would come up. I kept saying to myself, *Something will come up, something will come up.* It's probably the only thing that kept me alive.

I was fortunate at the time to be able to retire from the world like that and to have the time to build a life again. Everything had been so destroyed and ripped out from under me that I didn't have a world to have faith in anymore. But after a lot of time, life became

beautiful and precious again.

Sorry. I didn't think I would get into these things.

MD: And you didn't think this was going to be a good interview.

Neil: [smiles] Let's get back to drumming.

MD: Okay. Listening to *Vapor Trails*,

Andrew MacNaughtan

there are moments where it seems you're doing a good Keith Moon impersonation.

Neil: Great! I'm glad you picked up on that. In fact, I was thinking about Keith quite a bit. Interesting story: During the time I was rediscovering music, I was moving house and digging out old boxes of records, things I hadn't listened to in a long time. I didn't want to hear more recent music, because it made me think about things. But the older stuff from my youth brought some measure of happiness.

I went back and listened to some of the best of Keith Moon's playing. In listening to him on the *Tommy* album, well, I was full of admiration. Keith's playing on that record is sublime. The same with *Who's Next*. But *Tommy*, to me, is such a masterpiece of drumming. It shows how smooth and flowing Keith's insanity could be.

Around that same time, I read that biography of him, *Moon: The Life and*

behind a wife and daughter. I couldn't help but be struck by that.

But anyway, reexamining how great Keith was at that time revitalized that part of my drumming. And yes, there were certain parts on this record where I thought, *Let's do it the Keith Moon way.*

MD: In the past you always seemed to draw inspiration from music and drummers playing in the current scene. Were there any modern influences in your playing?

Neil: Hmmm. It's strange with modern music right now. As always, I find myself enjoying it. I listen to modern rock radio and like it, but it's not very

player's point of view. Maybe I'm wrong and maybe there are other examples that I'm not familiar with, but when I hear that music that's the one thing that occurs to me. I can't imagine it's very exciting to be a drummer in a band like that.

MD: Because it's more focused on laying down the time?

Neil: Yeah. There doesn't seem to be a lot of space for interesting things drum-wise. I mean, many of those drummers sound like good players. But the rhythms tend to be beat-oriented. It reminds me of something Tony Williams said about rock drumming: Rock drummers don't play drums, they play beats. I think that may be true now more than ever.

MD: There is a sense that, because of things like digital editing, drummers' parts are being heavily "adjusted" and processed.

Neil: Why is that happening? Shouldn't it be the drummer's decision? For instance, in the making of this record, we used editing to capture spontaneity. If there was a time when I was whipping out on a part or playing one of those crazy Keith Moon–inspired fills and only did it a certain way once, then we used that part. But there was no manipulation going on of moving beats or things like that to make me sound better.

Technology can be our friend in terms of allowing spontaneity and encouraging freshness and capturing it. But I would never be satisfied with having somebody take my drum part and correct it. I would do that myself with sweat and blisters. That's the nature of what you're supposed to do with practice: "Okay, I'll do it again and do it *better*." That would be my choice.

MD: Speaking of practice, you were away from drumming for such a long time. Was it tough to build back your ability?

Neil: I was thinking that it would be tough to "rebuild" my playing, but everything came back so readily and so naturally. Everything that I could play before I could play again. Of course, some transitions were rusty—getting one arm over the other, for instance. Physical dexterity like that took a couple of days to smooth out. But as far as actual playing, I think the muscle memory must be so deep after all the

Death of a Rock Legend. It's very well done. So I was thinking a lot about Keith, and looking at his life. And again, he was the total hero of my teenage years. But in the actual dynamic of his life, he was pretty much washed up as a drummer before he was thirty because of his insanities and his indulgences. He died at the age of thirty-two, leaving

much drummers' music right now. I love what's developed between rock and rap, like that Linkin Park song "In the End." I think that's a masterpiece of combining influences.

I enjoy the music, but I'm not hearing a lot of interesting drumming lately. Limp Bizkit and those types of bands are not really drummers' music from a

years I'd been playing—thirty-five years at that time. I've played a lot of drums in thirty-five years. It wasn't going to go away.

MD: At times you play so hard and in such a physical way. Did you have to build up your endurance and strength?

Neil: I kept up the stamina through other things. I did a lot of cross-country skiing and a lot of hiking. I stayed physically active. I've never turned into a slug, physically, so that wasn't a problem. The process of getting the calluses back on the hands was the only thing necessary to rebuild.

MD: After such a long break, I was wondering if, when you returned to the kit, did it feel comfortable? Or did you need to reposition things?

Neil: I didn't change a thing. In fact, I'm using the same DW kit I used on the last record and tour. The biggest change I went through occurred years ago, when I first started studying with Freddie Gruber. I completely changed my setup at that time to be more natural and more ergonomic.

The only thing I did experiment with this time while we were recording was my snare drum selection. I ended up using a combination of DW and Yamaha snare drums. I've always liked the DWs. And the people at Yamaha were very nice and gave me two very special drums that I used quite a bit on the record. One had a bamboo shell that was very bright sounding. It

worked well on the record. [For more info on Neil's snare drum choices, see the sidebar.]

MD: What about things like cymbals? Most drummers like to experiment with new models.

Neil: Yeah, but the classic Zildjians are simply the sound that I want to hear out of a cymbal. It's a very musical, controlled swell. There are other cymbal sounds I like and that I like to hear *other* people play. But for my voice, it's the Zildjians. I've been playing them for years.

MD: You're in the process of preparing for a long tour. And one of the highlights of a Rush concert is your extended drum solo, which is somewhat composed. What are you doing to prepare for it?

Neil: It's a good time to discuss this because I'm working on the solo now. I'm still trying to decide on an approach. I can look at the solo that evolved up to the last tour, which was a complete piece of music that expressed my influences, background, and explorations. It's my past and present all contained within one solo. I could easily go back to something similar to it.

Another part of my mind, though, is saying to not do *anything* like the previous solos. I'm thinking of other ways that I might approach it. Of course, I feel that I want to have some of the sections that I've used over the years. They've survived a long time

because they're autobiographical or close to me. They help me get across what I want to express musically in a solo in terms of presenting a complete array of things that a drum solo can be in terms of rhythm, dynamics, and expression.

MD: When most drummers take a break from playing, they come back to the kit with a fresh approach. Coming back to the drums after such a long break, did you find that you had a lot of new ideas?

Neil: Yes, I found myself going places that I hadn't been before. Some are tiny little baby things that I almost hesitate to recount because the principle is more important, the movement as a whole is more important.

MD: What would be a small example?

Neil: One would be in the song "Ghost Rider." I was looking for a subtle fill to lead into a verse. I ended up playing hits on a few cymbals. I'd never done anything like that before. It's nothing technically, but I was very happy with the effect. I didn't want to do a drum fill, and I didn't want to just come in with time on the downbeat, so I tried that, and it worked.

When I hear things like that, I secretly smile to myself, because it's something I don't think will impress a listener or another drummer, but it just pleases me to have gone somewhere different and accomplished something musically in a fresh way.

REMEMBERING NEIL

continued from page 76

The measure of a life is a measure of love and respect,
So hard to earn so easily burned
In the fullness of time,
A garden to nurture and protect
(It's a measure of a life)
The treasure of a life is a measure of love and respect,
The way you live, the gifts that you give
In the fullness of time,
It's the only return that you expect

Neil wrote these lyrics for the last song

on the last Rush album. To the last… you measure up, Bubba.
Chris Stankee (director of artist relations, Sabian)

While serving as an editor at *MD* in the 1980s, I received a letter from Neil regarding a contest we were administering in which the winner would be rewarded with one of Neil's old drumsets. At the top of the letter, where one would usually write the date, Neil wrote, "A rainy, leafy night in Toronto." It was October, and those few words beautifully captured the autumn season. As was obvious in his

lyrics, Neil was a master at painting pictures with words.
Rick Mattingly (*Modern Drummer* features editor, 1982–89)

Besides being a sad and staggering loss to drumming, Neil Peart's passing is an equally sad loss of one of rock's most literate lyricists—and a talented writer of prose as well. In fact, Neil was as proficient with his pen as with his sticks, which is saying something. I had the great pleasure of editing some of the articles he wrote for *Modern Drummer*, and I got to know him a bit in that way. We only

met in person a few times, and he was a gracious gentleman on each occasion—with a typically dry, witty Canadian sense of humor.

While many of Neil's fans have cited their favorite performance of his with Rush, my favorite of his performances was in a radically different setting. As a devotee of Buddy Rich, Neil was instrumental in making the *Burning for Buddy* tribute album and concerts a reality. And it was at one of those concerts that I saw him play. He was on a small drumkit, playing with a big band instead of a progressive-rock trio. He was obviously out of his element,

Neil on His *Vapor Trails* Snare Drum Selection

I have said before, notably in my instructional video *A Work in Progress*, that I like to have a wide range of snare drums available in the studio. The choice of a particular snare for a song is influenced by several factors: the character of the song I'm playing and the drum part I have created for it, my taste in sounds, and the sonic environment of the room in which I'm playing.

The recording of *Test for Echo* [Rush's previous album] was a graphic example, for I had chosen an array of snare drums during the pre-production process in a small studio, only to find that the big room at Bearsville Studios "required" a snare drum choice one degree brighter—i.e., a different drum.

For touring I use a versatile instrument that can cover all areas well, though even that is subject to change. For many years I depended upon an old Slingerland wood-shell snare for that purpose, but then it became supplanted by a DW Edge snare that combines wood and brass elements.

Now, as I rehearse for this *Vapor Trails* tour, I find that I've been favoring the DW Craviotto model, just because it sounds so good in the warehouse where I'm working. But again, that is subject to change when we move into full production rehearsals in an arena.

During the songwriting and pre-production work for the *Vapor Trails* album, as I played each of the songs to refine my part and its execution, I tried dif-ferent snare drums from my ever-growing selection. Listening to the playback, I could compare how each one worked in a particular song.

I am fortunate that my tech, Lorne "Gump" Wheaton, has good ears for what I'm after. While the recording engineer is busy with the overall sound as well as each of the other details of sound and performance, Lorne will listen for the nuances of the snare drum as I play. Then, between takes, he will give me a reliable report on what the current candi-date sounds like, and we'll discuss other options.

So given the above foundation, what follows is the selection of snare drums I used for each song on *Vapor Trails*. In that particular room, for those par-ticular songs, the Yamaha Elvin Jones model proved to be the most versatile, showing up on more than half the tracks. (Though the wooden hoops that are a standard feature on the drum didn't survive my abuse. We switched to metal.) From the driving dynamics of "One Little Victory" and "Peaceable Kingdom" to the more rooted timekeeping of "Ghost Rider" and "Sweet Miracle," this drum was a joy to play, and obviously gave great results in the studio.

A similar versatility applied to the Yamaha bam-boo shell, which sounded as crisp and bright as one would expect from that material, but still worked in the more sensitive role required in the song "Vapor Trail," for example (the intro to which also features "detail" work on a 13" DW piccolo, by the way).

I've always liked wooden piccolo snares, and it was a pleasure to find a use for the 14" DW model in "Earthshine," and the same with the 5x14 Craviotto snare that has become my current rehearsal main-stay, for it worked best on two of the tracks as well.

"One Little Victory"—Yamaha 7x14 maple Elvin Jones model (with metal hoops, not standard wood)
"Ceiling Unlimited"—Yamaha 7x14 maple Elvin Jones model
"Ghost Rider"—Yamaha 7x14 maple Elvin Jones model
"Peaceable Kingdom"—Yamaha 7x14 maple Elvin Jones model
"The Stars Look Down"—Yamaha 7x14 maple Elvin Jones model
"How It Is"—Yamaha 5x14 bamboo
"Vapor Trail"—Yamaha 5x14 bamboo
"Secret Touch"—Yamaha 7x14 maple Elvin Jones model
"Earthshine"—3.5x13 DW maple piccolo
"Sweet Miracle"—Yamaha 7x14 maple Elvin Jones model
"Nocturne"—5x14 DW Craviotto
"Freeze"—5x14 DW Craviotto
"Out of the Cradle"—Yamaha 5x14 bamboo

MD: It's great to hear you be so excited about drumming again. You seem very committed to the music.

Neil: Commitment is the word. I have a commitment to the music, and to Geddy and Alex. They've been such supportive friends to me through all of this. No one could have been more sympathetic, compassionate, and understanding. When we came back together to work it was because I had a commitment to them.

MD: You're turning fifty this coming September 12. What are your thoughts now that you're at the half-century mark concerning life, music, and drumming?

Neil: I guess my understanding of life has unwillingly been enlarged to a great degree, in that I've been to the blackest place that life can take you. With the support of friends and family, I've fortunately led myself through a lot of that dark time. I never knew how important people could be until I really needed them.

The age thing honestly doesn't figure in my thinking. I've read that everyone has an inner age that they think they are, regardless of their actual age. I really think of myself as being about thirty. In modern life it's a matter of keeping your prime going as long as you can.

Let's take that metaphor into the world of drumming. You go through the time of learning and experimenting, and you develop your voice as a musician. As long as you can sustain that prime of your life musically, mentally, emotionally, and physically, then that's your time.

MD: Hearing you talk about all of this, it really seems as if you still have the fire.

Neil: Well, I lost it for a while. But I have it back.

---

and very likely uncomfortable. But he still had the courage to put himself "out there" in front of a room packed with critical drummers. He had always had my admiration as a drummer, but that night he earned my everlasting respect as a human being.
Rick Van Horn (*Modern Drummer* managing editor, 1983–2008)

With an unwavering commitment to musical, rhythmic, and lyrical innovation and excellence, and an unabashed cynical attitude toward the mainstream music media in the face of radio-friendly rejection, Peart was an unstoppable intellectual force of nature, lyrically and rhythmically deep within his massive orchestral universe. "The Professor" left no artistic stone unturned. There will never be another like Peart to expand the rhythmic and musical boundaries of rock music so vastly.

"Tom Sawyer" will forever remain Peart's air-drumming epitaph. Neil unknowingly set the bar so high that it will take years to unravel and dissect just how deeply his musical impact will be on the future drummer/percussionist/lyricist. His majestic solos were ever-evolving, rhythmical, sculptured masterpieces. He was a prolific composer in every sense; everything had an artistic purpose.

I witnessed Rush on Peart's first tour with the band. He commanded the audience's attention with his relentless, fearless approach to drumming. With each tour, he became more focused and more artistic behind the kit. The last time I saw Neil was the R30 tour. His technique was flawless, and his approach was fresh and playful. His solo was the most improvisational that I had ever heard. There was a sense of accomplished freedom in his playing. It made me smile to think, He's done it all and now he's having fun, with nothing left to prove. Neil Peart's well-documented legacy and uncompromising body of work will forever be the standard by which artistic rock drumming will be measured.
Mike Haid (*Modern Drummer* contributor)

The first project I worked on with Neil was in 1991 for a video release of a Buddy Rich Tribute Show, and Neil was one of several drummers there to perform Buddy's music. At the time,

continues on page 92

Soloing In The Shadow Of Giants

In this first-person account, Neil tells the tale of
his attempt to preserve his soloing methods for history.

Brian Brodeur

Four score years ago (give or take), our forefathers brought forth the drum solo. The people watched and listened, danced and cheered, and it was good.

Prophets and pioneers like Baby Dodds, Chick Webb, and Big Sid Catlett passed the sticks down to Gene Krupa, and his showmanship and rhythmic grace brought the spotlight to the drum solo as a popular performance piece. Gene Krupa was the first and only drummer to have a movie based on his life, and more than forty years ago, before I ever touched a pair of drumsticks or knew what a snare drum was, I saw *The Gene Krupa Story* on late-night TV. To the boy I was then, the notion of being a drummer seemed exciting, glamorous, elegant, and dangerous, and my eyes must have been shining with inspiration and desire. I remember thinking, "I wanna do *that!*"

A few years later, when I did get a pair of drumsticks, and learned what a snare drum was, I began to get a sense of how much I had to learn. By the mid-'60s, *so* many giants had come before, pushing the frontiers of what had come to be known as jazz music. Buddy Rich's amazing technique and musicality had raised the drum solo to an even higher level of artistry and popular appreciation, and other inspired soloists like Louie Bellson, Max Roach, Joe Morello, Sonny Payne, Roy Haynes, Art Blakey, and Jack DeJohnette took the form in fresh, exciting directions.

And at the same time as I was starting out, drum solos began to bloom in rock music too, in concerts and recordings. Ginger Baker, Mitch Mitchell, Carmine Appice, John Bonham, Carl Palmer, and

Michael Shrieve brought audiences to their feet in theaters, arenas, stadiums, and festivals, and fired me with more inspiration and desire—"I wanna do *that!*"

Through the '60s and '70s, jazz remained vital and constantly changing. Its various mutations produced brilliant innovators like Billy Cobham and Tony Williams, who built a bridge between jazz

Brian Brodeur

and rock—a bridge that would later be crossed in both directions by Steve Gadd, Steve Smith, Peter Erskine, Bill Bruford, Terry Bozzio, Dave Weckl, and many others, all traveling with their own musical mastery and unbounded imagination.

The drum solo is a tradition handed down to us, our *heritage*, as it were, and

it is a heritage worth celebrating. Giants have come before us, and giants will come after, but even while we mere mortals play in their shadows, we can be inspired to aim just a little higher every day—or every night.

Drum solos are not for everyone, of course, whether they're drummers or music lovers. But even drummers who

choose not to *perform* drum solos can still enjoy and benefit from a *private* indulgence. Exploring and experimenting freely, and even just that kind of practicing on your own, can only nourish and improve your playing.

Go forth into the musical wilderness, and play well!

Anatomy Building

My first instructional video, *A Work in Progress* [1996], described how I created drum parts for new songs, then demonstrated the recording process. My directors and collaborators on that project, Paul Siegel and Rob Wallis, had already become friends of mine, first when we met at the Buddy Rich Memorial Scholarship Concert in 1991, and even more so in 1994, when they filmed the recording of the two-volume Buddy Rich tribute, *Burning for Buddy*.

In the weeks leading up to the May, 1996, shoot for *A Work in Progress*, at Bearsville Studios in upstate New York, Paul and Rob and I forged a close working relationship. The three of us exchanged ideas almost daily (by fax—*so* last century!), and together we developed and refined our program into points for discussion and demonstration in the show. I *love* that kind of collaboration: working with creative, dedicated partners to build a piece of work that grows into something I could never have imagined, let alone made, on my own.

For thirty years I have worked that way with my bandmates in Rush, Alex and Geddy, and their reactions and suggestions for my lyric writing and drumming not only elevate the *result*, they also elevate the *process*—the pleasure of doing business.

In the years following that first instructional video, Paul, Rob, and I discussed doing another project together, but I wasn't sure what it should be about. *A Work in Progress* had covered my approach to composing and recording drum parts, so the next obvious theme seemed to be live performance—but that was such a *big* one. I decided to start with something a little more modest (if that's the right word!), by making an instructional DVD about my thoughts and methods regarding drum soloing.

Anatomy of a Drum Solo is centered around a solo from Rush's thirtieth-anniversary tour, R30, filmed and recorded in Frankfurt, Germany, on September 24, 2004.

Our *Rush in Rio* DVD, recorded in 2002 on the tour for *Vapor Trails*, was (perhaps obviously) filmed in Rio de Janeiro. So I had titled that solo "O Baterista!"— Portuguese for "The Drummer." (Can't you just hear those words said so many different ways? A foreign movie with a terrified, goggle-eyed man backing away and screaming, "*O Baterista!*" Or a woman's soft, sexy whisper in the darkness, "O Bate*ris*ta!" Yeah…in our dreams….)

Anyway, because the centerpiece of *Anatomy of a Drum Solo* was filmed in Germany, I called it "Der Trommler." (You'll guess what that means.) It's a good example of my approach to soloing, which has built gradually over forty years of playing and performing. At the beginning of a tour, I like to build a framework, like any other piece of music, an architecture that will give me a certain level of consistency every night, but still allow me to experiment and express myself.

"Der Trommler" was composed from many of the same pieces as "O Baterista!"—elements, or "movements," woven together to tell a story that is historical, autobiographical, textural, and sometimes humorous. However, every tour I insist on rearranging the structure of my solo fairly comprehensively, making room for the natural, organic process of internally experimenting with new "fields of study" (as described in the DVD). Thus, over the course of a fifty-seven-show tour, the solo will always be a "nine-minute tour de force" (as Paul and Rob describe it on the DVD package), and hopefully always be entertaining and satisfying as a *performance*, but also remain an inspiring and creative vehicle for my own explorations.

Among a few other "bonus" solos in the program, there is one from Hamburg, Germany, performed a few nights after the Frankfurt show. We included that one to demonstrate that even though my solos are tightly composed and arranged, they can still vary significantly from night to night. I gave that one the title "Ich Bin Ein Hamburger," or, "I Am a Hamburger." This title owes something to Popeye's friend Wimpy, and also echoes JFK's famous statement in the early '60s, when he visited the newly divided city of Berlin and announced to the Berliners, and to the world, "Ich Bin Ein Berliner."

During the R30 tour, Paul and Rob and I got together a few times and discussed the notion of doing another project. Being in the middle of a long, hard tour, I wasn't very interested in thinking about another major undertaking, but Paul visited me before our show in Saratoga Springs, New York, and the next week both of them ganged up on me backstage at Radio City Music Hall. Unwilling to commit to anything, I did agree to let them arrange for some special "drum cams" for the Frankfurt show, which the band was already planning to film for a concert DVD.

Once the tour was behind me, the conversations among Paul, Rob, and me picked up in frequency and intensity. In early 2005, slowly, gradually, we began to circle around actually *doing* it. Plans were

made, people were chosen for cameras and technical crews, audio recording, and photography, and the studio was booked. Finally, my plane flight was booked, and I was on my way. (Hey—wait a minute! I'm not ready….)

In mid-July, it would have been an enjoyable adventure to motorcycle or drive from my California home to New York, but there was not time. Instead, I sent my car ahead by truck to Rob's house in rural New York. I would be able to drive the Z8 from there to the studio, then after the shoot, drive north through the Adirondacks to my house in Quebec, and to visit family and friends in Ontario. The expense was easy to justify, trading all those airfares, taxis, airport limos—and the sheer nastiness of air travel—for a beautiful drive.

And sure enough, after flying five hours to Newark and sitting in an airport limo for almost two hours from there to Rob's house, I was *very* pleased to be following Rob and the jovial Alfonse through the dark little roads of the Catskills.

Allaire Studios is located atop a mountain near Bearsville, New York,

where Paul and Rob and I had shot the previous video at Bearsville Studios, nine years before. Allaire's excellent recording facilities and cozy accommodations are built into a vast estate from the 1920s, once a summer residence for the family who owned Pittsburgh Plate Glass. The studio's website showed spectacular views in every direction, but I never saw them—the weather was foggy and/or rainy all through our three-day shoot.

But never mind; most of our business was indoors anyway. We tried to get outside between rain showers for some of my introductory, spoken pieces, and during one of those, I felt a few fat, heavy raindrops. I kept talking, Carlos kept filming, and even as the rain's tempo increased into a Buddy Rich single-stroke roll, no one wanted to say "cut." Then all at once everybody seemed to realize it was absurdly hopeless, and we made a comical run for cover.

In actuality, I was wet more from sweat than from rain, sitting behind the drums and working through the solo. Each part of "Der Trommler" was dissected (even "vivisected," hence *Anatomy*),

and I discussed themes, textures, and techniques, while demonstrating the pieces individually.

I have to say, it was the hardest three days of work I've ever done. Starting in the early morning, each day I stood or sat in front of the cameras for ten or twelve hours, either talking or drumming. There's a joke among comedians: "Dying is easy; *comedy* is hard." I would amend that to, "Drumming is easy; *talking* is hard."

Wanting most of the spoken parts to be unscripted and spontaneous, I had to exert all my powers of concentration to try to speak articulately, comprehensively, and smoothly—without drooling. That is a challenge for any drummer. (You know the jokes.) I found it demanded *so* much mental energy to remember what I wanted to say, in the order I wanted to say it, and not deliver it like a robot or a zombie.

At the end of each day I felt empty and drained, and at the end of three days, I felt truly exhausted—and yet, *exalted*, in the afterglow of all that creative and performing energy. The next day I drove from the studio to my house in Quebec, speeding north over the back roads of the Adirondacks in my Z8, and it was one of the great drives of my life. I felt ragged and fatigued, yet elevated, elated.

A few weeks later, after I had steeled myself to watch the first edit (fearing embarrassment and shame), I was talking on the phone to my wife, Carrie, and grumbled, "I guess it's going to be *okay*." She knew that meant I was very pleased.

Working with Paul and Rob and our excellent crew of artists, technicians, and assistants had been truly collaborative, with everyone contributing his or her bit of expertise and imagination. As each shot was being set up, Paul and Rob and I gathered in the kitchen to exchange ideas for talking points and demonstrations, roughing out a basic "script." Then off I went again—into the lights to try to *do* all that in front of the cameras.

Though difficult, the process was exciting and rewarding, truly *inspiring*. In those brief and fast-moving three days, all of us had forged a united team of people who worked toward a common goal—making the best show we could.

That being the case, of course we hope people are going to like it!

The first section of this article was pulled from the DVD booklet to Anatomy of a Drum Solo.

Brian Brodeur

Taking Center Stage

Right around the time of this, Neil's eighth *MD* cover story, the three-disc DVD *Taking Center Stage: A Lifetime of Live Performance* was released, putting fans throne-side with the Rush rhythmatist. Included in the set was an entire two-set performance on Rush's *Time Machine* tour, captured at upstate New York's Saratoga Performing Arts Center. And interspersed throughout the live footage was a conversation with Neil about each song, filmed at Death Valley National Park in California.

Interview by Michael Parillo

MD: Did the performance in Saratoga feel different because you were the focus of the cameras?
Neil: Fortunately we already used some cameras in the live show, on the rear screen behind us, so it was just a matter of adding a few more and then collecting all that exclusive footage of me. Later that same tour they filmed the whole band in Cleveland and took a whole different approach to lighting the band and the crowd.

The Saratoga one was specifically focused on getting the drums on camera, and then the mixes, as you know, are quite enhanced. Well, I think it's a normal sort of balance—that's about where I hear the drums! We always laugh about that in the studio, because I really do like loud drums. I think they're exciting, and not just because it's me. Yeah, I like that mix. I'll just say it.

There's such a purity of sound, whether it's the rehearsal footage or the performance stuff. The only effects are ones I actually play. I said to the engineer, Sean [McClintock], in

REMEMBERING NEIL

continued from page 87

I knew Neil was popular, but I didn't expect to see a line that ran several blocks down 8th Ave. in New York City. Almost everyone on that line was there to see Neil.

Over nearly twenty-five years of producing Neil's educational videos and books, I got to know him fairly well. Yes, we all know the power of his drumming, but if you asked me to sum up Neil in just one word, it would have to be integrity.

It ran through every aspect of his

being. His fans heard and saw his mastery at the drumkit, but what they didn't get to see was Neil's dedication to everything he touched. Working on his projects with DCI Music Video and Hudson Music, two of my labels, he was involved in every aspect of the product, from inception through editing, audio mixing, art design, all the way down to the quality of the paper we used for the packaging. And of course he was always right.

Neil had an old-school work ethic, and when he found people of similar mind, he stayed with them. He expected everyone to work and care

as much as he did. And working with him elevated everyone's game. Neil used to say that collaborating was like a 1+1=3.

He enjoyed selecting locations for our work, like filming our first project, *A Work in Progress*, at Bearsville Studio in Woodstock, New York, so he could snowshoe to and from his cabin on the studio grounds each day. For another project he had us film him in a row boat on a lake for some of the dialog sections, and for his last project, *Taking Center Stage*, we filmed him in Death Valley National Park, at Dante's Peak, as he rode his motorcycle up the

mountain in an winter storm.

I came to learn of Neil's intellect, infallible memory, rock-solid honesty, personal loyalty, and incredible kindness. Many of these acts of kindness were done away from the spotlight, as Neil was a deeply private person. He could have easily embraced the rock star life…he didn't.

The outpouring on social media of people sharing their stores about Neil's generosity of spirit has been remarkable but not surprising: how he sent autographs to young fans who wrote him letters; how he mailed cards or letters or made calls of support

Andrew MacNaughtan

these economical words, "It sounds like me playing my drums." That's the highest compliment. If you've done any studio work, especially years ago, it wasn't always like that. When you hear the playback, you go, "My drums don't sound like that!"

MD: It's a beautiful touch to have the interview segments set in Death Valley.

Neil: What a difference that made. It was so glorious how it came about, because in the previous two DVDs [1996's *A Work in Progress* and 2005's *Anatomy of a Drum Solo*] we had done

outdoor "talkie bits," but we'd filmed them at the studio in the Catskills. This time we were filming in January, which limited a lot of the outdoor possibilities. Winter in Quebec I've written about extensively and love so much. But you can't count on getting beautiful days when you pick two days in January. So Death Valley was the perfect place and one of my favorite places on the planet, and it gave us so much variety.

I have to see that I can live with everything over time, of course, but when I faced watching the revised edit of seven

to comfort people at times of need or grief; how he was generous with words of encouragement to friends, fans, and folks he'd never met. He used to tell me what a hard time he had saying "no" when people asked for something.

It is difficult to express the impact Neil has made on the lives of so many. He taught us about so many things, and his passing will leave a huge hole. It is still difficult to process. For now, all I can say is, "Thank you…and I'll see you down the road."

Rob Wallis (Hudson Music)

It's hard for me to overstate the impact that Neil Peart has had on my life. I play the drums because of him, and, incredibly, I was able to work with him and share a friendship with him.

When I was thirteen, I heard "Subdivisions" on the radio, and was inspired to play the drums. Soon my dream was to be a professional drummer like Neil. His intellect and creativity seem to jump right out of the speakers and affected me deeply, like so many others of my generation. My imagination was utterly captured, and I studied everything about Neil and Rush until it was part of me. I

went to see Rush dozens of times, memorized the drum parts, and even joined a Rush tribute band.

That part of my story probably sounds a lot like thousands of other guys my age. Then, in 2008, Rob Wallis told me that Neil might be interested in working on a new project with Hudson Music, and I was asked to write a proposal for Neil. My excitement and nervousness aside, I was able to craft something that engaged him, and soon I was brought by Rob to meet him, and then we created the *Taking Center Stage* DVD together. After that, Neil indulged my desire to create a

companion book, which was, quite literally, a dream come true.

Eventually, Neil and I became friends, and I gained his trust—a gift he guarded very, very closely. For all those who longed to meet him, I can tell you that he was a wonderful person, everything you'd imagine. With every trip to L.A., I'd ask Neil to have lunch, and make the journey to the hallowed Bubba Cave to hang and talk about life and drums. And every time I'd pinch myself a little, sitting there with my hero.

My hero became my friend, and my friend dealt with a lot of pain and

continues on page 94

hours of myself, that's very daunting. [laughs] But it was necessary to have the playing demonstrations and all that. I don't like watching myself on television or looking at pictures of myself, that mirror sort of thing. I like listening to the music, interestingly. Yeah, that is an interesting distinction—I like reading my writing, and I like listening to our music, but I don't really like *watching* me. It's the same self-consciousness, I think, that leads to a lot of other behavioral and character sort of things.

MD: The nature shots seemed like a good setting to reflect on your past as well.

Neil: [Hudson Music senior drum editor] Joe Bergamini had been urging me for the past few years to get historic and analytical, which didn't interest me at all. But in this context the overriding theme was live performance, which remains a main focus of my life, and it's not anything that I'm tired of talking about or feel is irrelevant.

So when I looked at the songs as *performances*… Like what happened where I just stumbled across that realization about myself—which happens a lot in interviews, and it's one reason I like to do them—the whole theme through the DVD of our songs being made to play live, I'd never thought of that before. It's just the way we naturally worked.

It's so obvious when I look back at "Subdivisions" or any of the *Moving Pictures* songs, in that they were absolutely made not to be played on the radio, not to be listened to on the floor with headphones, but they were made to be *played*. Yeah, "made to be played"—that's good! That makes our band so much of what it is, and it's what's sustained us as a live band. Those songs are so exciting for us to play that it makes the show a consistent expression of something real and sincere. I mention in the DVD too that we only play songs we really like playing. And I don't think that's true of all bands. I'll just go out on a limb and say that.

MD: You do hear bands say they *have* to play a certain song, or else the crowd won't let them out alive.

Neil: Yeah, I know. I feel very fortunate. That's a wonderful testament to the band being about playing music that we like: We *still* like it! Even those songs from twenty, twenty-five years ago, I like playing them. I was saying how a song like "Presto," like a lot of the older songs, feels better to me now than the record did. And Geddy pointed out that our internal clock, our rhythmic foundation, has shifted.

Of course, I've worked really hard on that, and my studies with Freddie Gruber were a big part of changing my whole orientation, not only physically but, I realize now, rhythmically. So I work much more to a rooted bass drum on a figure, and my tempo control is much more based upon the intricacies of the rhythm itself. That's an important part of the legacy of a teacher, because they put you on a path—and this is broadly applicable to teachers of all kinds—and all you have to do is stay on that path and you'll be alright.

I think about my earliest education in reading, for example—being taught to understand a novel, a play, a poem. Well, that ruined, like, Charles Dickens' *A Tale of Two Cities*, or Shakespeare's *Julius Caesar*. I can *never* read those again, because I was forced to dissect them. But it served me for a lifetime.

And my first drum teacher, Don George, same thing. Freddie, same thing. Peter Erskine, a few years back—studying with him continues to be part of what I do, because he put me on a path that I can follow *forever*.

As I get into later life, at fifty-nine, I still don't injure myself, and that's a big part of Freddie's teaching on a physical basis. He's saved me from the injuries that I know have plagued a lot of other drummers, especially hard-hitting ones who are getting older. [laughs]

MD: What's something you worked on with Peter Erskine?

Neil: I think Roland makes a drum pad with a metronome that plays two bars of click and then two bars of silence. Well, Peter gave me the assignment to get that little unit and play to two tempos every day, one very slow and one fast. You know how hard it is to keep time at a very slow tempo, but when you're up against the mathematical perfection of a *silent* click….

REMEMBERING NEIL

continued from page 93

tragedy in his life. For that, my heart is broken. I will forever treasure the inspiration he gave me and the time I got to spend with him.
Joe Bergamini (Hudson Music)

Of course I knew who Neil was when I was growing up, and I certainly realized his gift and influence. His impact on music is forever indisputable. But my deeper appreciation for him came later, when seeing firsthand how strongly he loved his family and his friends. His family truly was his core. And friendship was not a casual thing to him. If you were his real friend, he wanted to spend time with you—and not just once in a while, but all the time. Time was very important to Neil, and he gave it generously to those he loved. As intensely as the whole world admired him, he trusted and cherished his friends and family like gold. Even if he didn't know someone at all, he had a way of making them feel comfortable in the presence of a giant. When he spoke, with just one sentence from his smooth, mellow voice, you could immediately sense everything he was about: a man of honesty, intelligence, warmth, introspection, and hilariously quick wit. We are all fortunate to have lived during a time when he was here.
Juels Thomas (Drum Workshop education and events manager)

Neil Peart was about commitment and about sharing. After he'd penned lyrics for a song and chosen drums and what to play on them, he involved his constituency in the reasons for his decisions. Fans knew each note, phrase, and sound he uttered and how integral each was in spurring a song to its conclusion. Neil plotted out each drum, cymbal, and percussion instrument for good reason. As a result, many drummers took a second look at the nooks and crannies of the instrument—and at the drum and cymbal brands pursuant to Neil's well-publicized shifts every decade or two. The drum industry is a richer place for his presence.

Neil came up in an era where "playing for the song" often meant stripping down drum parts to basics. Neil begged to differ. He didn't toss off drumming and lyrics. He composed his parts, sweating the details that spurred songs forward, and he was proud to

I've heard other drummers just have gone crazy: "There's something wrong with that machine!" But what a great exercise. I was improvising in those tempos too, different ones every day, which also served me hugely.

Playing just the hi-hat like that, with no other responsibility but to keep to that tempo, continues to grow in a remarkable way that I feel in live performance now, in terms of time control in the tiniest increments, and of accuracy—getting to truly feel when it's right or wrong, and be right! How many drummers think they're playing the right tempo and they're playing too fast? Years of working with click tracks and metronomes helped, but they had a downside, and I found that in the mid-'90s I started to feel very rigid and mechanical—accurate, yes, but not the kind of accuracy I wanted. It made me want to study with Freddie. Having found Freddie and worked with Peter Erskine has served to let me be accurate and feel good inside, without feeling constricted and rigid. Yet my understanding of time and my control of it is *way* deeper than it ever was when I could do a mathematical, drum machine kind of accuracy.

MD: Where does improvisation come in?

Neil: Investigating improvisation has made me more resourceful, by necessity. That's such a great parallel with traveling. In my writing over the years I've done many comparisons between drumming and traveling and improvising and traveling. It's all about *adapting*. I love the fact that when I start improvising figures in the solo, I adapt to each one. That's how you keep going. You go, Okay, that happened, so then *this* will happen, trying to keep yourself out of repeating.

Improvising has helped me enormously in improvising *out* of trouble. That's an interesting insight right there. If you're wedded to a carefully arranged part, any, oh, mechanical problem that comes up to distract you or any loss of concentration means that an unrolling program gets interrupted. But when you're improvising there's none of that. Everything that happens is by nature and by intention unexpected, so it does prepare you to deal with the unexpected better. I noticed that on this last tour I was much more able to handle an error, whether it was mine or somebody else's or a

Andrew MacNaughtan

play them night to night as written. Without his ceaseless efforts, there would be no Rush.
T Bruce Wittet (independent performer, *Modern Drummer* contributor)

Neil's passing affected drummers from across the globe and will leave us with years of his presence as a master musician, accomplished author, and eloquent lyricist. Known the world over for his percussive innovations within the forum of Rush, Neil is indisputably the most influential drummer ever to come out of Canada.

We salute him.
Ralph Angelillo (Montreal Drum Fest and the Ralph Angelillo International Drum Fest)

As a young boy learning a new language and dealing with a new culture in my new country of America, my parents saw the kernel of drumming in me. A few years later, they bought me a drumset and got MTV. When I saw the video for *Exit… Stage Left*, I was hooked. I felt his lyrics were speaking to me. Bands, tours, and CDs followed. Fast forward thirty-eight years, I truly can say that without Neil's

influence on my life, I would not be a practicing physician today. Thank you. RIP, dearest Neil. You are missed.
Asif Khan (*Modern Drummer* contributor)

What can anyone say that hasn't already been said about such an iconic, world-class musician? I guess the only thing left to say is what Neil meant to me personally. I first noticed Neil when *Hemispheres* came out. A friend suggested I check out the band, knowing I was a fan of metal, prog, and fusion music played by drummers with huge drumsets. When I saw a

picture of Neil's kit for the very first time, I knew I was onto something. Needless to say, when I put the album on, Neil and the band did not disappoint! I was immediately drawn to his creativity and clever use of "all things percussion" on his kit. I thought, "Finally, a drummer with a big-ass kit that actually plays it all!"

Like many, I've followed the band throughout the last thirty-plus years. While certain musical periods are more appealing to me than others, there was no denying Neil was an incredibly influential drummer to the

continues on page 96

technological thing.

In the band's case, we just wanted to introduce more improvisation. We do like to arrange things, and we love to re-create recorded songs as well as we can do live, but on this tour particularly all of us were interested in getting outside and more interested in jamming. And as we get back to work on new material right now, we're talking in those terms. We collected a whole bunch of soundcheck jams, just like we used to do twenty-five years ago. Alex went through some of the ones he thinks are the most interesting, and he's encouraging us to use them as the basis of compositions. And the thing we've been doing live too, on the very last song of the show, "Working Man," is we just *go*. It's truly a jam session, in the time-honored way that I always did it as a kid and you probably did too: You get a cue. "When the guitar player plays this figure twice, we all come out." We're all inspired by that, and we're saying, "We're doing this in the studio." It's so exciting after all these years that we have these feels that inspire us, and the next record is not a question of "What are we gonna do this time?" It's like, "Look at all the stuff we're gonna do this time!"

MD: On the DVD, "Working Man" stands out as pretty much the lone example of straight-up 4/4 bashing.

Neil: Yeah, and it's one where Geddy and I are much more of the traditional rhythm section, playing the supporting role for a soloist who's going to the moon. Alex just goes completely out there. We talk about it later and he says, "I don't even know what I was doing there!" That's the kind of person he always has been—he's very spontaneous, out of the three of us.

So yeah, that's a neat role for us because we don't do it all the time. We figure it's free rein. We've always joked that when vocals are going on you're very respectful as an accompanist, but not when it's a guitar solo. [laughs]

MD: Do you ever think about the words and meaning behind the songs while you're onstage?

Neil: Sure, I do, especially when I see them reflected in other people's faces and see them singing along. An obvious example but a very good one is "Limelight." That so much reflects on live performance and "living on the lighted stage" and the sense of unreality. It remains just as true now as then. "Approaches the unreal." Yeah—how many times have those words been reflected back at me from an audience singing along? It's a feedback loop of my own reflection on the experience, and it's still true, so that's kind of cool.

MD: I've heard musicians comment on that unreality. Carlos Santana said something about how you're fawned over on tour but then you go home and have to take out the garbage, which is an important but often difficult transition.

Neil: Oh, yeah. And that's one thing I must say: I love traveling by motorcycle on tour because I come down to the everyday every day. I go to gas stations and eat in diners and travel through traffic. What could be more gritty, down-to-earth real than fighting through traffic every day? And I have roadside conversations with strangers or at a gas station or motel that are really lovely little exchanges, just human to human.

It's certainly true what Carlos was talking about, that dichotomy. Lift your finger and something's done for you. Then, when you get home, somebody else's finger is pointing at you, telling *you* what to do. I value that too, very highly. I love being at home, and I love doing the grocery shopping and the cooking and all that. But I've been able to keep touring fresh but also nourishing in the human sense. Every single day I feel a part of human life; I never feel as if I'm in a bubble. My life is so real on the road, much more so than it used to be, and it really helps me to keep my balance.

I think of Pink Floyd, and Roger Waters' famous essays on alienation in *Wish You Were Here* and *The Wall*, and I know what that feels like. I wrote to him years ago when I heard about the *Wall* performance in Berlin and just expressed the fact that it had been my autobiography as well. But you can't survive with those kinds of feelings. He had to change his feelings; I had to change my environment over the years. So between bicycling and motorcycling, it keeps me out of that bubble and keeps me engaged with real life. Gives me something to write about

Remembering Neil

continued from page 95

masses. In the early '90s, I remember asking the Zildjian folks who the most popular drummer on their roster was. I was expecting Vinnie, Dennis, Dave, or some other drumming icon easily recognized by a single name. Their answer: "Neil." I said, "Uh…Neil?" "Yeah, it's Neil—Neil Peart." I didn't quite expect that at the time. I was told, "If you add up all of the fan mail we get from every other artist combined, Neil's mail is a hundred times more!" I was blindsided. But at the same time, enlightened. Today I can't think of any drummer since Gene Krupa who has popularized drumming and captivated the masses as much. Thank you, Neil, for elevating the art form and broadening the spectrum. Hope you're playing a duo with Gene up there! Thanks for the memories of a lifetime.
Terry Bissette (vice president, retail sales, Maxwell Drum Group)

Being a fan of Neil's band, I always respected the group's musical and technical prowess, but I truly had no idea that Neil was not your stereotypical "rock star drummer with an attitude" until I met him backstage face to face some thirty years ago. His high intellectual level and great humility struck me like lightning, and we became instant friends.

Since that first encounter, I was lucky enough to share many conversations with him about being a lifelong learner and pushing musical boundaries. The latter point was where we shared a common passion with our groups: he being wildly successful in doing this with Rush and I being also able to break the traditional boundaries in music with my own group of over forty years, Repercussion. Neil was a fan of Repercussion (which was quite astonishing and flattering to me!), and after watching my group play in Toronto, he suggested that we record an album together. As fate would have it, 1997 turned out to be a life-shattering year for Neil, and the album never was realized.

Fast forward to one day in 2011, when Neil communicated to me that, since he would be in my neck of the woods, he would love to come out and make an appearance at KoSA. Nothing was really planned (except filming it); he just came onstage in front of our very emotional participants, and we just resumed one of our great conversations too. God, regular touring life—I'd have no stories! What an appalling thought. I never thought of that before, but that's one of the worst prices.

Caress of Steel

MD: You have a distinctive touch on the drums. On the DVD you explain your reasoning behind hitting as hard as you can. There's conviction behind every note, real clarity. Could some of that stem from working things out very precisely beforehand?

Neil: The conviction you describe was the confidence of: I really *know* this part now. I think of, just for example, "Tom Sawyer." I would've played that dozens and dozens of times and developed all those little figures to memory, such that they were played as a performance. There was an absolute knowledge of what I was doing and why, which would come through in that level of clarity and conviction.

MD: You also said something in one of your previous *MD* interviews along the lines of how indecision can lead to mistakes. What you're talking about now is essentially a lack of indecision.

Neil: [laughs] Absolutely so, yeah. That's the way I worked thirty years ago, and it has evolved over time. I love the fact that now I can approach that kind of conviction even when I'm making it up. It's true that I've become more confident about improvisation. I don't think it's well understood that it's something you can *learn*. I didn't know that. *Anatomy of a Drum Solo* was the perfect turning point, because I announced in that DVD that I am a compositional drummer. And then almost immediately I started thinking about that and going, Wait a minute. Why limit myself? I want to be improvisational. So I really did set out to learn how.

It's very interesting how I've built the confidence that I used to get from rehearsal. Studying how improvising works,

> "'Subdivisions' or any of the *Moving Pictures* songs were absolutely made not to be played on the radio, not to be listened to on the floor with headphones. They were made to be *played*."

and especially how my mind works when it's improvising, has served to give me the confidence where I can be much more free. The two newest songs, "Caravan" and "BU2B," were recorded that way—*much* less prepared, and consequently much less orchestrated than in the past, but certainly with no less power and conviction. I trust myself more now—that's what it is! A lot of good experience where I've managed to do it night after night for eighty-one shows just on this tour gives me the confidence that I'll be able to do it.

MD: So realizing that you're a compositional drummer made you want to become an improvising drummer. What if it's the opposite, if you're a drummer who isn't comfortable committing to specific parts but you'd like to learn to be more compositional?

Neil: Very interesting, and so likely to be true. I've talked to other drummers a little bit about that, about ones that *can't* play the same way twice, but there's more to be learned there. I've known guys like that, that just play great all the time. But you have to play so much safer then, generally.

There are a lot of reasons why I get away with being so active, especially how I got away with it in those days, and it was because of having carefully orchestrated drum parts that framed the necessary vocal parts of the song. I never got intrusive in that respect. And I know what the lyrics are and where the vocals are going to go. I don't know how many drummers I've talked to that had to record a song when the lyrics weren't written yet, and what a terrible handicap that is.

I love the fact that not only are the lyrics written, but because I wrote them I *know* them. [laughs] I know where I can punch up vocal rhythms and accents, for example. It's really lovely to be able to do that. I think a lot of drummers are forced to play simpler than they'd like to, just not to take a chance on being in the way. It's like a session musician thing—

"live," and then played music together like we were just jamming like crazy high school children. That day will be etched in my mind (and the mind of many) forever. The best thing was the email I received after, in which Neil said, "I smiled the whole way home in the Laurentians," and then asked, "When can we do this again?"
Aldo Mazza (KoSA)

Tom Sawyer was just a book by Mark Twain until Neil Peart got ahold of it.
I was in college when *Moving Pictures* dropped, and after that, in a way, Rush was over for me. I so loved that album.

They trimmed their excess, crafting some amazingly memorable songs complete with all the energy and element of surprise that made them Rush. I also distinctly remember the presence of the instruments on that LP. It introduced a new level of high-fidelity to our stereo systems and our ears. It was like being in the room with the band! For me it was their apex. I caught the *Moving Pictures* tour and was swept into the tribal joy of air-drumming along with Neil Peart in an arena full of the devoted. Big fun!

I think Neil was the harbinger of a new breed of rock drummers not

directly influenced by jazz/swing-based music, as were the first generations of rock drummers from the 1950s and 1960s. Besides the jazz/rock fusion of Billy Cobham's work with the Mahavishnu Orchestra, which was undeniably influential in fueling Neil's imagination, jazz was not originally a component of his approach. But, from a different direction, his approach to drumming was as forward thinking as Max Roach's was—putting the drums out front and adding to the vocabulary of the multipercussion kit. He was able, in the space of the trio setting Rush employed, to create compositional

parts beyond beats and—like Elvin did improvisationally with Coltrane—made the drums an equal voice in the music. And, like Buddy Rich, Neil too greatly inspired generations of drummers with his mindful, whirlwind approach to drumming. I couldn't help but notice that Neil passed on January 10, the same day Max Roach was born in 1924. Coincidence? Each possessed formidable imagination, leaving an indelible mark on our instrument and music as a whole. Let's make it a celebration day.
David Stanoch (David Stanoch School of Drumming, *Percussive Notes*)

you're supposed to be invisible. But in a band you're supposed to express yourself.

As far as the repeatability factor, that's something I don't know enough to comment about, but I'm interested in it. I know there are drummers like that, and the fact that they might want to be more compositional doesn't surprise me.

MD: You really do get away with being more active than most drummers, and it's certainly not an accident.

Neil: No. Absolutely by design, and that's something the three of us shared, again, from the outset: We really wanted to play, and we really wanted to play *better*. That kind of curiosity and willingness to experiment took us on some strange journeys, but it's served us well in the end and made us happy to this day.

We've done little things on our own. I love big band music and look forward to playing it, and I do things for my own amusement, maybe with hand percussion or melodic percussion. But for the most part—no, for the absolute maximum part—I'm *completely* fulfilled as a drummer by what I get to do in this band. And as a writer I love being the lyricist too.

MD: You have some pretty special bandmates as well.

Neil: Yeah. I like them. Don't tell them. [laughs]

Replay

MD: During the refinement period where you're learning a song and creating the drum part, you're playing along to a demo made by Geddy and Alex, I assume.

Neil: Right, yeah.

MD: Do you record yourself playing everything from the more straightforward to the more experimental?

Neil: Ah! Good point. No, I don't record everything. I experiment with the kinds of ideas that might work—finding good rhythmic patterns for verses and choruses, and working on transitions and all those things. If a part needs to edge forward and be propulsive a little bit, you learn to give it that feel; if a chorus needs to lay back a bit and feel more relaxed, you learn to do that. At a certain point I want to hear it, and that's usually after I've played it for a few days. So that's when I'll record it.

To record everything is too much information. And honestly, what I'm doing early on doesn't need to be recorded. I think this is important too: If you like it, you'll remember it. I'm one for jotting down notes from time to time, but I really don't have to. I don't recall ever saying, "Gee, I wish I'd taped that." There's a certain self-editing process that goes on in the early stages of a song that's absolutely reliable. If I think of a little phrase, like the title of a song, and smile, I'm going to remember that. If I play a little phrase on the drums and smile, I'm going to remember that. That's a good barometer—the smile factor.

MD: How has the process changed from the days when you were all together in the same room hammering out a song? I guess that's exactly the difference—that you're not all playing

at once.

Neil: Yeah, so much better. It wouldn't necessarily work for a band at the beginning, and of course I'm glad we did all that. But it was very slow going. Trying to sort out and learn your part and trying to adapt to the others when they're doing the same thing was so inefficient. And I bet a lot of good things get lost, because if you're trying to play for the other guys too, you're not going to go out on a limb too far, because then you're sort of sabotaging them. Whereas when it's just me playing along with the demo, there are no consequences. And there's no responsibility. That's the other word. I often talk about consequences in terms of improvising, but there's a perfect example—there's no *responsibility* to hold the band together.

Even in a rehearsing context, as a drummer it is part of your job. You always want to give the other guys that foundation. Well, on your own you can try out many more ideas in a much shorter period of time and take more chances and have the opportunity to refine an idea that may seem a little bizarre if you just played it for the other guys.

And I have to say my parts are way more intricate and daring now than they ever were in those days, if I think back to the *Permanent Waves/Moving Pictures* era. I can hear that I was focused on foundations and supporting the band. Whereas later, with my drum part on a song like "Bravado," for example, where it gets increasingly active and then sinks down dynamically and is very carefully constructed as a sensitive part of the song, I wouldn't have had the luxury in those days of refining something to that degree. Or something like the second chorus of "Leave That Thing Alone," where instead of playing time I play a Nigerian drum ensemble. That wouldn't have worked in the old way of doing things.

Or the fill in "Caravan" that I talk about on the DVD, where our coproducer, Booujze [Nick Raskulinecz], kind of air-drummed that part to me and I had to figure out how to play it. The figure and the triplet feel of it need a flamacue kind of sticking that I had to spend quite some time on, figuring out how to do it and then how to do it *well*. Those are two things: First I had to figure out how to do it, and then I spent more time refining it to do it well.

MD: And that can take a while. Maybe not for you, but…

Neil: No, I don't mind saying it did. And that's why I never mind telling people, look, our complicated songs take me three days to learn. I don't just sit down and play like that. I think it's important for people to realize that, and I never try to come off like some kind of a superhero. Nor the self-deprecatory kind of, "Aw, it ain't nothin'…" Yeah, it's something—it took me years! But I don't mind saying that it did take me years.

Traveling Music

MD: It could be simplistic to make too direct a connection between your travel experiences and specific drumming figures, but your roster of fills and rhythms is vast, and it's not stuff that can be acquired by just sitting with your drums in a room.

Neil: No, that takes years…and wheels. Oh, that's good—years and wheels. [laughs] But yeah, of course I learned a lot from West African music, from a distance. Some things from recordings, like King Sunny Adé from Nigeria. But a lot of it was hearing drummers play in Togo or Cameroon or Ghana. Ghana is probably the nucleus of the drum for the whole planet, I might venture to say. Those kinds of experiences are unforgettable. Or China—the chanting in the temples.

Here's a beautiful cross-cultural rhythm: just 1, 2, 3, rest; 1, 2, 3, rest… I've heard that rhythm riding my bicycle beside a church in Ghana, behind the choir singing. It'll be on a bell or a block: bum, bum, bum…bum, bum, bum… In Chinese temples, when they're chanting, I'll hear that exact same pattern, maybe on a metal disc this time, or on a temple block. And I ran into it in Western music somewhere, just by chance the other day, and I was thinking that of all the rhythms of the world, that might be the most prevalent. That simple little thing of three beats and a rest, because it's recognizably a repeating rhythm, but it's stripped down to its very essence. It's the [sings rhythmically] simp-lest syn-co-pa-tion, to leave one out. If you look at the book of syncopation, I bet that's page one.

Freewill

MD: One last question about playing live. Each member of the band fires his own sequences here and there during the show, so I was wondering: Do you get tempos for each song in your in-ear monitors?

Neil: No way. I object to that. First, [in drum rehearsals] I play along with the recorded versions, so click tracks and sequencers are inherent. During band rehearsals I use a metronome with two lights that flash alternately. That gives me enough information at a glance to keep me and thus the whole band on track. But no, starting with the final production rehearsals I put aside that crutch and just do it live. Very satisfying.

In the old days, in one film we used a click track behind it, and I was always terrified that it wasn't going to work. So this obviates that. I'd rather take freedom and responsibility in that sense than have something to rely on, because I can't trust that. There's a very important little metaphor going on behind all this. Yeah, freedom and responsibility are much more preferable to me than reliance on a machine.

The Deep Cuts

Neil Peart has left behind a gigantic body of work that ensures his legacy will live on in perpetuity. Here we dig into some of the deeper cuts from Neil's illustrious catalog with Rush.

Text and transcriptions by Aaron Edgar

"Cygnus X-1," *A Farewell to Kings*

This song opens with a tight and funky pattern that weaves through an array of time signatures (6/8, 7/8, 6/8, and 4/4). Each of the measures is identical for the first six 8th notes, with the open hi-hat repeated once in the 7/8 and twice in the 4/4. On the first pass, there's a bar of rest between each beat.

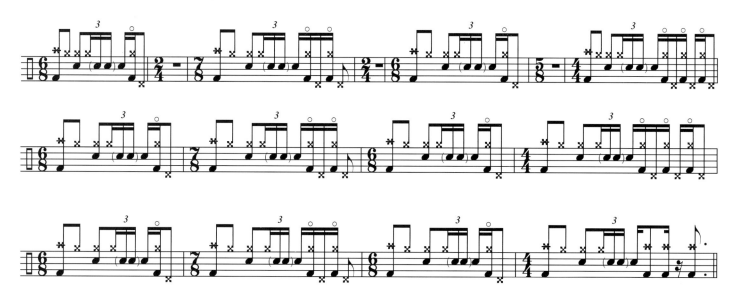

The song then explodes into a frantic 11/8 that's action-packed with cool groove and fill variations.

"Distant Early Warning," *Grace Under Pressure*

In the final pre-chorus of this track, the 7/8 section is doubled to ramp up the intensity even further as the song climaxes.

"Far Cry," *Snakes & Arrows*

Neil throws down an intense ending to this track as he solos over the hits. He starts with accents poking out of a quiet snare roll that progress into a flurry of toms, kicks, and crashes, until finally closing with a frenzy of gong drums and double bass.

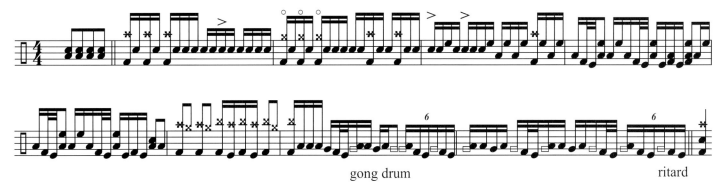

gong drum   ritard

"One Little Victory," *Vapor Trails*

The intro to this song features a driving double-bass groove where Neil matches his hands to his kicks with 16th-note singles. The right hand goes back and forth from the hi-hat to the snare as Neil accents a set of syncopated rimshots that poke through subtle ghost-note chatter.

"The Necromancer," *Caress of Steel*

In the middle of this epic track, Neil sets up a 12/8 section with a pattern that's based on a two-over-three polyrhythm. For every three 8th notes, there are two equally spaced snare hits, creating a hypnotic feel. Through this section, Neil plays grooves and fills that highlight both sides of the polyrhythm.

Deep Cuts continued from page 101

"Jacob's Ladder," *Permanent Waves*

At 5:15 in this song, the meter shifts between 6/8 and 7/8. (This section can also be counted in 13/8.) In the first eight bars, Neil dances around the pulse. As the section intensifies, he starts to play the China on the beat and then off the beat a couple of bars later.

"Natural Science," *Permanent Waves*

At 5:29, the feel flips from what seems like 6/8 to funky triplets in 4/4. The 6/8 feel is created with the ride cymbal. By playing every other triplet note, Neil ends up with three evenly spaced ride hits over two beats. That creates six evenly spaced hits through the measure of 4/4, which simulates a 6/8 ride pattern.

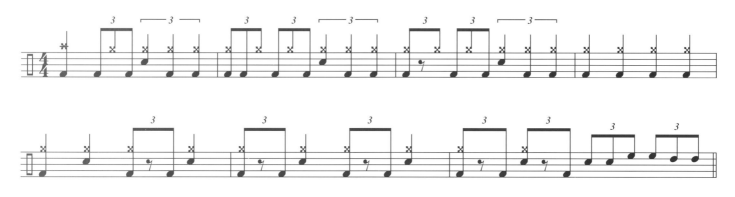

Neil On "Malignant Narcissism"

The Professor shares the backstory of how the
Snakes & Arrows instrumental cut came to be.

"The opening drum pattern of 'Malignant Narcissism' came about in some interesting ways," said Neil during a 2009 video lesson for Drumchannel.com. "As we were working through the arrangement, this song was maybe played three or four times before it was recorded. So it was definitely an on-the-fly, seat-of-the-pants situation. I was just tapping out time to the click track, and the producer, Nick Raskulinecz, said, 'I think you should start the song like that.'

"Then the sequence goes up to the verse pattern, where the bass riff shifts and the syncopation goes much more to a downbeat-oriented time," Neil continued. "There are three progressive treatments that all are based on tapping out the clicks and then responding to the bass player's interplay."

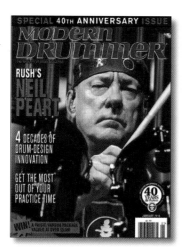
SPECIAL 40TH ANNIVERSARY ISSUE
MODERN DRUMMER
RUSH'S NEIL PEART
4 DECADES OF DRUM-DESIGN INNOVATION
GET THE MOST OUT OF YOUR PRACTICE TIME
40 YEARS

January 2016

Thinking Big, To The End

For his (record) ninth cover story, Neil held a typically fluid and intense discussion with *MD* backstage in his dressing room at the New Jersey stop of Rush's historic, career-spanning *R40* tour. The drummer greeted us, apologizing for being sockless and pointing to his feet, which looked like Father Time–affected, wear-and-tear evidence of half a century of bringing the power night after night.

Interview by Ilya Stemkovsky

Sustained Impact

Neil: [After discussing his injuries] At this point in the tour, you have no reserves. So a thing like this attacks, and it wears down your resistance in every other way too. And there's no getting better. I got tendinitis in one elbow on the '96/'97 *Test for Echo* tour, and then I didn't have it again for fifteen years—and it was the other elbow. For the rest of the tour I have to wear a brace to play, and I wear a brace at night. People say, "Oh, you just need to rest it." Okay, I'll do that. We'll just send these ten thousand people home tonight while I have a rest.

MD: You're certainly not back there playing "Peaceful Easy Feeling."
Neil: [laughs] As you can see, I often refer to what I do as athletic. It's not low impact. And through the teachings of Freddie Gruber, and through my own physical regimen and yoga, I've been able to sustain my peak for a long time and continue to get better and continue to study.

It's a revelation for me that at age sixty-two I can still be getting better and feel it and know it deep down. And move into a new area. Freddie had a transformational effect on my playing.

When I worked with him in the mid-'90s, he said, "You're a compositional player." And it's true. My drum parts all through the '70s and '80s were very carefully refined, partly by the nature of the way we worked in those days. We were all in the studio together, learning the song, playing it again and again, and one time I'd put in a little figure or accent and think, This would go with that, and, piece by piece, the architecture, the composition, would come together.

But when Freddie pointed that out to me, I thought, That's nice, but I want to be an improvisational player. So I set out

Craig Renwick

a bit on my own to work more in that direction and to use motifs in my solo and ostinatos that would allow me to expand more. I still have a framework, because I always felt a responsibility to present a composition.

When I was growing up in southern Ontario, the climate of the time was so healthy; I was seeing great drummers all the time. I loved the way some drummers played accompanying the band, but I didn't love their solos, because they had no vision, they had no story to tell. Some other drummers I'd watch solo, and I could see it was a composition, a performance.

Every band I was ever in, I've always played a solo. It became a part of my performing life from the beginning. It was such a great vehicle to learn, because there are so many technical aspects that I learned from soloing without the responsibility of supporting a band and being in the rhythm section.

That was just exploration. The same as my little warm-up drums here backstage. I can experiment on them without any consequences whatsoever. And I might think, Oh, I'm going to put that in my solo tonight. And I couldn't have known what Freddie was going to give me. I just surrendered myself to him and basically started all over.

MD: And Peter Erskine has helped continue your learning?

Neil: I loved the way Steve Gadd played "Love for Sale" on the Buddy Rich tribute album that we made [*Burning for Buddy*], and Dave Weckl playing it live. So I made that my summit. I wanted to aspire to

Craig Renwick

that performance.

Don Lombardi from Drum Workshop and I agreed that Peter Erskine would be the right teacher to take me in a better direction for big band drumming. And he lives ten minutes from me. So I started going to his house for lessons, and he started me on a course of practicing with the Quiet Count feature in Roland's V-Drums brain, which is a metronome that gives you two bars of click, then two bars of silence, and [so on].

Freddie was about motion. He'd say that when you hit the cymbal, it was that, but he also liked these gestures. And Peter had studied with Freddie too. Peter asked me to play quarter notes on a ride, and I was putting in this little curl. He asked what that was, and I told him it was timekeeping. He said, "No," and pointed at my chest and told me the time is *there*. He wanted me to play those quarter notes with laser accuracy and linear motion. And he had transcended Freddie's teaching, as I learned to. That feeling, that curl that Freddie had put into timekeeping, I intuited it. And I worked on it for months and went back to Peter to play those quarter notes. Like any student, I was nervous about the teacher. And at the end he said, "Perfect," and I was so happy.

MD: Did you feel your internal clock change?

Neil: Rush was on a hiatus and I had a year and a half where I could practice. Later, when the three of us got together, I started putting down drum tracks for the demos. Geddy and Alex said, "Well, it still sounds like you. It doesn't sound any different." And I was kind of disappointed. But when they went to play with it, it *was* completely different. The clock had just changed, altered that much. And that remains to this day. If we revive one of the older songs from prior to that time, I play it as I would play it now.

One song we revived, "Presto," we play so much better now, and Geddy said, "We have a different clock now." So they got it. There was something fundamental and seemingly intangible, because they couldn't hear it. It was more of the freedom now.

On the last two Rush albums, I haven't composed the drum parts—I've performed them. We worked with producer Nick Raskulinecz on the last two records, and I would play through

the song a few times, see what would work, and then he'd come in and we'd start recording. And he would conduct me, because our arrangements can be obtuse, and it used to take a long time for me to learn them.

I used to say it took me three days to learn one of our songs and put together a drum part. I don't like to count. I don't like to write notes. I want to play this thing like music. On this tour we're playing a lot of our older stuff from the 1970s with bizarre times. Why did we do this stuff? Because we were kids. We were learning how to do it. Because we could. I play that stuff completely differently now, with a much better lilt and feel and natural flow.

MD: In your last *MD* interview, in 2011, you said that studies with Gruber and Erskine helped you retain accuracy but feel good inside. Has anything changed? Is that even better now?

Neil: I'm still evolving in the ways that they have guided me. Sometimes I'll do an interview with non-musicians and they'll ask why I practice so much and take lessons. Well, I have the privilege of being a professional musician. It's my responsibility to devote myself to being all that I can be to the people that have given me that opportunity.

MD: Not everyone thinks that way.

Neil: I know, but they should. [laughs] I live by example. As a drummer, set a good example and don't work the audience. And when other drummers tell me I've inspired them to play drums, I tell them to apologize to their parents. [laughs] Like for this tour, I started preparation three months earlier. I'd play along with tracks all day and work on solo ideas, five days a week. So by the time we get to band rehearsals, I'm ready.

MD: How did the reverse chronological order of the R40 set list come about?

Neil: Alex and I were excited to find the deep tracks, the songs we never play live. And we wanted to do a theatrical presentation where the show devolves back in time. So then we started thinking of how the songs should be chosen, and you've got two responsibilities—set one and set two, like two sides of an LP. So they'd have to start and end somewhere, and carry the audience dynamically.

Years ago we were talking about a certain order of songs, and Alex said we couldn't do that because they were all

in the same key—something no one would think about. And I'm conscious of that tempo-wise. And for Geddy as a vocalist, he might not want to sing certain songs in a row.

A Tale of Two Kits

MD: Let's talk about your drumsets on this tour.

Neil: The kit in the first set evolved as an instrument of perfect comfort. I can play it with my eyes closed. The musicality through the cymbals and the toms. Everything is carefully chosen and put where it should be. I tell people: Don't look at those forty-seven drums. It's a four-drum setup. Look at the middle—everything spins off from there.

In the '70s, things evolved from the '60s. Ginger Baker [Cream, Blind Faith] had his ride off to the side with a crash on top of it, so he could have three or four toms across the front. That's around the era when I started playing, so I gravitated that way. When I first switched to the double pedal in the early '90s and DW really refined the first proper double-pedal setup, I went to it willingly right away—just ergonomically to free up the space. But I couldn't believe the sonic aspect. At the time, I half-noticed that the toms sounded cleaner and everything sounded more discrete.

This second kit was modeled after my 1978 black chrome Slingerland set. I had the notion that wouldn't it be great if, instead of having the rotating set I've had for years that kind of contrasts the acoustic and electronic drums, I went to a whole second drumset. I went to Drum Workshop and said I wanted that exact setup.

I always say this about old cars and motorcycles, and old drums: I love them, but new ones are better. There's no argument. And both sets are made from one tree in Romania that fell in the river, got buried in silt, and lay there for 1,500 years. In 2014, John Good from Drum Workshop bought that tree and made a few prototype shells that I tried.

Of course the wood gets super-dense over that time, with pressure. And the resonance and timbre of the note were superior to even the best shells DW makes, which have evolved over my twenty years with them. And playing two bass drums and open concert toms again was fun.

MD: Was it tough at first to play that old setup again?

Neil: It was tough. The ergonomics of it all. I used to make everything so close and under me. But it was counterintuitive thinking. I used to think the closer it is, the more power I can get on it, but that's not true. You have to get it the *right* distance. Close or near

doesn't matter. And the way the set list works out, I had to solo on that set. I'd much rather solo on my modern set in every sense, musically and physically.

But there are cool things as well. I used to have timbales on my left side, so I got those again and they're fun. That's part of the solo. But it grew organically and naturally by what excited me to play. And I never practiced this solo the way that I used to. I used to really compose the solo, and this one never went that way. And there are things in my solo that have been there since I was sixteen, that always thrilled me and still do.

MD: The snare stuff.

Neil: Yes, I can vamp on a snare drum all

day long. And the four-on-the-floor. It feels exciting to me. And in the solo it's all spontaneous. There are places I like to get to, like the waltz, because I love that. And I'll go up on the concert toms over the waltz, because I like how that works. And I want to get the cowbells in because they're funny. And there's a little Brazilian ostinato I love, though it's not in there every night.

MD: I'd figure you'd have the fearlessness to improvise a solo like that back in the day, but you're doing that now, later in the game.

Neil: I didn't have that fearlessness. And it was a responsibility thing. I wanted to make sure the performance was consistent. And I don't want to use tricks, but tools. There's a very important distinction. The quarter-note bass drum can be a terrible cliché. But if you use it at the right time in a complicated arrangement or something, there's nothing more powerful. I don't ever abuse it.

To me, my solo has become a soundtrack to an imaginary movie. When I want to build up the excitement, it has to be organic. When I build up that rudimental snare part and I bring the bass drum in, as soon as I start stomping on the hi-hat, it starts glancing, it's more exciting, and it's more exciting to play.

And for years I had 13" hi-hats, clamped down tight. Peter Erskine said he used to be like me—he had his hi-hats super-tight and super-controlled. He said to just try to let them slosh for a while and see what happens. I did, and sure enough I learned that when they're moving like that, your velocity has to be exactly right and it helps your time sense. I got used to it, and it has this whole other benefit. Like in "Roll the Bones," the part with the sloshy hi-hat. I play that so much better now, and the feel in my bass drum foot is so much better for the quick hits. As is the time control, because I have to play to that moving hi-hat. Rhythmically, the velocity

of my stick affects when it's coming back and the interval in between. And it's funkier. It's not just a sloshy hi-hat—it's part of the time.

MD: It's a shame you can't have all this fun on the kit you'd rather be playing.

Neil: Old things are nice, but new things are better. And I just know so much more through all the learning and evolution. The newer kit is just such a comfortable instrument, while the second one is ad-hoc. It came together bit by bit. Playing it now, I have to sit at it differently. My posture. And think about it and look where I'm going. The first time I tried to hit crash cymbals without looking, I was bleeding. And very many times I would finish something and go to where the ride cymbal should be and there's a tom there. So the map is different.

But I was able to compensate. It's not a compromise, it's a limitation, and one that I decided on for all good reasons. And I noticed quite a few of the songs

Craig Renwick

had chimes. I have that as a sample on my malletKAT, but I thought, You know what: Real chimes—it's suitable for the theater. Century Mallet in Chicago made these beautiful-sounding black-nickel chimes.

The one factor that connects all this is the second bass drum. All the toms sound muddy on that side. And I'm told by the sound guys out front that a good thing is the main bass drum resonates in the other one, and it gives it a certain sonic quality out front that's all right. But it's the little subtle things like that that are a challenge.

Making Trades

MD: You've been celebrating the fortieth anniversary of the band on this tour. How do you choose what to play?

Neil: We don't have any songs that we hate, and there's none that we get sick of. They all have their charm to us, because they were all written from the heart, so there's none we feel reluctant to play. We came up with alternate sets, so it allowed us to not have to drop things but just play them every three or four shows. And that served us well on the last tour, and it was the first time we dared to try that. We usually hesitate to take on more work than we need. [laughs] And that's true even on the records. We've never written and recorded a song that we didn't put out. Why go through all that trouble?

Our benchmarks are really organic ones. I always think if I have a good idea, I'll remember it. If we play something that we like, we'll remember it. So there were songs that never got played, for one reason or another. We also wanted to fix on what we thought were high points along the way dynamically. But all the ones in the first set are killers to play, physically.

MD: They look demanding on you, right away.

Neil: On an album, you'll typically have a couple of slower, easier, gentler songs. But live, we don't. So it's an hour sprint for me. Full power from me.

MD: So if you never played "Limelight" again, that'd be okay?

Neil: Yeah, we've done it. We still like it. And there were lots of songs like that. We said, "Let's do *this* instead." We had to make those kinds of trade-offs.

MD: With your new feel and clock and maturity, do you ever think about how you might do something differently from these iconic parts and fills that you wrote long ago?

Neil: I do play those songs very differently. I've evolved into a different, more improvisational player. The clock on "Tom Sawyer" or "The Spirit of Radio" now…they're very different from what they were. I'm happy to play the composed parts the same every night. "Tom Sawyer" remains that way. If I can play that right every night? Fine. I don't change very much, and I don't feel like I want to. "The Spirit of Radio" is another great example. Since 1979, I don't think I've changed anything except the feel.

For songs in those days, we were just starting to do a very formative technical thing, which was to put sequencers in the middle of a song. For that song, I'd have to play the intro and the first verse, which already have two different tempos, and then get to the chorus, with that sequence [sings the synth part], which was going to be the same every night. But I learned from that, to get set up and to get there and to flow through it and out of that. At the end, this piano sequence comes in, and typically toward the end of a song you might be speeding up—that's human nature. But I had to learn to train myself to know that thing is going to be coming in, and I want that to feel great. *That* should be the lift; that can't be the drag. So my time feel on those songs is that subtle difference that doesn't sound different but absolutely feels different to play, and better to play.

The Nature and Nurture of Change

MD: Back in the day you were part of a movement of idiosyncratic drummers who had a "sound." Stewart Copeland, Billy Cobham—if those names were on a record, it was going to sound a certain way. Guys who imposed brilliantly on the music, like Jack DeJohnette.

Neil: One of the masters. I've said of Jack that he's the one who best bridges classic drumming and modern drumming.

MD: Beautiful player, but he's not going to appear on a Katy Perry pop session.

Neil: [laughs] Let's hope not.

MD: And country records all sound quantized. Is it a healthy time for drummers? Where's the individuality? Where is the instrument going?

Neil: It's difficult. We were rehearsing in Toronto and I was driving back and forth and made it a point to listen to Top 40 radio. And it was fine. I love the R&B/hip-hop combo—it's very healthy for what it is. And I've always loved pop music if it's honest. Don't pretend you're a rocker in a leather jacket if you're a pop star. What is *pop* short for? Popular. It's not the same thing as being in a rock band, where I think a certain amount of integrity is inherent with the definition.

Over the two weeks, I didn't mind the music, but I did not hear one drummer or one drum. But all of these acts have real drummers live, because the difference onstage—the theater of a live drummer—is enormous. The hope for the future is as performing drummers. It's hard to encourage young musicians now, because my rote advice is so useless, because I say, "What you have to do is play live." When I was a kid, we used to get gigs at the high school or the roller rink on the weekends, and during the week I could get paid $20 to jam at the coffeehouse with other musicians. There were a lot of opportunities to play live if you were willing to ride in a van and pay your dues that way. There's no better way to learn.

For this band, when we got together in 1974, when we went out opening a tour, if the headliner took a day off we would go back to Akron, Ohio, and play the club. We would play anywhere and do anything. It was a slow build, and we worked so hard as an opening act. We were all supply and no demand. So later, when the demand grew, we eventually had to learn to say no. To not play ten shows in a row. Those were lessons along the way.

But we had the opportunity to play, and together. First, to build that unity, and then, over making subsequent albums, to learn how to write and arrange songs, and to learn to play and have a thing like "La Villa Strangiato (An Exercise in Self-Indulgence)." We knew what we were doing. Yeah, we were playing all this stuff because we could, but that's what we were supposed to do.

MD: Your music demanded the audience to invest in it.

Neil: We built our enduring reputation by live performance. Our albums would sell up and down, but people would still come to the show: "I didn't like that album so much, but I know that they'll play the rest of them, and the show will be good and they'll give it all they have." There was a trust factor there. So that's the hope for the generation of the future—the passion for the instrument. That people would want to play, whatever it takes.

And now people are finding avenues to communicate their music other than coming up through clubs. Not to publicize it or to brand it or sell it, but just to get people to hear it. If a band can get heard and seen on YouTube, then they can get gigs and start playing live. It's different, all right, but I still see people making it.

The Write Way

MD: You've said that sometimes you'll change lyrics so that Geddy can sing them more easily. Do you ever collaborate on the rhythmic delivery of the vocals?

Neil: Yeah, we often discuss phrasing. Plus it's kind of in-built. I have an advantage there, in that words are always rhythm to me. A line comes into my head and it has a rhythm, automatically, because I hear it as a drummer and pattern my phrasing that way. But sometimes I'll take liberties so that one should be longer and the next one should be back-phrased. And I might explain that to Geddy, or when he's doing his vocals I'll be around and if I hear him having trouble, I can rewrite something.

MD: And he's open to your suggestions?

Neil: Oh, mostly asking for help. [laughs] "I'm having trouble with this line" or "I need two more lines like this." Great—I can do that.

A lesson I learned is not to try to write one whole song and give it to the guys, like, "Here's my precious masterpiece." I just write a whole bunch of stuff and give it to them. They'll sit and jam and record it all, and Geddy will sift through it and make an arrangement out of it. And when he likes lines, I'm inspired. Just the fact that it's been accepted and found worthy to be a song. If anything gets rejected or left out, it's not a negative.

"Caravan" from *Clockwork Angels* is a good example. We had the "I can't stop

> "When I worked with Freddie Gruber in the mid-'90s, he said, 'You're a compositional player.' I thought, That's nice, but I want to be an improvisational player."

thinking big" line. Geddy made it into the chorus and asked if he could have one more line to wrap it up. And somehow it came out to be "In a world where I feel so small, I can't stop thinking big." I don't know where that came from. It was just spontaneous.

It was a puzzle to solve. I'm really good at crosswords, and that helps a lot with that kind of thing. I have this many syllables. A song, even in our case, without much repetition, is only a couple hundred words. So you have to become super-economical with them and choose the word that conveys the meaning the best and that sounds the best being sung, and that bears repeating. I didn't write "I can't stop thinking big" to be repeated. It was just a line. That's one example where the problem-solving can suddenly be inspiring. I don't know where that came from, but thank you. [laughs]

MD: What's more gratifying, seeing fans

singing your lyrics or seeing them air-drumming?

Neil: Singing. One of the keys to our longevity is that I know in many bands there's a great envy of the singer for getting all the attention. It causes a lot of ruptures and conflicts and all this pure ego. But all these people singing along with Geddy, they're singing my words. How can I feel bad about that? So that's very gratifying.

And the air-drumming is the same thing. It's a level of engagement, just sheer exuberance. That's the energy you feel. It's truly spontaneous and it's a feedback loop. We energize them and they energize us. It's a palpable, sincere thing, and it's not just about [the musicians] putting on a show, but [the audience] being *in* the show. And I always say, I am the audience. I'm not a performer by nature. The choice of drums drove me into being a performer. I'm really a one-on-one talker. When I'm onstage, I watch people a lot. And the world too—on my motorcycle rides on my days off, it's the show coming at me. I'm the audience for it, and I try to absorb it as deeply as I can and hopefully share it with others later.

And that's the big appeal with prose writing, the urge to share. And this just occurred to me, but I bet the excitement I get in playing particular songs of ours [comes from the fact that] it communicates, "This is real." The energy that I'm giving this, the fact that this excited me when I recorded it and that became the drum part I wanted for that song—that meant something, and it still means something.

MD: Induction into the Rock and Roll Hall of Fame, the cover of *Rolling Stone*… what's going on here?

Neil: [laughs] Persistence! Just keep going. You can eventually earn people's respect. It's easy to be dismissed in the beginning. And I've done that myself as a reader. Just dismissed certain writers. And then they earn my respect over time. That's persistence.

MD: What's in the future? If Rush isn't touring, will you still record? Write prose? Be a dad?

Neil: You just answered it. There's no strict answer, but those possibilities are all there.